IN MY OWN VOICE

Christa Ludwig about 1972

Christa Ludwig
IN MY OWN VOICE

Memoirs

Translated
with Reference Material
by
Regina Domeraski

LIMELIGHT EDITIONS
New York

In My Own Voice: Memoirs by Christa Ludwig

Originally published in German as ... *und ich wäre so gern Primadonna gewesen*
© 1994, Herschel Verlag, Berlin

English translation © 1999 by Regina Domeraski

First Limelight Edition October 1999

English translation published in the United States by Proscenium
Publishers Inc., New York.
All rights reserved under international and Pan-American copyright
conventions.
Printed in Canada.

Library of Congress Cataloging-in-Publication Data

Ludwig, Christa.
   [Und ich wäre so gern Primadonna gewesen. English]
   In my own voice : memoirs / by Christa Ludwig ; translated with a
      discography and chronology by Regina Domeraski.
     p.   cm.
   Discography: p.
   Includes index.
   ISBN 0-87910-281-0
   1. Ludwig, Christa. 2. Mezzo-sopranos—Biography.
   ML420.L932A3   1999
   782.1'092—dc21
   [B]   99-43233
                                           CIP

Text design by Jeff Fitschen

Contents

Another Costume, Another Role

Surviving Rehearsals and Stage Directors

Conducting Styles

Lieder

Singing Is Hard Work

(in alphabetical order)

The Men in My Life

A Fast Foreword
by Regina Domeraski

As I was driving Christa Ludwig to one of her master classes at Ravinia last summer, I asked how she felt about the idea that 100 years from now, when we were both long dead, people would probably be listening to her singing in some colony on Mars. Christa seemed rather startled, and said, "Oh God, never! . . . Maybe you should turn left here."

But I persisted. Certainly the *Fidelio* she recorded with Otto Klemperer and Jon Vickers has been considered a classic for 30 years and probably always will be. Then, as I obediently turned in the designated direction, I reminded her of the huge success of her Dyer's Wife in *Die Frau ohne Schatten*, and bolstered my argument further by bringing up the recent enthusiasm for her Marschallin recordings with both Leonard Bernstein and Karl Böhm, especially among younger critics. And who can forget the *Das Lied von der Erde* recording she made so many years ago with Klemperer and Fritz Wunderlich?

I could have continued, but didn't because I'd missed the turn into the parking lot, and Christa hates being late. Still, the conversation started me thinking about what exactly made Christa Ludwig such a great singer. There's a long list: a beautiful voice; an incredible degree of musicality; theatrical instincts; her mother's determination; historical circumstances; her own personality; and a touch of genius. And since I've promised Christa that she can read this foreword before I send it to the publisher, I know she will only let me get away with "a touch of genius" if I qualify it by saying a very, very, very small touch of genius, if any. But I can defend my opinion!

What attracted me to Christa Ludwig many years ago was her ability to create a complex, living human being onstage. Like most Americans, I first heard Christa at the opera. I became a faithful fan for life on a night when she sang one of her greatest roles at the Met, Kundry in *Parsifal*. I can even give the exact date (November 21, 1970), and, if pressed, I can probably give the exact time, too (it was on the words "Dienen . . . dienen" in the beginning of the third act).

I left the theater that night amazed. Christa Ludwig's Kundry was a deeply moving, highly emotional experience, and it was also a theatrical tour de force. In the first act she was a lowly household slave for the Grail knights, and in the second, an enchanted seductress. Yet throughout, the audience had a sense that Kundry was neither of these things, but a suffering human being fighting against the two roles that fate was forcing her to play. Then, on the words I've already mentioned in the third act, Kundry miraculously became that suffering human being—her real self. It was an incredible performance. In my slightly overwrought undergraduate diary that night I wrote, "This is my birthday in opera. Christa Ludwig has opened the door of my understanding. I *know* now." I knew in my soul, but I certainly didn't know in my head. So on that night began a personal 20-year odyssey during which I tried to answer two questions: how did she do it, and why was that performance so powerful? Many of the answers are in this book.

For example, I mentioned that Christa's Kundry seemed to be three different people, and in her book, Christa talks about how Karajan wanted three different women to play the role in his Vienna production. Aha, but then how to explain that, while Christa was playing the roles of slave and seductress in the first two acts, you also felt deeply the presence of the suffering Kundry who was trapped in those other guises and who would only emerge as herself in the third. That I can only ascribe to Christa's musicality, that is, her sensitivity to the music, the text, and the psychology of the character she was playing. This sensitivity started to develop at birth, or as Christa suggests in her book, perhaps in the womb, since her mother was pregnant with her while she was singing Carmen and other major roles. Both Christa's parents were professional singers, and they ran their own opera school. Her father taught her a respect for words while her mother taught her almost everything else.

How Christa could give such powerful performances is a more perplexing question, because to meet Christa Ludwig is to meet a gentle, warm, very low-key woman whose favorite comment about herself is to say how lazy she is. I would point to at least two motivators in her book. The first is the poverty Christa and her family faced after their home was fire bombed during the Second World War. When her parents divorced shortly after the war, Christa and her mother were left with nothing but Christa's talent and her mother's ability to teach singing. Still, that probably wouldn't have been enough without her mother's vision and determination. Eugenie Ludwig was, by all accounts, quite an extraordinary person, and the chapter about her ("Singing Is Your Destiny") is understandably one of the most extraordinary in her daughter's book.

But why did Christa decide to write a book? She tells us her initial reason in the first chapter, "How I Started to Write This Book": she had to. She wanted to tell her story herself, not through interviewers and public relations people (you'll find out what she thinks of PR in due course), but honestly and openly. She's written a series of short pieces, a collection of thoughts about her experiences that touch on every aspect of singing.

The catalyst we all have to thank for Christa's book is Peter Csobádi. He encouraged Christa to keep writing, and he was the one who took all her handwritten sheets and, with the editors at Henschel, put the original German version together. A year or so later, when Christa was approached about an English version, she asked me to be her editor and translator. She told me she wanted her ideas to be clear and understandable for the American audience she loves so much. We spent nine days together laughing and crying and working very intently at her home in France, and later we discussed revised sections at Ravinia where I had the great privilege of watching Christa teach. We also discussed things in our usual way—in innumerable faxes.

Of course, we had the predictable tussles about what certain German words meant in English. For example, we had a long debate about whether the word "Geheimnis" in the *Winterreise* chapter meant "the secret" or "the mystery." Some things are simply not literally translatable. And for some things in music, there simply are no words.

Mentioning "Geheimnis" reminds me of another evening when I was driving. In my quest to understand Christa's "Geheimnis," I found out that the best time to get her to speak freely was in the ten minutes it took to drive her from the Met stage door to her apartment building after a performance. On this particular evening, she had been singing the *Rheingold* Fricka, which was not one of her favorite roles because Fricka has very little to sing and spends most of the evening "just standing around," as Christa put it. We stopped at a light, and I asked her what on earth she did on Tuesdays in other parts of the world when she had to "stand around" and the conductor wasn't James Levine and the Wotan wasn't James Morris? What did she do when the conductor and the other singers and the production were—well, boring? Feigning complete innocence, she turned to me and said, "When I am on the stage, it is never boring!" And we both laughed so loudly that we startled quite a few of the pedestrians crossing the street in front of us.

As you begin reading this book, I'm sure you'll quickly see that Christa can also truthfully (but modestly) say, "When I am on the page, it is never boring!"

For My Mother

I learned discipline and dedication from my mother, who guided my professional development for more than thirty years. Her wise words are always with me, and not a day passes when I don't say at least once, "My mother always said. . . ." Here are some of her thoughts:

Singing is spiritual. Physical technique is the base,
but you must also be in spiritual harmony with yourself and
with your surroundings.

Love must flow from you when you sing.

Having a good voice is only a small part of talent. Discipline and
sacrifice are more important.

Never think, "I wish I were like this singer or that one."
Only be yourself. In this way, you can develop your
own special personality.

Readiness is all (as Shakespeare said).

You must use your talent wisely. Remember the parable of the
wise virgins. Protect your talent as they did the oil for their lamps.

Vocal cords are like raw eggs. Once they're broken,
they can't be repaired.

Try to avoid singing when your voice isn't healthy.
Cancel immediately.

Breath, vocalization, and overtones are the pillars of good
singing technique. Everything else comes from differences in
body structure. Different cavities resonate differently from
person to person.

Never strive to sing loudly. Only aspire to make a beautiful sound.
Practice singing every note smoothly from pianissimo to forte, and
back, at least forty times every day.

Always remember that your voice is a gift only for a short time.
You must have other interests.

Don't take any success or failure too seriously. You can learn best
about yourself from honest friends—or honest enemies.

Be like a sponge, but absorb only the best influences from
the world around you.

Never prejudge, or repeat what other people say.
Always form your own opinion, and always look for
the good in people.

Don't give advice. Just give your opinion.

Give yourself entirely to life.
Everything you give away will come back to you.

My mother was a very wise woman, and I am grateful for all the wonderful
advice that she gave me about singing—and about life. This book is dedicated
to her.

Starting at the
Beginning

How I Started to Write This Book

"I can't write a book!"

"Of course you can."

That's how I awoke from my nap on the afternoon before a performance in Paris. I had rented a tiny apartment in the center of the city near the Church of the Madeleine, one of the many "cells" I occupied during my professional life. I know dreams often burst like bubbles, but the idea of writing a book took hold of me, so much so that I bought myself many pads of paper.

"Maybe they'll never become a book," I thought, looking at the huge pile of blank pages. Nevertheless, I began. I did this in spite of my bad experiences writing essays as a child. I remember to this day the time I had to do an essay on German fairy tales at school. I wrote for weeks about the morals of fairy tales and about their bloodthirstiness. I thought about the hacked-off horse's head that could talk ("O, Fallada, there you hang"), and about all the evil stepmothers. I was inspired, and what happened? I got a D. Not good enough!

And now I'm presuming to write a book? But because my subconscious keeps saying to me, "Of course you can," I'm presuming to do it, even though there's the possibility that I'll never find a publisher, or, worse yet, a reader.

Since organizing my writing in a logical way has always been a problem for me, I think I'll make things easy for myself. I'll put everything in alphabetical order. But how can I concentrate even on this simple scheme when I'm always distracted by some cat or other (we have seven), or the dog, or the telephone? Or suddenly I realize how I can best sing a note. I stand up, go to the piano, and try it out. Meantime I've forgotten what I was writing.

But since I've always welcomed a challenge, I've decided to persevere. OK, fine, I'll go from A to Z. But then I can't decide if I should write about Karl Böhm under "B" for "Böhm" or "C" for "Conductors." And, for heaven's sake, what about X and Y?

And if I write the truth, will people find it too heavy? I don't want to write only about the spiritual side of singing and my successes and the "God-given gift of the voice" and the "calling" to give people joy. No, I also want to write about the fears, pains, failures, and difficulties. I want to write about how I sometimes would have gladly thrown away this "gift from heaven" to lead a normal life as a woman, wife, and mother.

Women's Lib! I know what it's like to be "free" to do what you want, to earn a lot of money, and to spend it on fancy hotels and expensive automobiles. Free? Not true. The singing profession is slavery! It only looks easy and enviable from the outside. You are showered with bravas and blossoms (aha, I'm up to B!), but from the beginning, the sword of Damocles always hangs over your head. After a certain age, you no longer have the ease, and your voice is no longer as radiant. Indeed, you must stop singing just at the time when you've finally know what singing is all about. When you've finally gained experience (and also, one hopes, worldly wisdom); when you can dig more deeply into the character of the roles you perform; when you finally grasp the full meaning of the poetry in the songs you are singing—then your voice isn't there anymore! Isn't that a real tragedy? All other professionals, except for athletes and dancers, mature and do their best work later, as is so beautifully said, "in the prime of life." But singers stop singing in the middle. Naturally, I'm speaking in particular of female singers. The men have it better. They easily retain their vocal abilities well past the age of sixty. A big exception is Birgit Nilsson, the great Isolde and Brünnhilde of our time, indeed of our century, who, in her mid-fifties and later, continued to sing demanding roles.

It's not even the voice as such that gives out, but rather the breath, and in the breath lies a large part of the secret of singing. These tiny vocal cords, scarcely half an inch, how they must be cherished and protected. But I see I'm beginning to get into a subject that belongs under "V" for "Voice," so I'll hold off for a while. Order must be maintained. Back to my story!

My thoughts for this book continued to take shape. Instead of sleeping, I relived the past. Memories came, and I often lay in bed at night, turning things over in my mind. Then, in the morning, I would write everything down that I'd remembered during the night.

Oh God! I have an interview today on TV in Paris! I've got to look fresh with no dark circles under my eyes! And I have to speak French too! Languages don't come easily to me, and I didn't learn French until after my second marriage (to a Frenchman, my beloved Paul-Emile Deiber). It's such a beautiful language, and I'm always trying to speak it properly. But with my accent and my mistakes, the result is sometimes very comical.

Only half awake, I search through my closet for a dress to wear, and then I glimpse my hair in the mirror with horror. Later, with hair freshly washed and curled and with make-up in place, I'm in a better mood. I enter the studio with its glaring lights for a short interview.

"Which country do you prefer, Austria or France?"

"Naturally, both." (What questions!)

Then on to the Marschallin in *Rosenkavalier*. This part of the interview goes better because I love the role very much, even though it's a soprano part and I'm a mezzo. (But wait! That subject belongs under M!) After a few more pleasantries, the taping is finished.

Hundreds of times over the years, professional duties like this TV interview in Paris have interrupted my attempts to write my book. Nevertheless, I haven't abandoned the project. I wrote when I had to be quiet before my entrances at the opera and at concerts. I wrote in hotels. If I was alone, I wrote during long flights. And more and more, I was drawn into the past and into the experiences I had to come to terms with.

Still, because of all my travels and the time I needed to study new roles and songs, my notebooks, with their virginal white pages, often gathered dust in the closet. For many months, I didn't write down anything, nor did I make much progress in ordering my thoughts from A to Z. But finally I began to deflower new pages once again. I began to write in earnest.

Growing Up in Germany, 1928-1945

My mother, Eugenie Besalla-Ludwig, came from a poor middle-class Berlin family. Her father, a man of few words who always found everything "just fine," was born in East Prussia. Her mother was a Rhinelander, and she sewed men's vests at home. She sold these to earn extra money so that all her children could have music lessons. In this way, she made it possible for my mother to have private instruction with Professor Niklas Kempner, one of the most famous teachers at the Berlin Stern'sche Conservatory.

Voice lessons were, and still are, very expensive. Even then, from 1915 until 1920, twenty minutes of private instruction cost the equivalent of about $25. But since my mother had an unusually beautiful voice, she quickly received a scholarship. At the conservatory, she met a fellow student who later became the wife of Max Lorenz, the famous heldentenor, and also Claudio Arrau, who was prized as a piano prodigy. But it was wartime, and my mother told me how scarce food was in Berlin. If a horse collapsed from hunger on the street—there were still many horse-drawn carriages then—in a very short time only a skeleton was left. That's how desperate people were for something to eat.

When my mother was 21 years old, she was engaged as a beginner at the municipal theater in Aachen, singing mezzo-soprano roles. Here she immediately fell in love with the stage manager and opera director, Anton Ludwig— my father! Unfortunately, he was married and had three children when they met. But he was the first man in her life, and Anton, who was from Vienna and eleven years older, threw a net of Viennese charm around the young Prussian from which she could not free herself. Later as an adult, when I accused my mother of having destroyed a marriage, she would remind me that I wouldn't have been born if things had gone differently. But since I saw, as I grew older, that great sorrow came from my parents' actions, I always fled whenever I found a married man too attractive. Thank God my sister from my father's first marriage and I became good friends, and we are still friends today. (My two brothers are dead.) When we were younger, both Annemarie and I had a problem realizing that all men didn't act like our father.

For my future profession, having my father and mother as parents was a stroke of genetic luck. Vocal gifts seem to be hereditary on my father's side of the family. My father was related to Anton Schittenhelm, a singer from the Austrian Imperial Opera, and he began to sing very early. He studied with Rosa Papier-Paumgartner, whose son, Professor Bernhard Paumgartner, later became president of the Salzburg Festival. For the first 19 years of his career, my father was a baritone. He sang Papageno at the Vienna Volksoper at age 18, and in 1909, at age 21, he was engaged at the Metropolitan Opera in New York, where he sang Bajazzo and Silvio in *Pagliacci* with Caruso. Caruso thought my father was a tenor, and so, on Caruso's advice, my father trained as one. My older half-brother, Heinz, was born in New York. He became a well-known set designer and worked for a long time in Düsseldorf and Graz, and at the Hersfeld Festival.

Vocal talent and musicality were part of my heritage from both my parents, and it seems as though, to paraphrase Adorno, my musical training began "nine months *before* birth." Indeed, my mother told me that as she sang

Carmen, I zealously boxed in her belly in time to the music. My mother also told me that when she sang to me as a tiny baby, I was immediately fascinated with the mouth from which the beautiful sounds came.

I was not born in Aachen, where my parents were engaged at the time. As a Berliner, my mother wanted her child born in her parents' house in Berlin, and that's where I came into the world on March 16, 1928. My parents had a school in Aachen where they taught singing, acting, and public speaking. There my father trained preachers to project their voices clearly, since they had no microphones on their pulpits then. Because I often listened from the adjoining room, and was also permitted in the studio, I could recite the whole diction phrase book from memory as a very young child, and I still laugh when I remember how comical my father sounded when he exaggerated the difference between things like the open and closed German "o" vowel in nonsensical diction exercises. Yet to this day, I still take the basics of proper diction my father taught very seriously.

Naturally, I was fascinated by opera arias. According to my mother, I sang loudly and without a mistake the Queen of the Night's aria from *The Magic Flute* with its high F, bird-like ornamentation, and high E-flat ending—at the age of three! Then, when I finished, I'd always crawl under the grand piano and hide very shyly. After the students left, I'd say, "Now it's my turn," and I'd sing and act out what I'd seen the others do, regardless of whether it was Azucena or Marie from *Der Waffenschmied*.

I also became a true opera addict. As interim opera director in Aachen, my father had a box at the theater, so I could go whenever I liked. When I was about seven years old, I saw my mother as Fidelio and Elektra with Herbert von Karajan conducting. Then in his late twenties, the young maestro was also engaged in Aachen. At home, I wanted to learn these roles too, and since I had studied piano from the age of six, I could do it with the patient help of my mother. That's when I learned to count beats! I memorized the operas in German, of course, and I still immediately translate any operas sung in another language into my own German version.

I was at rehearsals when my father managed a production, I was backstage during the scene changes, and I constantly attended performances of operas, operettas, and plays. I practically lived in the theater, and I saw everything as theater in my imagination and in the real world, too. For example, if we went on a picnic and I saw a meadow surrounded by a forest, it immediately became a stage set for me, and I patiently waited for the characters from the fairy tale operas *Christeflein* or *Hänsel und Gretel* to appear.

I can still see my father before me acting fire-like as Loge in *Rheingold* in a costume of shredded red and yellow fabric with a red flame wig. I also saw him in the title role of the Hans Pfitzner opera *Der Evangelimann*. Marcel Prawy, the eminent Viennese musicologist, knew my father during his second engagement at the Vienna Volksoper in the 1920s, where he sang helden-tenor roles like Tannhäuser and Lohengrin and also Eisenstein in *Die Fledermaus* with Leo Slezak as Alfred. My mother was also engaged at the Volksoper at that time, and she sang Prince Orlofsky in the same production. My mother told me that my father and his colleagues added so many improvi-sations in the second act one night that the prompter got mad, closed his score, turned out the light in his box, and whispered, "The last tram leaves in five minutes!" Also in the second act, Slezak came to Orlofsky's party on a long chain led by Frosch the jailer, and sang Felix Weingartner's "An ihren bunter Flügeln" with Weingartner conducting.

Unfortunately, I only know this period in Vienna from the stories I've been told, because all of my parents' pictures, reviews, and the other memen-tos were burned in a bombing during the war, and I have only been able to obtain a very few things from friends. The Volksoper at that time was a pri-vate enterprise and had many financial problems. Often an especially good role was given to a female singer only because she had a friend who would clean her costume for free.

But my father really preferred stage managing to singing. As he grew old-er, he hated to make up his face and put on a costume, because he considered it unmanly. My parents always tried to find a double engagement at a subsi-dized theater, since that made their financial position more secure. One of the two would have to take a smaller salary—and that person was never the man of the house! My mother told me that a well-known Viennese agent once promised them such a double engagement in Braunschweig. My mother signed her contact as "first dramatic mezzo-soprano," but the contract for my father as "senior stage manager" was supposed to come later. It didn't, and my mother had to go to Braunschweig alone. However, first she ambushed the treacherous agent, thrashing him with her umbrella. Naturally, she was given a summons and had to pay a fine. In order to get another double engagement, she had to go back to Aachen, where she remained for many years as a singer while my father acted as stage manager and temporary opera director, as I've said before. But since the very young Herbert von Karajan was engaged there as general music director, the house was extremely interesting artistically.

For my parents, it was a very difficult time financially in spite of the dou-ble engagement. Aachen only had a seven-month season, so they had no income the other five months. That meant that my father had to look for summer theater jobs in the elegant spa cities, since the only festivals then were Salzburg and Bayreuth. The Salzburg Festival was very new, and today's festival halls were not yet built. When my father didn't find summer work, we always had severe financial problems during the five months without an income. Among my mother's old letters, I found a thank you note for a pair of stockings that I received as a gift. The note said that they were exactly the right thing because "Christa only has one pair"!

In elementary school, I wore the same dress every day. Once an old dress of my mother's was altered to fit me, and the teacher called me up to the front of the class to show the other students what a pretty new dress I had. I still remember a blue wool dress that became too short for me, so it was lengthened with a piece of material with a checkered pattern. When I was invited out, we added a starched white collar to this dress. Once one of my female classmates asked me if that was the only dress I owned! From that moment, I was clothes crazy. I only wanted to be friendly with children who were beautifully dressed, especially with the girl who owned a red coat with a white hood and zipper. One day a girlfriend of mine forgot her blue rain cape at my house, and I proudly wore it for a walk—in the bright sunshine. Then the war came, and once again I had nothing to wear. I desperately wished for beautiful clothes throughout my childhood.

I vaguely remember Kristallnacht in Aachen in 1938. I was only 10 years old, and as my mother and I walked to the theater, we could see the smashed shop windows on which "Jew" had been scrawled over and over and the burning synagogue. My mother was indignant, but at whom? It was just like today when wild demonstrators turn over cars and set them on fire, or when right-wing radicals destroy foreigners' apartments. The propaganda was so powerful that many families believed the lies of the Hitler regime, which claimed that "the people had been justifiably stirred up." Hitler himself seemed to stand outside of the turmoil, as if he were merely listening to the opinion "of the people."

Today it's almost impossible to understand those terrible times. News was strictly controlled by the Nazi propaganda machine and came to us only through the "Volksempfänger" or "people's radio" broadcasts. Foreign newspapers were unavailable, and many respected intellectuals described Kristallnacht as "the healthy wrath of the people against the controlling Jews." Minds were poisoned by such words, and the common sense of popular poets and thinkers vanished. My father was only afraid of losing his job. How do I judge him for that today?

My mother was a different case. One day, when she refused to join some political organization or other, I think it was the State Society of German Women (Bund Deutscher Frauen), the organizers who came to our house threatened her with the words, "Just be careful. You have a daughter!" But my mother was not a woman who could be intimidated, because she was very religious and had an unshakable trust in God. She still said no.

Meanwhile, my father became director of a charming little theater in the small city of Hanau, near Frankfurt. He produced three very good seasons there, and was particularly successful with Mozart operas, for which the small house was very well suited. My mother stopped singing completely during the war, because she didn't want to be separated from her husband and child, and also because she didn't want to sing in such a small house. In addition, she had developed the feared "hole" in her middle voice from which many mezzo-sopranos suffer.

In Aachen under Karajan, my mother often sang dramatic soprano parts, since she was a mezzo-soprano with a good upper register. But in between these roles, she always had to go back to singing true mezzo-soprano parts, and this constant changing from dramatic soprano to mezzo-soprano and back again was not good for her voice. When a female singer pushes the "chest voice," which is used for the lowest notes, higher into the middle range, the register change from chest voice to middle voice becomes very obvious. This can cause the notes in the middle register at the change to lose their ring and fade away to almost nothing, creating the dreaded "hole." Because of her experience, my mother always warned me about the dangers of singing dramatic soprano roles for the kind of voice that we both had.

In 1943, we moved to Giessen, where my father became the director of a larger theater. My parents were no longer unhappy about their financial situation, but they soon faced other, greater sorrows. One of the worst was the death of my brother Rudi, my father's younger son from his first marriage, who was killed on the Eastern Front.

My father's success as a theater director did not last long. Every day it was becoming more obvious that the war was nearing its end. There were daily air raids, which usually began at about 11 in the morning, so we children knew that there were certain classes we no longer had to study for. When the sirens sounded, some students went down into the air-raid cellar, but my girlfriend and I went to a neighboring cafe where the proprietor served us sweet, heavy southern wine in coffee cups. At the beginning of 1944, in this central German area, we didn't take the air raids very seriously. We saw the squadrons fly overhead on their way to other, more important targets.

Aside from the air raids, which we children saw as an exciting game, the war didn't disturb our lives very much. I was confirmed in the Protestant

Church, and later took dancing lessons, but my great passion then was horse-back riding. I was in love with both my riding instructor and my chemistry teacher, and because of my love for the latter, I actually considered studying chemistry at a university instead of becoming a singer.

Food was rationed with coupons, so everyone got a very small allotment of groceries, and, for Christmas, an eighth of a pound of coffee. We ate "Lohengrin Liverwurst," which we also referred to as "the gray mystery." This concoction was named after the romantic hero Lohengrin because he cautions his beloved Elsa never to ask his identity, nor where he comes from, with the famous words "Nie sollst du mich befragen" (You shall never ask!). We also had floating soap that never sank, but disappeared after only two washings.

Because everything could still be had "under the counter," household items were readily available. But money had little value, and bartering became popu-lar. I "sold" my most beloved baby doll for a pound of lard, and my father gave out "comp" tickets to the theater in exchange for meat. We constantly ate pota-toes with gravy and gravy with potatoes, and many young people took to calling their dates "roast-potato relationships" because they always ate so much of this ubiquitous vegetable—before! Most families took their valuables to the country because they were afraid their houses in town would be bombed. But my father, who didn't want to live without the beautiful things of life, refused to do this, and so we really lost everything when the bombings finally came.

Like all young women, I was in the State Society of German Girls, which was called the "Bund Deutscher Mädchen" (BDM) in German. At age 10, everyone joined the "Jungmädels," and at 14, the BDM itself. We were kept busy with school lessons on the one hand, and marches and home meetings on the other. We had a uniform: blue skirt, white blouse, white socks, brown shoes, black neckerchief with knotted leather slide, and a "Kletterweste," which was a vest made of a leather-like material that reached to the waist. We had to participate in parades where we were forced to stand for hours with our right arms raised in the Hitler salute, and we tried every possible position to relax our arms because they hurt so much.

We were sent out in the street with canisters to collect money for all kinds of war relief programs, and we also had to collect old rags and paper. Warnings were issued to the parents of girls who didn't collect enough. One time, the Hanau police chief, who always backed the Hitler regime, received a letter from the director of his daughter's school with just such a warning. The police chief answered indignantly that his daughter was preparing to take her university qualifying exam, not for a career as a ragpicker.

The home meetings and trips were fun for us children—if the group leader didn't care too much about political ideology. We sang songs accompanied by a guitar or flute, knitted mittens or socks for soldiers, and took overnight trips to youth hostels. We learned to make beds, and to cook over an open fire. We said "Heil Hitler" instead of "Guten Morgen" or "Guten Abend," and we didn't think much about it. In my parents' house, the political situation was not mentioned.

Today, I can't understand my parents' apolitical attitude. But since my father still had to provide for both his first family and my mother and me, his primary consideration was his profession, his income, and his position. In a provincial town, the tension was not as great as in the large cities. However, my mother told me later that she did wonder why she suddenly didn't see any of her Jewish friends around town, and the common belief was that they'd left the country. Probably people didn't want to investigate these stories because of their own great fear.

In the small city of Hanau, where we lived from 1940 to 1943, I saw some of our neighbors wearing the yellow Star of David on their coats. One neighbor in particular I often saw working in her garden with her daughter. This Jewish woman also shopped at our grocery store, and, while greetings were exchanged, there was no real contact. I was a little afraid of her and her daughter because they were so quiet and serious. In our little city, I never saw any aggression against our Jewish fellow residents, but there were small incidents. For example, in my class at school, there was a picture-perfect, blue-eyed blond girl whom I took with me once to sit in my father's box at the theater. The next day, my father received an extremely unpleasant letter from some Nazi party boss, asking if he knew that this girl was half-Jewish.

Before Hitler marched into Czechoslovakia, a monstrous propaganda machine began to run, spreading the idea that Germans living abroad were being massacred and that other atrocities were taking place. For example, we heard that the tongues of German children were being nailed to tables. Later, stories were told about German soldiers who smashed the heads of Czech children against walls to kill them. A normal person can't imagine such abominations, and doesn't want to believe they could happen. Once, in 1944, I remember my father coming home from the theater deeply upset, and he repeated to us what a female singer had told him. Her brother, on leave from the front, said that he saw Jews forced to dig a large hole, after which they were shot from behind so that they fell into it. My father could only say over and over, "That didn't happen. No, no, impossible."

We had no idea at all about concentration camps, mass murders, and gassings. I know that people can't imagine this today, but definitely my family didn't know. After the war, when there was no more censorship, we heard about everything for the first time. Silence during the war was the rule, even within the closest families. Large billboards everywhere warned, "Shh! The enemy is listening." Friends were afraid of friends, and fathers were afraid of their own children. For this reason, people didn't talk, even when they knew something. At the beginning of the war in 1939, we had a cleaning lady whose husband was sent to the Western Front as a civilian laborer. When we questioned him about what he'd been doing there, he said that he'd been looking for potato beetles, but really he'd been building the Western Wall.

Now and then, my parents listened secretly to the BBC German language news reports, and one time I created a problem for myself at school because of this. During "Current Events," I innocently reported that Strasbourg had fallen, which was the news that my parents had heard the night before. "Indeed, and where do you know that from?" asked my teacher. German news broadcasts always reported such setbacks much later—if at all. Since I'm now married to a man who was born in Alsace, I know what a difficult time they had because they were under French rule one day, and German the next. During the occupation, people were forbidden, under threat of severe punishment, to speak French or Alsatian. Even in school the students suddenly had to speak German instead of their mother tongue, French.

In 1944, all-out war came to Germany. All the schools and theaters closed, and everyone became part of the war effort. My father acted as streetcar conductor, which at least was better than working in a munitions factory. He looked very chic in his uniform, with freshly pressed creases in his trousers and his cap set at an angle. Every time he passed our house, he rang the bell on his streetcar and announced "Central Station—Cemetery," and this was a role he played, just as if he were in the theater.

Even we children were forced to become part of the war effort. Some of my girlfriends and I were ordered into the country to work on farms. The farmers were very skeptical about having city girls helping out, because we knew nothing at all about farming. We were assigned the lowliest jobs which were almost impossible to botch. I, for example, was assigned to clean potatoes that were stored in a damp, dark root cellar. This cellar was not a sparkling clean, tiled room like the cellars of today. It was a filthy pit, full of slippery, rotten, smelly potatoes. As I searched around for the elusive vegetables in the semi-darkness, I accidentally stuck my hands into all sorts of horrible things, such as nests from heaven-only-knows-what-kind of terrible creatures. At other times, I had to gather up pears that had fallen from giant pear trees, or clean the farmyard.

During this time, I lived in a house, which was about a 45-minute walk from the farm where I worked. On the way, I had to pass through a very dark forest. Of course, my operatic imagination conjured up all sorts of Alberichs and Samiels lurking behind the trees, and I was terrified. Since I desperately wanted to go home, I got the wonderful idea of complaining of a terrible pain. I found a sympathetic doctor, and he wrote me a note saying that I absolutely had to return to Giessen to be examined at the university clinic. Perhaps this was truly the start of my acting career.

So I joyfully packed my backpack and went home. After arriving at the train station, I took the first streetcar. And who was driving? My father, of course. He dropped me off right in front of our house, which was not a sched-uled stop, and rang the bell on his streetcar as loudly as he could.

Slowly, the air attacks on Germany increased. Members of my mother's family, who had been living in Berlin, were homeless because of the bombings there. My grandfather had been living with us for some time, and also my cousin from Cologne. Her parents had been burned to death in their cellar dur-ing an air raid while she was in a hospital with her leg in a cast. During her hospital stay, a bomb dropped just on the other side of the wall next to her bed.

At first, Giessen was apparently too unimportant to be bombed, so the city was quiet. But, then, on December 6, 1944, destiny caught up with us. We were celebrating St. Nicholas Eve when we saw what we then called "Christmas trees" in the sky. These were lights that marked the areas where bombs would be dropped. We said, "They are over us!" and ran into the base-ment. Oddly enough, the noise of the bomb blasts, the crashing down of the walls over our heads, and the terrible rushing sound of the fire from the incen-diary bombs made us neither frightened nor hysterical. Instead, we were para-lyzed, and stood emotionless, leaning against the cellar wall, resigned to our fate. When the bomb attack passed, we ran out of the basement as quickly as possible into the open, because we knew about the danger of being trapped by a fire, which might start in the coal that was stored there.

We lived on the edge of town, near the cemetery, where the houses stood separately, and were surrounded by gardens, so there was less danger of fire spreading quickly from one house to the next. Behind our house lay an immense field which was part of a game preserve. We fled to this field, taking only a trunk that had been stored in the basement. Because my father had refused to put any of our possessions away for safe keeping, everything of any value had been in the house itself, which was now burning out of control. The contents of the trunk were laughable and completely useless to us. It was full of my parents' theatrical paraphernalia—wigs, theater make-up, castanets, embroidered silk evening shoes, Spanish shawls, and even a crown.

So we sat on this trunk in the field, while a few horses from the neighboring game preserve ran around neighing in fear. What I saw then was so vivid that I've never forgotten it. Around us a drizzle of ash rained down, and we saw the entire town of Giessen in flames. The sight must have been as majestic as the one that surrounded Nero when all of Rome burned. We tried, of course, to rescue some things from our burning house, but this was impossible because of falling objects and collapsing walls. Our little one-story home was reduced to ashes and useless rubble. My father broke down completely, but only after "rescuing" two bottles of wine. My mother kept saying positive things like "most important of all, we have ourselves" over and over. And so we sat until dawn.

The fire burned all night, and the sky was as red as blood. In the distance, we could see many shadowy outlines of people carrying stretchers. I remember how odd everything sounded, as if the whole world was wrapped in cotton wool. All we heard was the muffled crackling of the slowly dying fires. All we saw was the ashen rain, and the soundless silhouettes of men, carrying the dead to the nearby cemetery.

Since we had just moved to Giessen in the fall of 1943, we didn't have any friends or acquaintances who might take us in—if they weren't bombed out themselves. What to do? Where to go? Suddenly my mother said, "We'll go to Bitsch." My father had never heard the name. Mrs. Bitsch, a talented painter, had studied voice with my mother for pleasure, and my mother liked her very much. But all my mother knew was that the Bitsches lived in the nearby village of Oppenrod. Luckily, we saw a handcart in a neighbor's yard, which we borrowed as transport for our idiotic trunk. Since my grandfather was 80 years old and my cousin was crippled, this cart was a godsend.

We soon found the road to Oppenrod and were on our way. For the first few miles, we walked on a highway full of refugees like ourselves, along with Red Cross workers and many other people. There was complete chaos, and, since it was December, the weather was very cold. Slowly, everything calmed down, and the landscape, as well as the villages we passed through, began to look normal. We entered a world that was untouched, and it seemed as if nothing extraordinary had happened. After a few hours of walking, we arrived at the tiny village of Oppenrod, which probably contained no more than 150 residents, and we asked around for the Bitsches. Mr. Bitsch was the district school teacher, and what we didn't know at the time was that he was using this obscure village as a hiding place, because his wife was half Jewish.

The teacher's house was near the school. We knocked at the door, exhausted and filthy with the soot that marked us as victims of the horrible event of the night before. The door was opened to us by Mrs. Bitsch, who immediately grasped the situation, and, without a moment's hesitation, said, "Come right in. My house is your house." I'll never forget that moment and this wonderful woman's completely natural goodness. My parents stayed in the teacher's house, while my grandfather, my cousin, and I were placed with different farmers.

On December 11, 1944, Giessen suffered another fire bombing, which this time we watched from a distance. It was only then that all the stored-up horror of what we had experienced poured out of us. We sobbed, and our whole bodies trembled uncontrollably. For years afterwards, I couldn't look at fire without suffering an overwhelming nervous reaction.

Except for the incredible love and goodwill of the Bitsch family, I passed an ice-cold winter in Oppenrod. The farmers with whom I lived were not at all gracious. They ate breakfast secretly, and told me every morning that I hadn't earned the right to eat because I hadn't done any work yet. The money we paid them was worthless, and they preferred valuables, but, of course, we didn't have any.

In March 1945, the end of the war was very near. We heard now and then of deserters, who were driven off or who were hiding in the countryside, because desertion was punishable by death. The roads were full of retreating soldiers, filthy, starving, dead tired, sick, and embittered. The defeated army came on foot, without proper shoes and sometimes with feet wrapped only in rags, crowded on trucks or in broken-down cars. In this mass of humanity, I suddenly recognized one of my girlfriends from school. In desperation at the end of the war, the government had created what was called the "Volkssturm" or "People's Army," and they drafted everybody. The boys (and even some of the girls) were given soldier's uniforms, but the girls usually went along as cooks. The chaos of these hectic times was like a drug for us young people, and we found everything very exciting. In his Christmas speech of 1944, Goebbels announced that there would be a triumphant conclusion to the war because of the use of a powerful new weapon. We made jokes about the "Christmas trees" in the sky, and Goebbels' Christmas fairy tale.

When the American troops marched in, we knew we were saved, and everyone cheered. Because we had nothing, we followed along after them, scavenging their discarded provisions—cans of corn, bits of chocolate, cigarette butts, and packages of instant coffee, something we had never seen before. The American soldiers were good-natured and didn't harm us. For the first time in my life, I saw a black man, and my three-year-old nephew was so frightened that he hid under a table.

Because my parents thought about moving back to Giessen, we traveled there a few times. In the hope of being given a place to live and citizenship papers, we had to fill out mountains of paperwork. Of course, there were the usual bureaucratic foul-ups. My father, a native-born Viennese, was declared a German citizen, and my mother and I, both Berliners, suddenly became Austrian. Thank God this didn't cause us to be separated, as happened to many families who received mixed-up papers.

One day we were assigned an undamaged but filthy apartment whose former occupant had fled to the country. In the apartment was a piano that soldiers had used as a toilet, and, of course, there was no flush! Cleaning it was a terrible experience, but we didn't care. We had a piano, and that was the important thing. My mother had already begun to give me voice lessons at the home of one of the farmers in Oppenrod, who had a piano in his "good" back room. This "Sunday parlor" was, of course, only heated one day a week, and never when we used it, so I was always cold. But we were now delighted with our new apartment and smelly piano, and happy to have a chance to make a new start.

Because of his former party membership, my father was forbidden employment until his denazification, but my mother provided for us fairly well by giving voice lessons. Studying singing was a wonderful way to forget the wretched way we lived, the ruins, the still-smoldering coal cellars, and the stink of ashes. People had plenty of money, but all of it was worthless. The black market blossomed. The lucky ones were those who had something to sell—carpets, silverware, dishes, jewelry—everything was exchanged for food. People made pilgrimages to the country for eggs, meat, lard, and other basics. Since we had nothing to sell or barter, I pilfered food wherever I could. Oddly enough, in those days when people had almost nothing, they were far more willing to share than today, when people have so much.

Thank heaven, the American soldiers needed entertainment! I was asked to sing Gershwin songs and other popular American tunes in the American Officers' Club. With tremendous dedication, I learned "Stormy Weather" and other songs in a language I could barely pronounce. But where to get a dress? Even though I'd gotten only passing grades in school in sewing, I'd knitted a turtleneck sweater during the winter in Oppenrod to keep myself warm, and I'd made a coat out of an old gray horse blanket. Although now I see myself as stupidly impetuous, I got a brainstorm and decided to sew an evening dress out of an old Nazi flag. They weren't useful for anything else anyway. I took the flag with its red background and white circle and black swastika, and made a red dress with black sleeves and white puffs. Since I was very slender, everything fit fine, and none of the soldiers ever guessed what I was wearing. For each performance, I was paid in cigarettes, which was the real currency at that time. As I recall, a carton of Camels was worth about $500 on the black market.

Naturally, I pinched everything in the former casino where I sang that wasn't nailed down—candles, matches, paper napkins, anything I could lay my hands on. Once I came home heavily laden with a small bucket. We opened it, and inside we found some sort of mysterious light brown grease. Carefully I stuck a finger in, smelled it, and tasted it. Amazing! It wasn't half bad, but what was it? Peanut butter—something totally unknown to us in the German provinces.

Doughnuts and instant coffee were the items I coveted most, and I could exchange a carton of cigarettes for a half pound of lard. Lard was a treasure, because we had no proper fat for cooking. We were forced to fry in rapeseed oil, which stinks terribly, or in castor oil, which has a predictable laxative effect. Now and then, we even browned roasted potatoes with ersatz coffee. The real coffee that we got "under the table" was usually green, and we had to roast it ourselves in a frying pan. The other residents of the house would smell it and ask, "Who is roasting coffee?" Conjuring up all our acting powers, we'd answer, "Well, I wonder. Certainly not us!" Black market trading was forbidden, and we didn't want to get caught.

Finally, after my father was denazified, he was again permitted to work, and he was restored to his position as director of the Giessen Municipal Theater. I received an apprentice contract from him, and he organized variety shows in which I took part. Thus my professional life began in the fall of 1945. I was only 17.

A Ten-Year Apprenticeship

When I received my first contract in 1945, my professional life as a singer truly began. I performed in variety shows, which took place everywhere in Giessen—in taverns (where the tables were moved aside), in small auditoriums, and even in factories. At these shows I usually sang "O schöne Jugendtage" (Oh, Lovely Days of Youth) from *Der Evangelimann*. This nostalgic aria was an odd choice for a 17-year-old girl, except that it fit my voice perfectly at the time, and one critic wrote that I was "ein junges Mädchen, das Alt singt" (literally, a young girl who sings old). I'd also sing "Mon cœur s'ouvre à ta voix" from *Samson et Dalila*, in German, of course. Unfortunately, that aria has a high note where I usually cracked, since I had scarcely any formal training, and sang only with a beautiful natural voice.

Finding toilets (if I dare use such an elegant term for the facilities usually available) at the variety show venues was often a problem. I remember once jumping out a window to avoid squeezing myself through a crowd of people with the same pressing need as myself. Another time, I asked to use the toilet during the intermission of a show, and was told that there was none in the dressing room area. I'd have to use the same one as the audience. So, in my evening gown, I stood in line patiently with everyone else, only to find that it was a pay toilet. With great embarrassment, I had to ask the other people in line for a ten-pfennig coin because, of course, I didn't have one with me. Such experiences taught me that the first thing I must ask before every concert—whether I am in Boston or Bologne—is, "Where is the. . .?"

As is normal for teenagers, I soon had a crush on someone. In my case, it was a comic dancer named Jochen. We sang and danced operetta duets, and we would snuggle up very close on the bus trips to the places where we performed. My father didn't care much—but my mother! When she found out, she never let me out of her sight for a minute. If I wanted to go to the movies with Jochen, she went along—and sat between us. But too much strictness doesn't always work, and I soon vowed to run away. Secretly I fled with my beloved Jochen to his parents' home in a nearby city so we could make love more easily—or so we thought. His parents were surprised, and not at all pleased, and we were so nervous that we never consummated our passion. Soon my mother arrived at the door with a police car and took me home. Naturally, I was very unhappy and angry with my parents, but my mother gave me daily voice lessons, and this distraction helped me get over my broken heart.

Before the end of the war, I had already taken a so-called performance-qualifying test, without which you couldn't get a theater engagement in Germany under the Hitler regime. My mother kept the note I wrote to her about it:

Frankfurt, during the exam
15 September 1944

Passed!
Dear Mama!

I left Hanau for Frankfurt at 7:30 in the morning with my friend Ria Steffen. After walking through the debris and ruins, we waited at the school until 9:15. I warmed up my voice, and the women who were already there told me that I would pass. I did pass the first time, and I sang Erda up to "Urwala Erda mahnt deinen Mut." The examiner said "Thank you, that's enough, you passed. May God be with you, my child," and I was the only one to finish so quickly. He asked no questions about theory. I said that papa was my father (naturally), and he asked for news of Muschi [Christa's sister Annemarie from her father's first marriage, also a singer at the time], and that was all. Tomorrow I must go to the civil service office. I don't want to do it, but I must. Brigitte has to go every day as a replacement to Darmstadt. She found herself in the middle of an ambush, had to climb over all the dead, etc. It must be horrible. Ria Steffen also passed the exam, and I asked if it went well. That's enough for today. Greetings to all.

Kisses, Krista (overjoyed)

P.S.: Telephone and telegraph are not always working.

But, after the war, passing the qualifying test meant nothing, and I was condemned to doing the variety shows. My mother didn't like my appearing in them at all, because she thought my talent deserved better. She wanted me to have "proper" engagements, and perform in different theaters throughout the country. But Germany was divided into several zones by the occupying armies, and it was not very easy to travel from one zone to another. Once I was engaged to sing in Göttingen, which was in the English zone, and we were living in Giessen, which was in the American zone. Since I didn't have the necessary papers, I had to get off the train when it arrived at the border, and I was ordered to return home—which, naturally, I didn't do. Railway travel in those days was not at all as it is today. The trains were over-crowded, and traveled very slowly because people stood on the steps, and even sat on the roofs, of the cars. But I was forced to leave the train, so I walked quickly across the countryside, without really knowing where I was, and crossed the military border without the necessary papers.

After the performance, I tried my luck on the train again with a borrowed pass. But the photo on the pass didn't look at all like me. While the military policeman was studying the pass more carefully in his guard booth, I bolted and resumed traveling on foot, through forest and field, to reach my home in the American zone.

My real career began at the Frankfurt Opera. The Manager and General Music Director Vondenhoff gave me a beginner's contract there with a monthly salary of 400 Reichsmarks (about $100). I was overjoyed to have a job that allowed me to leave home, as the relationship between my parents had become very tense. My father was depressed, his despair growing blacker every day. He was unhappy about the impoverished way we lived; he missed the beautiful things of life very much. His work didn't satisfy him, his theater was too damaged to be used, and he considered the variety shows a torment. Since he was almost sixty, he didn't believe he would ever again have a beautiful home. My mother, on the other hand, escaped into excessive optimism and piety, and both my parents looked as if they were starving. So my life at home was not a happy one, and, on top of everything else, there was my sad experience with Jochen. After that incident, I just wanted to leave home and be on my own.

So I moved to Frankfurt in September 1946, and found myself in a city that was almost totally destroyed. In the western part, where a few houses were still standing, I found a lovely large room to sublet in the house of a very nice woman who lived with her two children and her mother. The grandmother was wonderful to me, since she often stood at my door with a little kettle of something, and said, "Miss Ludwig, would you perhaps like to eat this? My babies don't want anymore, and, otherwise, the dog will get it." In my furnished room stood a splendid old Frankfurter armoire, and it was this piece of furniture that began my lifelong love for antique cabinets. I slept on neither a bed nor a sofa, but a mattress laid on top of a wooden board held off the floor by four bricks. There was also a corner sofa with a table, and an iron stove for heat. The only thing I owned in the room was a tiny electric hot plate. According to the rental contract, I had full kitchen privileges, but I was always corrected or criticized whenever I dared enter there. Today, I understand this perfectly. It's really not easy to share a kitchen with an 18-year-old girl.

So I depended on my hot plate for my meals. I would set a pot of potatoes on it before I went to rehearsal at 9:30, and when I came home for lunch at 1:30, they would just be done. Food was still rationed then, and the rations were supposed to last four weeks. As I generally ate up everything else in the first week, I almost always had only potatoes after that. Once, in a restaurant, I had sauerkraut *only* because I had no more ration coupons. It took me more than an hour to eat it, since it had just been pulled from the brine and was extremely sour. Thank God the stage hands at the Frankfurt Opera took pity and shared their bread soaked in drippings with me, which they received as a special allowance for doing heavy labor.

Since I was an opera addict from early childhood, I lived more or less in the opera and for the opera at this time. As the opera house had been completely destroyed in the bombings, we performed in a room at the Stock Exchange, where, of course, no business at all was conducted at the time. There was only one dressing room, about six feet by nine feet, for all women, solo singers, and solo dancers. Around the walls were make-up tables with chairs. Whenever the dresser was helping someone put on a costume, the rest of us had to sit down at the tables, or there wouldn't be enough room. But none of this mattered to me, because, as a beginner, I sang only very small roles. When my more mature colleagues got dressed, I thought to myself, "You'll never look like that," since I was very vain about my slim 18-year-old figure.

I had many new parts to learn because I couldn't use any of the ones I had memorized during my childhood—at least not yet. My very first role was sung from *behind* the stage, as I was the shepherd in the third act of *Tosca*. For my *onstage* debut, I was given a fairly large role, Prince Orlofsky in *Die Fledermaus*. Before the first rehearsal, the stage director said to me that the first thing I had to learn was how to walk properly on stage, and he was quite amazed to see that my stage movements were already completely natural since I'd gained so much experience in my parents' opera school. Walking around on stage was simple and natural to me, for I had no inhibitions at all. It was much more difficult for me to walk through a restaurant—there, I had inhibitions.

Because my training period had been so short, I totally forgot one of the most important rules of singing opera: vocal technique must be seamlessly combined with acting technique. The voice must always be supported by a column of air. When he taught, my father always used the example of a ping-pong ball dancing on a column of water, like the fountains in the gardens at the Hellbrunn Castle near Salzburg. As long as the column of water is strong and high, the ping-pong ball dances beautifully. But if the pressure drops, so does the ball. When a singer "drops the ball," the result is a very unpleasant break in the sound. I moved well on stage, I didn't make any musical mistakes, and I could even deliver dialogue very well. But when I had to sing even a single high note, my voice simply collapsed. The audience made an audible "ah," and I was extremely embarrassed. Because of this, I grew very nervous onstage, and the problem was that I simply hadn't learned enough technique yet. I visited my mother in Giessen for lessons whenever possible, or she came to teach me in Frankfurt where I managed, in spite of my very limited salary, to have the luxury of a rented grand piano. Because I had the piano, I could study roles myself, and besides, it really looked good in my room. I have to admit that I probably inherited the desire to be surrounded by beautiful things from my father. To this day, I still hate ugly hotel rooms.

During those early years at the opera, I played all the smallest parts. One time I made a count, and realized that I had been in 250 performances in 10 months. Included in these performances were some operetta roles, and once I even played an angel in a Christmas pageant. Old people, young people, both sexes—I played everything. Oh yes, one day my old beau Jochen suddenly came to visit me. But I had no time for him; he was ancient history to me. My life was dedicated completely to opera, with almost a religious fervor. Sometimes, I was saddened when girlfriends from my school days, who were going to the university in Frankfurt, would stop by and tell me about parties and dances and ask me to go with them. But I always had either rehearsals or performances. And so began my long renunciation of normal life and normal friendships.

Perhaps the best thing that happened for my voice at this time was the divorce of my parents. It allowed my mother to visit me more often and, eventually, to move in with me in Frankfurt. But the divorce turned me against my father completely (and, unfortunately, against men in general for awhile), because he chose to abandon my mother at a time when she had nothing left. She was no longer young, she could no longer sing to support herself, and she was no longer attractive. He abandoned her to marry a former pupil of his who was 28 years younger than himself . My new "stepmother" had a very beautiful voice, and my father gave her a contract at the theater where he was the director. To add insult to injury, he engaged her to sing all the roles that my mother sang when she was younger. And what seemed worst of all at the time: this woman's family home was never bombed, and her parents owned a grocery store! A chance for a better life—that was something my father couldn't resist. Today I understand what my father did. He was 60 years old, and hoped to rejuvenate himself. How many men, when they feel themselves growing older, marry girls the same age as their own daughters? Understand, yes. Approve, never!

My mother was too proud to ask for alimony, so we lived on her income as a voice teacher, and on my small wages. At that time in Frankfurt, barter and the black market still flourished, and the stores were almost entirely empty. You couldn't buy anything with money, not even "under the table," and everything was even more expensive than it had been during the war. A pound of lard now cost 1200 marks (three months of my salary), a loaf of bread 10 marks (almost a day's wages for me).

I saved most of my salary for wood, since a little over half a cord cost 2000 marks (five month's wages!). I stacked the precious stuff in the corner behind the sofa, and since it came only in large pieces, I had to break them up myself with an ax. My large northern room was fiercely cold in winter, and I always went to bed fully dressed without washing. I only made a quick "lick and a promise" wash in ice-cold water at my sink in the morning. My neck always stayed dirty because I refused to remove my turtleneck sweater. I sat by the stove in my homemade horse-blanket coat, and firmly laid another piece of wood on the fire. My front side was warm, but my backside was nearly frozen. I never got over colds, and in the little diary I kept then, which I still have, I repeatedly wrote, "Sniffle, Sniffle!" In order to have something of value, I would knit gloves or socks and barter them with friends. Mittens were relatively easy, but gloves with fingers were extremely intricate, as were the heels in stockings. But making these items gave me something to trade. For a pair of stockings, I could get a quarter pound of lard.

My mother moved into my room in Frankfurt shortly after her divorce, and we lived together in that one room. In a way this was good for me, because it gave my life a certain routine, and, best of all, daily voice lessons with an experienced teacher. My mother also went with me to all important rehearsals, and she attended every performance. She criticized me and praised me, and, in short, she was the only person whose opinion I could really trust. She explained to me what I could accomplish and urged me to work harder, perhaps because of her own frustrated ambitions. She made it clear to me that she felt that I'd inherited a great deal of natural talent, and that it was my duty to make good use of it.

Later in life, I had doubts that living only to sing had been worthwhile, and I sometimes accused my mother—unjustly, I now think—of encouraging me to concentrate so much on my profession that I missed out on a great deal in my private life. But, back in that ice-cold room in Frankfurt, when we had almost nothing, the sacrifice necessary to build a voice, earn money with it, and really try to accomplish something seemed worth it without question.

At the opera, I finally was given a larger role, and, at the tender age of 18,

I sang Ulrica in Verdi's *Un Ballo in Maschera*. But only once. I must have been terrible, since I played the part of the old gypsy woman with ferocious intensity—and, as usual, forgot completely about vocal technique. My voice broke on all the high notes, and I was quickly put back into the tiniest roles. But the director of classical music at the local radio station had his eye on me. Since he was also a pianist, he invited me to sing lieder with him on the radio. He accompanied me in Dvořák's *Zigeunerlieder*, which was my radio debut. So, from the very beginning of my career, I did concert and recital work in addition to my opera engagements. If I couldn't sing the big roles at the opera because I was too young, I could succeed very well in concerts, because I didn't have the added strain and distraction of acting a role. I got a lot of engagements singing lieder, and even orchestral works, because my voice was beautiful, and had its own special character.

In the currency reform of 1948, 100 Reichsmarks (RM) suddenly became 10 Deutschmarks (DM). In the first week after the reform, everyone received 40 DM instead of "normal" money as a start. In this same week, I sang two or three concerts, and, since RM fees now became DM fees, I received about 150 to 200 DM per concert. Suddenly I felt rich! The shops, which the day before the reform had nothing in their display windows, were suddenly overflowing with food, clothing, shoes, hats, handbags—everything anyone could wish for. It was like a miracle, and I hardly knew what to buy first. For the first time in my life, I could, as the Americans say, "shop 'til I dropped." I bought things not only for myself but also for all my girlfriends and, naturally, for my mother. I was ecstatic. I bought myself mountains of material to sew my own daytime clothes and new evening dresses for my concerts. Since I was tall and thin, everything fit me. I sat on top of the piano, cut the fabric with my shears according to my best judgment, and sewed everything by hand. Somehow everything fit! Since I knew no one would see the inside of my outfits, I didn't care how sloppily I sewed them—outside, "Ooh!" but inside, "Pooh!" My obsession with clothes, which started in my school days when I was frustrated by having only one dress to wear, could now be satisfied.

In addition to my obsession with clothes, I also love to buy new houses and apartments. Perhaps this obsession came from the homelessness my family suffered during the war after the bombings when my greatest wish, next to having beautiful new clothes, was to have a beautiful house and garden. Even today, I still dream of houses with large gorgeous rooms. Throughout my career, I've owned many beautiful houses and apartments, but I've never really lived in them, except for a few days between engagements. Instead, I've almost always lived a homeless gypsy life in hotels all over the world.

Early in my career, I was often asked to sing contemporary music. Only established singers were asked to sing the great classic works, but I was much sought after to perform works by Liebermann, Boulez, Nono, and others. New and experimental music, which had been banned under Hitler as decadent art, could now be performed, and there was a big demand for concerts of this kind of music to make up for lost time. Darmstadt and Donaueschingen were important centers to which all the great contemporary composers traveled, and I was always singing there. I learned the music of composers like Egk, Fortner, and Maderna easily, I sang it beautifully, and I didn't have to be paid very much. In this way I became known to the important critics of the day, well before I made a name for myself as an opera singer.

My opera career developed very slowly. It wasn't until 1950, when I was 22 years old, that I was finally entrusted with the role of Octavian in *Der Rosenkavalier*. But it was still too soon. After the second act, I actually prayed that an earthquake would come and destroy the theater. I was overwhelmed. I totally forgot my vocal technique while I was acting, and I cracked on all the high notes. I was absolutely terrible, and, as a result, I went back, like a good girl, to the smaller part of Annina.

My upper register always caused me enormous difficulties. My natural range was narrow, and stopped at F in the middle register. It took me a year of hard work to develop each additional half-note. But one good thing resulted from these difficulties with my top. I had so much to learn technically that I couldn't use my natural voice, and so I couldn't just sing without thinking. I always had to be aware of what I did. Mezzo-sopranos have it especially difficult, I think. We really have three different voices: the low or so-called chest voice, the middle voice, and the high or head voice. These three voices must flow together smoothly and seamlessly, and there must be no "hole" like my mother developed from alternating mezzo-soprano and dramatic soprano roles. Even the chest voice must have the overtones of the head voice, which is not to be confused with falsetto, a kind of "fake" voice. And one must occasionally carry the richness of the middle voice into the higher range. A singer must take all these technical details and develop a sound Singer-Intuition. The details must sink in so deeply that they become instinct.

During this time, I had to learn the soprano part of Siebel in Gounod's *Faust*, a part that was much too high for me. Siebel has a very high note where, of course, I always cracked, and after which the audience (as usual) always made its audible "ah." Because of this, my mother advised me to go to the director of the theater, and tell him that I didn't want to sing this part anymore. His response? "But Miss Ludwig, you have plenty of time to develop yourself while you're here. And, besides, you have such pretty legs!" (Siebel wore a medieval doublet and tights.) So I continued to "develop" myself in the role of Siebel. I sang, I cracked, and I became increasingly nervous on stage. When one newspaper critic wrote, "whether she will succeed in controlling her faltering top notes or not is questionable," I was crushed, but my mother was indignant and said, "He doesn't know anything. Of course you will learn the top. You're just too young yet." Because of my constant and pervasive fear that I wouldn't eventually learn to overcome my problems, I lost all interest in leading the life of a normal 19 year old girl.

Since it was impossible for me to continue to live with my mother in one room, I looked for new lodgings with two rooms and kitchen privileges, but still as a sublet. Postwar rebuilding had begun, but an apartment of our own was out of the question, especially because we had no furniture or bedding. During the years between 1948 and 1954, whenever I'd get a concert booking outside of Frankfurt, I'd wonder where I'd get the money for the train tickets. Thank God I had a well-to-do aunt in Frankfurt who always lent it to me. My concert fees were not high, and I usually made just about the cost of two pairs of shoes.

I stayed in the cheapest boardinghouses or in private homes, and looked with longing at the great hotels that were still standing. I swore that I would stay in them someday. I was known as a "young talent with a beautiful voice," but my mother wasn't satisfied with that, because she felt that I didn't work hard enough on developing myself. I just sang, and she told me that there was more to it than just singing. I had to put more into my voice than mere sound, especially when I sang lieder. I had to put in my soul. It's simple to say, and I understood what she meant, but doing it was another matter altogether. It would take me many years to master this art.

My mother gave me some tricks to use to make my singing more expressive while I was learning. I had to sing my consonants very distinctly, three M's or five F's instead of one. For example, in order to make the M in "milde" really sound mild, I would have to hum the initial M slightly, and delay the vowel sound a little. Or to make "feindlich" really sound hostile, I had to begin with lots of F's. These little tricks would make my diction clearer, and fool the audience into believing that I'd really grasped the meaning of the text, even though I'd only absorbed it superficially. Real inner development eluded me. When I remember how young Grace Bumbry was when she first sang Venus at Bayreuth, I am amazed. Oh God, at that age I was still an absolute bumpkin!

Slowly we began to buy furniture for our two rooms after my mother received a payment of 5000 DM (about $1000 today) as compensation for the total destruction of her home during the bombings. It was enough to buy two used armchairs, some drapes (which I still had until recently) and some ugly, thick net curtains. We sat admiring these things, astonished by our sudden good fortune. Most important of all, we bought a grand piano, which, as we soon discovered, came to us with a very strange ailment. Of course, we had looked for a piano at the best price we could find, and we saw a classified ad in the newspaper that read: "Blüthner piano, privately owned, good condition." It had been stored on a farm during the bombings, and we were assured that it was in perfect shape. And it certainly looked it. The piano was brown and shiny, and had a beautiful tone.

Everything was fine, until we were awakened in the middle of the night by something that sounded like ghostly harp playing. At first, we had no idea what the source of these strange and delicate sounds was, but then we noticed that they were coming from the piano. We opened the lid, and several terrified mice sprang out at us—a mother with her children. The mother had made a little nest between the strings, and now that they had been disturbed, the terrified mice ran around the room, until they somehow found a hole in the wall and vanished. This didn't surprise us, since the shocks from the bombings had left cracks and holes everywhere.

The mouse family made our lives very difficult, since their favorite activity was roaming around in our kitchen cabinets. Finally, we couldn't take it any longer, and we resolved to get rid of our annoying guests. We set up a mousetrap, offering a precious bit of bacon as bait. In the morning, the bacon was gone, but the trap wasn't sprung, since the baby mice simply weren't heavy enough to trip it. We continued to bait the trap (and only succeeded in feeding our roommates very well) until one night the trap snapped shut. We turned on the light, and saw a terrible sight: one of the poor mice had lost its tiny leg in the trap. With its three remaining legs, it was dragging itself slowly, and with enormous effort, across the floor towards a hole in the wall. The injured mouse left behind a delicate trail of blood, while it looked at us accusingly with eyes that seemed ripped wide open with pain until it disappeared into the wall. I shall never forget that pathetic sight, and since that time, I've been acutely aware of the suffering that we humans, who consider ourselves lords over all the earth, inflict on animals of all sizes and species. We forget that we are all one—we all live as a part of nature and we all share the same world. And I myself have never again been able to set another mousetrap.

Things got progressively better at the opera. The theater was rebuilt in order to give us a new home, and, with light hearts, we left the Stock Exchange and the terrible 6-by-9 foot dressing room. The opera management also now had much more money to spend on its productions. But it has always been true that spending a lot of money on lavish productions is no substitute for imagination. At that time, there was a very good theater director based in Darmstadt, Harro Dicks, who had staged very exciting productions in the Stock Exchange. He later developed the famous Darmstadt style, which was highly praised as a synthesis of music, text, and movement. Productions in this style became much more popular than traditional productions, where singers are interchangeable, and one singer could just drop into a role in a production today, and another tomorrow. Also in Darmstadt at this time was Gustav Rudolf Sellner, who managed the temporary theater in the Orangerie. He became one of the most important theater managers in Germany, and later led the Deutsche Oper Berlin during a high point in its distinguished history.

Dicks convinced me to come and work with him in Darmstadt. He valued my talent, and wanted to set me on the right path. Since singers make great careers as much by using their heads as by using their voices, I decided, with my mother's full support, to work with Dicks. We continued to live in Frankfurt, since Darmstadt was only an hour away by train, and I began a kind of pendular existence. To swing into Darmstadt for rehearsal at 10 in the morning, I'd have to catch the 7:30 train, and follow it with a half-hour's walk to the theater. After work, I'd "swing" back into Frankfurt again.

From Harro Dicks, I learned one of the most important lessons about singing on stage—concentration. He taught me to forget everything that was going on around me, as if I were in a trance. Since my singing technique was now much stronger, I could hold the audience's attention, at least for part of the time I was onstage, but he said I must concentrate so hard that the audience's attention never wavered. This is the essence of the performer's art. If you can't hold the audience, you can never hope to reach their hearts. This is also the secret of a great recitalist. You can never break the tension during the prelude and postlude of a song. You can't move a leg or even raise your shoulders when you inhale on stage. This is something you are never supposed to do anyway, because you are not supposed to look as if you are singing. Typical "singing" gestures, such as raising your arms to heaven while you are "reaching" for a high note during an opera aria, were strictly forbidden by Harro Dicks, and by all good stage directors.

I also learned to observe my own movements and gestures in daily life, and those of others. I studied how someone opens a door, comes through, and closes it. I studied exactly how people reacted to bad news, and what they did when they were frightened. I studied how inhibited or self-conscious people sit, and what gregarious people do. I observed a thousand such details so that I could mimic them on stage and master the naturalistic acting style that was in fashion then. I also had to learn the kind of stylization that Dicks taught.

Stylized movements only suggest normal human behavior, and an occasional grand gesture stands out like a mountain among hills. Harro Dicks was a master of such techniques.

Since the Orangerie where I performed in Darmstadt was a small room, I had to make sure that every tiny movement would command the audience's attention. Unfortunately, because of the size of the room, I couldn't properly expand my voice and develop it. So my mother championed the idea that I should be engaged at a proper opera house with a very good conductor. In Darmstadt, I sang Eboli in Verdi's *Don Carlos*, Giulietta in Offenbach's *The Tales of Hoffmann*, as well as the composer in the opera *Ariadne auf Naxos* by Richard Strauss, all with success, so it was obvious that my technique, along with my top, had become much more secure. But because I still had to be careful not to overextend myself, I passed up financially attractive contracts where I would have been expected to sing heavier roles, such as Ortrud in Wagner's *Lohengrin*, and continued to search further for the right situation.

My mother wisely selected Hanover, which at that time was administered by the outstanding opera conductor and general music director Johannes Schüler, who earlier had conducted in Berlin. Marie in Alban Berg's *Wozzeck* was planned as my debut role, but before I began to sing in Hanover, I received one of the famous yellow letters from the important German agent, Ballhausen. He wrote that Dr. Karl Böhm, the new director of the reconstructed Vienna State Opera, was looking for a young Elisabeth Höngen. Ballhausen had thought of me, and asked if I was ready to sing for Böhm. I really didn't want to do it!

Vienna was notorious as a hotbed of all sorts of intrigues, and I felt that I was too young and inexperienced at 26 to survive there. Furthermore, I was engaged to be married to a doctor (he was always at the hospital, so neither of us had much time for a private life), and I had no intention of going far away. I even considered, at that time, giving up my singing career and having a large family instead (my fiancé was a gynecologist). But I wanted to get a variety of opinions before I made a final decision, so I asked a few people high up in musical circles what I should do. Their advice universally was to "go for it." So I took heart, and walked nervously up the steps of the Hotel Frankfurter Hof, where Böhm was staying.

"So, my dear, you want to audition with me for Vienna."

"No, no, really I don't. I think I'm too young and unprepared."

"Well, you must let me be the judge of that. Sing for me tomorrow."

So I packed up my music for various arias, all from heavy warhorse roles like Amneris and Azucena. When I finished singing, Böhm said thoughtfully, "Uh-huh, you still need to work on your top, but in my house we'll start you as Cherubino."

Although I auditioned for Böhm in the winter of 1953/54, I wasn't free to go to Vienna until the summer of 1955, because first I had to fulfill my contract at Hanover. I was called to audition for Böhm twice more, once for the role of the Composer in *Ariadne auf Naxos* at the Salzburg Festival, and again for Cherubino in *Le Nozze di Figaro*, which I had never sung. In Frankfurt, when I was just starting out, I always sang old Marcellina, Figaro's mother, and, when I would hug the fatter and obviously much older Figaro and sing "Figlio amato (Beloved son)," the whole audience would roar with laughter. My round face made it very difficult for me to look old, even with the heaviest makeup. When I sang Orestes's old nurse in *Das Leben des Orest* by Ernst Krenek, a special tulle mask was made, painted to make me look old. There were holes cut for my eyes, but, since the nurse is supposed to be blind, heavy gray bushy eyebrows were attached to cover the holes. The mouth area was open, so I could sing. The result was that my chin looked twenty, while the rest of me looked seventy. And, of course, I didn't sound very much like an old nurse either.

When I auditioned for the Composer with Böhm, I had to fly from Hanover to Berlin, which, in those days, was a blockaded city. I hoped that my return flight would be paid for, but nothing of the kind occurred. The little money I had would only buy me a railway ticket, and shortly after my departure from the station in Berlin, the border guard on the train looked over my papers and saw that I had traveled to Berlin by plane. In those days, the rule was that if you went somewhere by plane, you had to return by plane, so I had to fly. I was put off at the next station and had to wait five or six hours for the next train back to Berlin. When I arrived again, I still, of course, didn't have enough money for the return flight. Thank God I at least had enough money to telephone my mother, who explained my plight to the opera management in Hanover, and they arranged for my return flight.

My audition for Cherubino was in Salzburg, and included the stage director for the production, Oskar Fritz Schuh. I felt faint from nervousness, and I had good reason to be afraid. The two arias were difficult for me, I didn't have much experience performing in the Mozartean style, and I didn't know Italian. Furthermore, I was called for the audition in the middle of my vacation, and I wasn't properly prepared vocally. Since my mother always told me that when I sing for men, I should dress attractively, since they see first and hear second, I put on a very pretty dress with a generous décolletage. I added a pair of high-heeled sandals to show off my legs (remember Siebel!) and proceeded to the festival hall. There I encountered Böhm immediately, since punctuality was one of his many virtues. I coquettishly admitted to him how nervous I was, to which he said, "But why, dear child? You're already hired."

Vienna (Finally!)

And so came the big move from Hanover to Vienna. In spite of all our money troubles my mother and I had a three-room apartment all to ourselves in Hanover. What progress! Before we left, we bought some more furniture to take with us to Vienna, along with our now mouse-less grand piano. But we didn't have enough furniture to fill an empty apartment, so we rented a furnished one with the help of Professor Wobisch, the first chair trumpet and, at that time, member of the board of directors of the Vienna Philharmonic. We easily fit our small collection of household treasures into our new living space. I had a three-year contract as a soloist which didn't specify my vocal classification, and that was something new for me.

A newly engaged singer in Vienna couldn't lay claim to any particular role, and I didn't have one of the larger salaries, as had been the case in Hanover. As a result, we had to worry about money again. So, after my first very good review, I went to the general secretary, Dr. Egon Seefehlner, and told him that I was really hard up. He looked into the situation, and raised my wages before the end of the first year of my contract. Later, I experienced two other generous pay raises. Once in Wiesbaden I sang a gala performance of *Der Rosenkavalier*, and received twice the fee I'd asked for! Later, at the Metropolitan Opera in New York, Sir Rudolf Bing told my first husband, Walter Berry, and me that he thought we were underpaid, so he doubled our fees after our great success in "FroSch" (a.k.a. *Die Frau ohne Schatten*).

When I came to Vienna, I had very little experience singing major roles, even though I'd technically been singing for a decade. I'd done one Amneris in Hanover (without rehearsals), Eboli in Darmstadt (with rehearsals), the Wozzeck Marie in Hanover (with rehearsals), Brangäne (again without rehearsals), and my first Ulrica at 18 (without rehearsals). I was simply tossed into the great sea of the Vienna State Opera and expected to swim. Fortunately, in such must-swim situations, I usually manage to stay afloat, and my first Eboli and my first Amneris in Vienna were successes. As is customary at the State Opera, I had one stage rehearsal for each role, and, in the case of Amneris, an orchestral rehearsal with Karl Böhm, which went well. For this rehearsal the orchestra played only the parts of the opera where Amneris has to sing, and I sang the part with no Aida and no Radames in sight. Altogether, the rehearsal lasted about an hour.

I was now the right age for the parts I was performing. Eboli, Amneris, and the Wozzeck Marie are all in their late twenties or early thirties, so finally I didn't have to disguise myself with heavy makeup or tulle masks. I first sang Ortrud when I was 33, and I didn't need to think very much about the story. My figure, the music, and my costume all worked in my favor. And, of course, there was also a little bit of talent. But, in spite of everything going my way, I had terrible stage fright. I could only sing Dorabella in Così fan tutte with ease, because that part suited both my voice and my personality perfectly. Many other roles made me very nervous, because each one had a trouble spot in it for me to worry about. Because my vocal cords are very pliable and also small and delicate, they are especially vulnerable to any strain. Still, I always sang every role without holding back. Once Vladarski, the impresario, came back-stage after a performance of Aida and said, "My dear Miss Ludwig, what you are giving to this role shouldn't be seen on stage until you are making at least ten or twenty thousand a night, not ten thousand a month." To which I answered, "I can't do otherwise." On stage, I always gave everything, and I think I was a convincing singing actress because I never did hold back.

With my first Cherubino in the Redoutensaal, I became part of the famous Mozart ensemble in Vienna, which included Irmgard Seefried, Sena Jurinac, Paul Schöffler, and Erich Kunz. I especially remember how Paul Schöffler liked to play Almaviva both on stage and off. He invited me to din-ner and ordered a very sweet southern wine. When I expressed surprise at his choice, he said, laughing, "That way, things progress faster." But a man can't make progress with me that way, and so, when he invited me to "go fishing" the next day, I politely declined and went out and bought myself a dog.

As I was a newcomer, or "Pifkinesin," as Germans are called in Vienna, I was made to feel that I was a foreigner in this homogeneous ensemble with its special, refined Mozart style, even though the public and most of the critics immediately liked me. On top of everything else, I didn't like singing the role of Cherubino. Trained in Darmstadt in a modern style, I found the way I was expected to play the role absolutely too superficial. To present Cherubino as only a rococo, demimondain charmer seemed to me to show too little of the real character of this poor boy. He had problems that were too obvious for me to play him as merely comic and cute.

What fascinated me was the musical experience. The first time I heard the Vienna Philharmonic's sound and the beauty and elegance of its phrasing, I felt that I was hearing perfection, conveyed in utter simplicity. In Germany, all the performances were thoroughly rehearsed, and I felt that everything was definitely under rehearsed in Vienna. Yet the performances were of the highest quality, and couldn't compare with anything that I'd heard in the past. However, I was deeply disappointed by the stereotyped stage movement of the singers. Such formula acting was forbidden in Darmstadt, and it was only Vienna's complete musical superiority that made me forgive what I considered serious dramatic deficiencies. I experienced charismatic singing personalities for the first time, and I gradually became Viennese, not by nature but by nurture. In many ways, I became more Viennese than the Viennese, and I came to feel perfectly at home in my adopted city. I found new ears to hear and new eyes to see, critically, but with love.

I began to appreciate the Viennese way of life, often slandered and very difficult to understand, especially if one can't distinguish the subtleties of language inflection so as to know, for example, whether a "yes" is really a "yes," or if it's a "no" or a "maybe." My upbringing had been very black and white, but now I was finally learning to see the gray in things, which makes life far more interesting. I came to love the subtleties and to understand them, just as I learned to love the toughest critics in all the world, the Viennese public. People noticed that I was happy in Vienna, and had decided to make it my home. And Vienna returned my love. However, my fiancé, as a German doctor, couldn't establish himself in Vienna, so we broke our engagement, and he went back home.

When I made my first phonograph record in Hanover, it was as part of the quintet "Noch ein Weilchen, Marie" from *The Bartered Bride*. At the recording session, I met Erna Berger and Rudolf Schock, who sang a duet from the opera. When I told them that I'd been hired in Vienna, Schock said, "Then nothing stands in the way of your international career." I didn't know at first what he meant. "When you debut in Vienna," he explained, "you'll be introduced everywhere." And that's exactly what happened.

Singing Around
the World

"My" Opera Houses

Because I sang mainly in four opera houses, I consider them "my" opera houses: the Vienna State Opera, the Deutsche Oper Berlin, the Paris Opera, and the Metropolitan in New York. I'm often asked which of these houses I liked best, and without trying to be diplomatic, I say that I liked all of them equally. But I must admit that I preferred Vienna and the Met, because I sang most often in those two houses.

Vienna

After many years of singing in small provincial houses like Frankfurt, Darmstadt, and Hanover, I felt that the Vienna State Opera was my first "real" opera house. When I made my debut, the house had just been rebuilt, and it shone brilliantly in red and gold, rededicated to the curious genre called opera, just as it had been for more than a hundred years before the war.

I remember my very first performance at the State Opera as Octavian in *Rosenkavalier* on December 26, 1955. At the beginning of the second act, in brilliant white spotlights, I appeared beautifully dressed with a white wig in a richly embroidered white silk costume. With the silver rose in my hand, I hesitantly sang the words "Mir ist die Ehre widerfahren," accompanied by the magical, silvery sound of the music of Richard Strauss. It was then that I first realized what it was like to sing in a huge, grand opera house, and I truly felt that singing in such a place was a great honor. I was overwhelmed with reverence and pride. Here I was, permitted to sing in the same place as the most celebrated singers of the past, singers whom my parents had always spoken of with the utmost admiration: Maria Jeritza, Rosette Anday, Lotte Lehmann, Leo Slezak, Alfred Piccaver, and many, many others.

But as I stood there, I also knew that I had to prove myself in front of the Viennese public, something every singer fears. And, worst of all, I had to be judged by the highly critical listeners in the standing room places. But I loved the house immediately, from the moment that I walked through the stage door for the first time. "Here you'll be able to sing well," I thought. I breathed more freely there, and my spirits lifted. Perhaps this sounds like an exaggeration, but it isn't. That's exactly how I felt. For me, the Vienna State Opera lives, and isn't a temple for a dead muse, even though some people feel that way. And the audience seems to feel as I do since they dress festively when they go to their opera house, which makes it seem that they want to show that they are worthy, too.

But the most important thing to me at the Vienna State Opera is what is in the pit—the Vienna Philharmonic, an orchestra I sincerely admire. But "pit" is definitely the wrong word, since in Vienna the Herr Professors in the orchestra don't want to be heard only, but also seen, and they want to be able to follow the action on the stage themselves. So the orchestra pit in Vienna is not the kind that you would normally find in an opera house, and it's certainly not covered as it is in Bayreuth. The musicians sit only a little bit lower than the audience, and because of this, the sound of the orchestra in the opera house is unique. The audience can actually see the individual musicians play. For us singers on the stage, it's a joy to hear the wonderful sound, which comes in such a huge wave to our ears that we have a tendency, until we've gotten used to the unique setup, to try to drown it out. That is definitely the wrong thing to do, because the acoustics are excellent, and a singer can be heard easily by the audience—when the conductor tells the orchestral players that they must listen to the singers. (More than anyone else, Karajan used to do this.) If the orchestra doesn't listen, we poor people on the stage can easily be covered by the sound of the huge number of players required for a Richard Strauss or Wagnerian opera. One human voice versus one hundred instruments. It's not fair! But a singer making music together with one hundred musicians—that is a wonderful collaboration.

Everyone who works at the Vienna State Opera is first-class, from stagehands to dressers, and everybody is friendly and helpful. Their ways are what we might call "southern" in Europe: they prefer to improvise and not do things too rigidly. But this "laissez-faire" or "mañana" attitude, off-putting though it sometimes seems to foreign stage directors, is only on the surface. The Vienna Opera has its own working style, which the "Zug'rasten" (foreigners) often don't understand. For example, singers sometimes don't appear at rehearsals, yet they give a better performance than many singers at other opera houses who rehearse a lot. Every position in this big opera company is filled perfectly, and every person is a master of his or her craft.

It was always a pleasure for me to return to Vienna after a longer period of making guest appearances in other opera houses, because the atmosphere in Vienna is so friendly and charming; for example, the dressers wait after the performance until a singer is fully dressed, instead of disappearing quickly once they have the costume in hand with an "I guess you don't need me anymore." The backstage crew is also a very knowledgeable audience, and a "Schön war's" (It was beautiful) from them means a lot. Also, the rehearsal rooms are wonderful, with huge windows that look out on the Ringstrasse. The coaches, who often practice with the singers up to six hours a day, are very relaxed. In short, the Vienna State Opera is a dream place to work.

I should mention the Vienna State Opera's version of what we Austrians call the "Beamtenlaufbahn," the hallways and offices of the management. These are also located high up in the opera house and also have huge windows, through which light floods in. The surroundings aren't the most important thing, but rather the work of keeping the wasp's nest, which an opera company is, under administrative control. The offices open on a long hallway. At the beginning are the offices of the people who oversee day-to-day operations, and at the end is the office of the director. And here I come to the most awkward subject of all: the position of "artistic director" at the Vienna State Opera.

When I was first hired in Vienna, a colleague warned me immediately: "The main thing is to outlast all artistic directors." Back then, as a newcomer, I didn't have a clue that a favorite game of the Viennese is to appoint opera directors only to fire them again as quickly as possible. The game has always been the same, whether the director's name was Gustav Mahler, Karl Böhm, or Herbert von Karajan. It sometimes seems that Vienna wouldn't be Vienna if no one took pleasure in firing opera directors, so that new gods could be enthroned one day, only to be sent tumbling down to earth—or lower—the next. The selection of an opera director is far more important than any political election. Vienna is a city where every saleslady in every shop knows whether or not the Queen of the Night in *Zauberflöte* the previous evening hit the high F. Because people are so passionate about it, operatic politics is far more interesting than anything else. In Vienna, all that's wanted is bread and circuses—or rather pastry and opera.

But these "circuses" can sometimes go too far. The management now and then receives letters, either unsigned or attributed to "the public," which declare that a particular performer will be booed off the stage because he or she is simply not wanted. Once this happened to a tenor who sang Tannhäuser. Not only was he booed off the stage, but people waited for him at the stage door after the performance just to boo and jeer at him again. After this experience, the poor man couldn't sing anymore, and he really wasn't a bad singer. He was unpopular simply because some people in Vienna decided that they wanted to hear someone else.

I'll never understand why people boo. If a performance isn't good, all that's necessary is simply "to sit on one's hands," as they say, and not applaud. We singers have very sensitive ears, and we can tell immediately by the amount of applause whether an audience is pleased or not.

By my count, I've survived eight different directors at the Vienna State Opera. This was relatively easy for me because, after my first six years as a permanent "employee" who was paid monthly and who received benefits like a paid vacation and health insurance, I had a contract for thirty performances a year, paid by the performance. Sometimes I sang more, sometimes less, but because I sang only individual performances and wasn't a permanent employee, I had little contact with the internal workings of the opera house and the quarrels and petty jealousies that arise when people work closely together all the time. I flew in, I sang, and I flew out again. During my last years as a singer, I sang less and less in Vienna, and this wasn't the wish of the management, but my own choice. I had to (and wanted to) give up "my" parts to younger singers, and there weren't many roles that I really wanted to sing.

When Dr. Claus Helmut Drese became director in 1984, he asked me to come in to discuss my roles. He asked "What do you want to sing?" and I countered with "What do you have in mind?" He read me a list of the new productions he was considering, and I didn't hear any parts that would suit my age and vocal possibilities at the time. So I simply sang a few repertory performances in productions which he inherited from his predecessor. That's just the way life is, and I didn't shed any tears for my lost youth.

But opera was not the only thing I sang. I also sang a great many concerts and recitals everywhere, and because my contract at the Vienna State Opera was very loose, I was never fixated on singing in this one opera house. I enjoyed a certain freedom and didn't feel tied down all the time. If a singer has enough offers, he or she can play one opera house off against another, and say "At this opera house I get this fee, and if you want me, you'll have to pay the same." But, on the other hand, this freedom comes at a price, because one lacks security. "Ka Musi, ka Göd" (No music, no money), as they say in Vienna. A "free" singer has no paid vacation, and sometimes can't even afford to be ill or have a baby. But Vienna has something that is very much in demand—a pension! I don't think any other theater in the world pays a pension, as the Volksoper, Burgtheater, and the State Opera in Vienna do. Since only Austrian citizens qualify for this pension, many foreign artists try very hard to get Austrian citizenship. They sign contracts, and for the sake of the pension, commit themselves to Vienna for many years to sing, act, design scenery, stage, produce, conduct, or even become artistic director! Even though they complain a lot about the Viennese mentality and about the "Kammersängerei," they all want a pension!

The title of Kammersänger is really quite funny, because every singer at the Staatsoper is addressed as Herr or Frau Kammersänger (never Frau Kammersängerin!), even before a singer has officially been given the title. This is considered polite in Vienna, but it also means that you will sometimes hear someone say "Have you heard that Herr Kammersänger X has become Kammersänger?"! Erika Köth, who received the title of Kammersängerin at both the Vienna State Opera and the Munich State Opera, said to me once that this was "ein Titel ohne Mittel" (a title without means). Nothing is tied to it except honor, and the honor is doubtful sometimes, since singers can acquire the title through great achievement, or they can "ersitzt" (sit and wait) for it, or, to put it nicely, the title of Kammersänger can be given for "loyalty" to the house. Many singers, who can't make a big career and who stand in the shadows, can, in the end, have the satisfaction of being put on the same level as the most famous stars.

But I was happy to become an official Kammersängerin, because in Austria this title opens many doors for you. When you introduce yourself on the phone, you can say "This is Kammersänger X," and the person on the other end of the line knows immediately how to treat you. But this doesn't always work in countries outside Austria. When I called an office in Berlin about the government pension I was entitled to when I celebrated my 65th birthday, I introduced myself as Kammersängerin Christa Ludwig, and the man on the phone said, "Anybody could say that. Sing something for me!" So I sang a little bit, and then he believed me. In Germany the title of Kammersänger is useful now and then, but that's it. But in Austria, where the craving for a title is strongest, everybody is addressed with a title, and even nobodies are addressed as "Herr Doktor" with the same ease as people in other countries address women as "Darling" or "Chérie" when they don't know their names. My husband, a French actor and stage director, comes from a country where even the doctors in a hospital are addressed simply as "Monsieur," and he was astonished when the groundsman at the tennis court in Austria addressed him as "Herr Regisseur," and if he had read a good review in the newspaper, called him "Herr Oberregisseur" (literally, Chief Stage Director). My husband found this especially amusing since a regisseur in French theaters is the stage manager, not the stage director.

I'm not only a Kammersängerin in Vienna, but also Ehrenmitglied der Wiener Staatsoper (Honorary Member of the Vienna State Opera), and I was especially happy about that because I always envied my husband who is an Honorary Member of the Comédie Française—now I can compete properly! I felt exactly the same about membership in the Legion d'Honneur, which both my husband and I received. I was gleeful when I was given the honor, and I must admit that it did the Austrian part of my soul good. And, as Ehrenmitglied der Wiener Staatsoper, I have special privileges. When I die, I can be laid out in the foyer of the State Opera, and I get a beautiful grave in the Zentralfriedhof, the main cemetery in Vienna where Beethoven, Brahms, Schubert, and Hugo Wolf are buried, free of charge! In the old days, my body would also be carried in procession around the opera house, as what the Viennese call a "scheene Leich" (beautiful corpse). I think this is a terrific idea, even if I don't "live to see it." I can already imagine how festive the ceremony would be with all the speeches, and the choir could sing something for me, perhaps the famous Nestroy couplet set specially for the occasion, "und's ist alles net wahr, 's ist alles net wahr" (and it's all not true, it's all not true).

Berlin

The years when I sang in Berlin were marred by the Berlin Wall, which was put up on August 13, 1961. As the Deutsche Oper opened, that ugly monster stood in the middle of the city. Families were split, and the windows and doors of houses were bricked up. And with the houses, also the hearts. Since I was born in Berlin and my mother was a Berliner, I had lots of relatives there, and the audience received me as one of its own. I also felt at home immediately, because I have always liked the commonsense and cheekiness of Berliners. Despite the wall and the great poverty in the East, Berlin remained a very cosmopolitan city. The inhabitants are open-minded, free-spirited, and generous, but not as charming and amiable as the Viennese.

At opera performances and rehearsals, the tone was completely different than in Vienna, very precise and Prussian, rough but warm-hearted. As I was always used to questioning everything, doubting everything, and wanting to know why and how, my German colleagues were quite astonished at me. They said yes to everything that the conductor or the stage director wanted. They didn't complain that there were too many rehearsals or that they started too early, which is what I was used to in Vienna. In Vienna one just says "no" for the sport of it. In Berlin one says "yes" as a matter of principle.

The Deutsche Oper Berlin was built in a modern style, a box on the inside and on the outside. It is cool, functional, matter-of-fact, and without charm. To be fair, I must say that the people who work there, compared to the Viennese, are a bit colder, but also straightforward and honest. In Berlin, there really is a pit for the orchestra, and the musicians sit quite far down, and, of course, they are not the Vienna Philharmonic. The people in the audience don't dress as smartly as in Vienna, but that fits the style of the opera house. I remember attending the opening performance of Mozart's *Don Giovanni* in September 1961 under the wonderful, but already fatally ill, conductor Ferenc Fricsay, with Dietrich Fischer-Dieskau in the title role and my then husband Walter Berry as Leporello. I was sitting in the audience in a big evening gown and my wide tulle skirt flowed over my neighbor (that's how narrow the seats are). So, during intermission, I tore out a few of the tulle petticoats in the ladies' room.

Wonderful avant-garde stagings were always done in Berlin, and the house has continued in the tradition of doing such forward-looking productions. During the years 1961 to 1963, Wieland Wagner's stagings of *Aida*, *Lohengrin*, and later *Salome* with Anja Silja were much talked about, and I had a guest contract in Berlin during those years. After that I appeared only occasionally.

When the Berlin Wall was taken down in 1989, I sang in Berlin and felt very happy, as if I was joined with all those who still remembered Berlin when it was one city. But how disappointed I was that many young people were completely indifferent to the reunion. Of course, they had never experienced an undivided Berlin, and I thought it was horrible that almost two generations knew only a divided city. When it was divided, the feeling of being confined in a tight spot depressed me a lot, and I thought how unjust it was that only one side of the city could prosper. Many Berliners were unhappy because they could no longer freely visit their relatives on the other side of the city, or, as happened to one of my aunts, they lost their homes when some houses were bricked shut. But despite everything, the citizens of the city kept their witty Berlin-style sense of humor. Immediately after the war, concerts were held in an oblong bare hall in the Hochschule für Musik. But later the "Zirkus Karajani" (Circus Karajan) or "Musikschuppen" (Music Barn), as the

Berliners affectionately called their new Philharmonic Hall, was built. Berliners always have apt names for things. In front of the old airport in Tempelhof stands a modern monument, which is meant to represent the airlift that the Americans used to bring relief supplies to West Berlin when the Russians blockaded the city. This odd-looking structure the Berliners call the "Hungerharke" (Hunger Claw) because that's what it looks like.

I find the large Philharmonic Hall fabulous for big concerts, but extremely problematic for lieder recitals because it is built "in the round," and there are always people sitting behind the singer who only see the singer from the back. I never knew where to turn when I sang in such halls. Now to the left, now to the right, now forward, or should I turn my head around and glance behind me? Certainly it depends on the song. During a cheerful one, it's easy for me to turn my head back and forth, but during a serious song, I always faced forward to keep my concentration. But what to do about the poor people sitting behind the stage? I always sang at least one encore facing them, out of politeness, as I saw Elisabeth Schwarzkopf do.

Aside from Philharmonic Hall, I also sang at the rebuilt Schauspielhaus at the Gendarmenmarkt, which is a wonderful concert hall. And I also sang later on at the historic State Opera on Unter den Linden. I had the good fortune to sing in all of Berlin's major houses, although never, regrettably, in an opera at the State Opera. The audience in Berlin is a typical big-city audience like in New York, Tokyo, London, Paris, or Rome, a very open-minded audience, capable of great enthusiasm.

Perhaps because I have roots in Berlin, I always had a feeling of belonging whenever I sang there.

Paris

During the years that Rolf Liebermann was in charge of the Paris Opera, I was a constant guest there. Liebermann had previously done Regietheater (opera productions where theatrical values are emphasized over musical ones) at the State Opera in Hamburg, where star singers appeared only as guests on exceptional occasions, and ensemble was emphasized. In Hamburg, Liebermann organized extremely interesting productions with almost no world-class singers, but these productions nevertheless stimulated a lot of animated discussion. In Paris he organized his productions quite differently, and, in a few years, made the Paris Opera, which had never been a world-class opera house because of limited funding, into the most interesting opera house in Europe. First, he demanded a far bigger budget, which I believe was the highest of any European opera house at that time. He invited the greatest conductors, stage directors and designers, and the most famous singers of the day, and he made what is called grand opera, but without ever forgetting, even with popular operas, to offer interesting, exciting productions.

I had the good fortune to sing many wonderful roles in Paris during the Liebermann era: the Marschallin, the Dyer's Wife, Klytämnestra in Richard Strauss's *Elektra*, Fricka in Wagner's Ring Cycle, and Ottavia in Monteverdi's *L'Incoronazione di Poppea*. Since my husband was living in Paris at that time, it was very pleasant for me to be able to spend time there. But Paris wouldn't be Paris without the Parisians! There were strikes and more strikes at the Paris Opera, sometimes the stagehands, sometimes the orchestra, sometimes the ballet. A few performances had to be canceled, or sometimes we played totally without stage sets in front of black curtains. And the discipline, which I was used to in Vienna or Berlin, was far less evident. I was surprised that, in spite of everything, premieres of new productions took place on schedule, and most of the time they were of exceptional quality.

"No Smoking" signs were posted all over, but everyone smoked, and there were cigarette butts everywhere. But the worst thing at the beginning of the Liebermann era was the toilet. I'm talking about the old opera house, the Palais Garnier, which, by the way, smelled wonderfully of powder and make-up. Everything backstage was very old: the offices, the dressing rooms, the rehearsal rooms—and the aforementioned place, since the building had been opened in 1875. As you can still find frequently in France even today, the toilets could only be used standing up. This may have been very comfortable in earlier times, when ladies didn't wear panties but only long skirts. I know my grandmother had cotton panties, which were open and didn't have a strip of material in the middle. But can you imagine using such a "standing toilet" while wearing the Marschallin's huge costume with all its crinolines? Managing this was a great feat!

Dressers and hair stylists were a scarce commodity at the Paris Opera, and it was best to do everything yourself. The situation reminded me a bit of the days when I sang in Chicago, where the singers had to bring wigs from their home opera houses and style them themselves. I can still see myself when I sang Helen of Troy in Boito's *Mefistofele* there. I brought a red-blond wig that I had used when singing Kundry in *Parsifal* in Europe, and I had great difficulty restyling it so that it looked Greek. Because the wig didn't have hair long enough for me to gather it in a roll at the back and bring it up on top of my head, I added yellow fabric and styled the hair over that. Paris was not quite as bad as Chicago, but it was certainly very different from what I was used to in the other opera houses where I sang regularly.

As with the Viennese, one needs a special talent to get along with the Parisians and understand their "merde" (I don't give a damn) mentality. They are extremely freedom-loving and individualistic, and they don't like to be forced to follow rules or say yes to everything. De Gaulle is supposed to have asked himself how he could possibly govern a country in which people eat a different kind of cheese every day of the year. As I'm born under the sign of Pisces, I swim along easily with the attitudes of people from many different cultures. I always adjust well, and it's easy for me to take on the unique customs of a country. I behave like the natives, dress like them, always try to speak their language (out of politeness), and even eat like them. Of course, the last thing is not at all difficult in France. Once when I was in a restaurant in Santiago, Chile, I heard an American woman order cottage cheese at the next table. When the puzzled waiter brought her order, I heard—she spoke very loudly—"Oh, that's not cottage cheese!" The waiter, more and more puzzled, let the woman explain to him at great length exactly what American cottage cheese was, and he took her plate and reappeared after a while with another "cottage cheese," or something he thought was cottage cheese. "Oh, that's no cottage cheese!" she said again very loudly, and at this point, the maître d'hôtel appeared and assured the woman that in Santiago, this was cottage cheese. So I'm always careful never to ask for "cottage cheese" in Paris!

I wanted to live, as we say in Austria, "wie Gott in Frankreich" (like God in France) because the food and wine is so wonderful there. Singers always like to sing in Paris, and this was especially true when Rolf Liebermann managed the Paris Opera. He and Sir Rudolf Bing of the Metropolitan in New York were two of the last great opera managers. Both were always present in their opera houses during performances, and both were extremely witty and clever, and sometimes a bit wicked, although always in a very charming way. They were two men who truly knew how to run an opera house. Liebermann would wind everyone around his little finger, and, most important of all, he knew a lot about voices and loved them. I also valued him as a composer. Once when we were talking, he mentioned that I had sung many of his compositions, and then added, "The only thing I regret is that I never asked you to marry me"!

Today, now that the new Opéra Bastille is open, everything is different. I only sang *Die Winterreise* there once, and that performance almost didn't take place because of the famous Paris traffic. Everyone who knows Paris also knows that the traffic situation there is almost catastrophic. At times, the traffic stands totally still, and you can't go forward or backward or even sideways. I got caught in this terrible traffic when I took a taxi to my *Winterreise* recital. I knew that if I allowed myself to get excited, I would lose my voice, so I stayed very calm, even when it was five minutes to eight, the time my recital was supposed to start, and the taxi was still stuck in traffic quite far away from the Bastille. I thought to myself, "They have to wait. Without me they can't do anything." But I didn't mention this to the driver because I didn't want to make him nervous.

When we finally arrived at the Place de la Bastille and again everything was standing still, I got out, squeezed through all the motionless cars in my evening gown and fought my way to the stage entrance. There everyone was waiting, very agitated, and I heard the bell sound over and over again, signaling that the audience should take their seats, even though they were all sitting already. I remained very calm. I absolutely couldn't get excited, or my voice would tremble during the recital. And this is how I entered this huge new house for the first time.

As a rule, I never practiced in an empty hall before a recital, unless it was absolutely necessary (for example, if the performance was being recorded for a radio broadcast). Without an audience, a hall has a completely different sound, sometimes better and sometimes worse, but always different. Because of this, I'm always shocked at the sound when I sing the first song, so why practice beforehand in the hall since I'm going to be surprised anyway? Often I have to take a step forward or back to find the spot where I can hear myself best.

The Opéra Bastille is gray concrete everywhere. I took an escalator up to my dressing room, and everything looked very modern, like a department store. I thought that my evening gown, which was wide at the bottom, might get stuck in the rolling mechanism, but I couldn't worry about that because of my voice. Then I saw the very modern dressing room, and there was even a leather chair before the dressing table that I could use as a recliner. Super!

Sadly, the room didn't smell of powder and make-up, but there was no time to think about that. I quickly met my accompanist Charles Spencer for a last "toi-toi-toi" (break a leg), and we were on! From the stage I looked into the new hall, all gray and black with no trace of red and gold, which are the colors I loved so much in old opera houses. The somber setting fit the mood of *Winterreise* perfectly, but I couldn't keep myself from whispering to Charles during our entrance bow, "How hideous!"

The vistas of Paris, a city with millions of inhabitants, are well known. Since people in the audience at a musical performance must often travel long distances or come straight from their work by Metro, they can't wear beautiful clothes. Still, sometimes I'm astonished at the kind of clothes they do wear.

At which flea market did they pick *those* up? Surely one has to search for a long time to find something that ugly! Strangely enough, this way of dressing seems to suit this city, just as it seems right for people to crumple their raincoats under their seats in New York. As Leonard Bernstein said, it doesn't matter what the audience wears. The most important thing is that the audience is interested, and comes to a performance. In the elegant old opera houses and concert halls full of red and gold, many people are too intimidated to walk in the door, in the same way they are afraid to enter elegant, expensive shops. In a place full of red and gold, an audience feels that it must dress in a more refined way, and they might not go to a concert or an opera because they feel they don't have the right clothes. I heard that the Bastille is an opera house that was deliberately built for the "common people," but, of course, the ticket prices are not the kind that "common people" can afford.

At the Opéra Bastille, I saw Mozart's *Idomeneo* for the first time, and the French translation of the Italian text appeared in lighted letters on a screen that hung over the stage. I believe this technique called "supertitles" was first tried at Lincoln Center by the New York City Opera, which is more a "local" opera company than the Metropolitan Opera, which is more "international." I know that some people are against the use of such supertitles, but I think it helps the audience to understand the opera, especially if the stage direction is not very helpful. Still, it's very comical to see the same translation repeated over and over again when the same words are sung over and over again on the stage.

The Met

In New York, as in Paris, I got to know two opera houses: the old Met, which stood in the middle of a row of buildings on Broadway between 38th and 39th Streets; and later, beginning in 1966, the new Met on the plaza at Lincoln Center, farther uptown.

I didn't like the old Metropolitan Opera at all. I know that some Americans will be angry at me for saying this, because the old Met was the venerable house where Caruso sang, and many other great singers, too. And because the wealthiest people in New York had gilded boxes there, the dress circle was nicknamed the "diamond horseshoe."

My father sang at the old Met in 1909 and told me about the "hallowed boards" there. He sang with Caruso on the old Met stage when he was only twenty-one years old and immediately got a contract for ten years. But being a real Viennese and a man who made difficulties, he managed to get his contract canceled after only one season. I have often noticed how Viennese colleagues behave in foreign opera houses, especially in America, where they love to complain about the working conditions, the hotels, the weather, the food, in short, everything. It's just like the American who demanded cottage cheese in Santiago.

To me, the old Met looked like a dusty old box. It's true that the auditorium and the foyers had an old-fashioned beauty, but behind the stage everything was dark and depressing, and the dressing rooms were awful. I had a toilet enclosed in a kind of wooden crate, which was open at the top and in the middle of my dressing room! Please don't think, "What's with Christa and her obsession with toilets?" But just imagine, you are nervous, and sometimes you have to stand on the stage for a whole act. All you want to do afterwards is quickly and comfortably. . . .

In the old Met, we actually held rehearsals in the Ladies Room. Now it's true that this Ladies Room was very luxurious, because, of course, it was meant for the audience, and not for us "entertainers." There was a big entrance room, where elegant ladies could powder their noses, and this powder room was filled with stylish sofas and comfortable chairs, and had a red carpet and thick curtains. And there was also a piano, which we used for rehearsals. Well, at least, the room smelled wonderfully of powder and make-up!

Also, the administrative offices were tiny, dark, very narrow, but cozy, although not cozy in the same way as the original offices at the Salzburg Festival. Everything was very spare and American. At the Artists' Entrance (really Servants' Entrance would have been more appropriate), there were huge garbage cans which we all had to squeeze past. And the part of Broadway near the opera house was not a wonderful neighborhood either. When I was hired for the first time in 1957, Hilde Güden advised me to stay on 38th Street, but "across town" on the East side, past Fifth Avenue, on the corner of Park Avenue. She recommended a very small apartment hotel which was like a private residence. She also told me that I should buy a few dishes and pots and a small broiler, so I could cook something for myself in the kitchen, which every apartment had. That was when I first discovered American frozen, ready-to-eat meals, which today are known all over the world.

Back then, everything about New York fascinated me. The European countries, destroyed in the war, were slowly being rebuilt, and America seemed like the land of milk and honey to me. With money you could buy anything. The exchange rate for the dollar was about 4.25 German Marks, but I quickly realized that my buying power in America was only about two marks per dollar. Because of my tiny fee, I couldn't afford taxis, so I walked everywhere, but I didn't get to know New York. My forced marches were only from the hotel to the Met, and from the Met back to the hotel again. I didn't even know there was a Central Park!

My schoolgirl English didn't help me much either. Although I could ask a question, I didn't understand a word of the answer. And the city frightened me. The traffic, the crowds of people and their diversity: Blacks, Puerto Ricans, Asians, and many others. Apparently crazy people talked out loud to themselves and slept on the streets, all mixed in with singing Salvation Army people, young men with shaved heads in yellow gowns who were trying to look like Tibetan monks, fortunetellers, and frustrated tenors who sang opera arias out loud. I found all of this overwhelming, and since I was completely alone, I was very nervous. Yet this is the city for which I always feel a kind of homesickness today, exactly because of all this diversity!

When the new Met opened in 1966 and I saw its location in the middle of the spacious Lincoln Center Plaza, I was overjoyed. It's true I signed petitions to ask that the old Met be maintained as a museum, but Americans are not sentimental. The old Met was torn down, and today in its place there is a huge office building. The new generation doesn't even know that there was once a mecca for opera lovers on Broadway near 38th Street.

The new Met is a magnificent building with windows about seven stories high, through which one can see paintings by Marc Chagall. To the right of the Met is the home of the New York Philharmonic, today called Avery Fisher Hall, and farther in the back is the New York Public Library at Lincoln Center and the Vivian Beaumont Theater, and, across the street, the famous Juilliard School of Music. To the left of the opera house is the New York State Theater, home of the New York City Opera, another huge building. Creating this cultural center in a rundown residential area was an enormous undertaking, but it made the entire area prosper. I think that the new Met is extremely grand for a modern building, and it has a relaxed elegance. And even though it is modern, my favorite opera house colors, red and gold, dominate. Huge crystal chandeliers, donated by Austria, adorn the auditorium, and public and private donations from all over the world helped to build the house, and little plaques on some seat-backs have the names of contributors inscribed on them. And, as in all big American opera houses, there is a real restaurant in the new Met, where operagoers can have dinner before the performance.

LEONARD BERNSTEIN

I always thought Christa Ludwig the
greatest Brahms singer among her peers, but that
was only until I heard her sing Strauss. Then
she was the greatest Marschallin until I heard her
do Mahler. Again I had to reassign her to
another throne. But then I heard her sing Wagner
and the same thing happened, and when recently
I heard her incredible interpretation of the
"Old Lady" in my operetta Candide, then I had
to give up.

She is simply the best, and the best of all
possible human beings.

2 March '90

Leonard Bernstein writes about Christa Ludwig

Anton Ludwig as Siegfried in 1926

Eugenie Besalla-Ludwig as Ortrud
in 1926

Christa Ludwig's parents,
Anton Ludwig and
Eugenie Besalla-Ludwig

At 9 months

At age 6

At age 15

Variety show publicity photo taken in Giessen, 1945. Christa Ludwig is seated on the far left and her father is standing behind her.

As Orlofsky with the Frankfurt Opera,
1946

As Marina in *Boris Godunov*, Hanover,
August 1954

Guest appearance as Octavian with the Frankfurt Opera in Paris, February 1956. Georg
Solti conducted with Maria Reining (Marschallin), Hanni Steffek (Sophie), and Kurt
Böhme (Ochs)

As Miranda in Frank Martin's *Der Sturm* at the Vienna State Opera in June 1956

Publicity photo taken in London about 1956

As Waltraute in *Die Walküre* at the Vienna State Opera in February 1958

Lieder recital with Ernst Krenek at the Vienna Konzerthaus in May 1956

As Dorabella with Hermann Prey
(Guglielmo) in film of Così fan tutte
about 1969

As Amneris at the Vienna State Opera
in 1958

As Cherubino backstage at the Roudentsaal (Hofburg) in Vienna with Dr. Karl Böhm,
Erich Kunz (Figaro), and Irmgard Seefried (Susanne) in April 1955

With Maria Callas and Franco Corelli during *Norma* recording sessions in 1960

Recording Adalgisa with Callas as Norma in Milan, 1960

First Carmen at the Vienna State Opera in November 1956

With James Levine in *The New Yorker*, April 17, 1989

Rehearsing with James Levine for *Die Winterreise* recording in 1986

Farewell recital at Carnegie Hall with Levine on March 20, 1993

With Zinka Milanov (left) and Maria Jeritza in New York, 1971

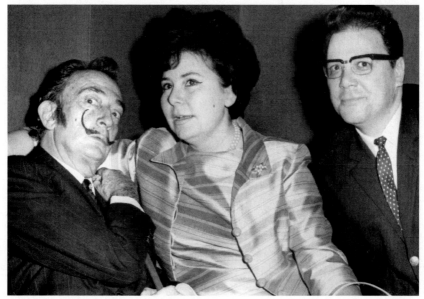

Public relations photo with Salvador Dali (left) and Walter Berry in New York about 1966

As Kundry in *Parsifal* at the Metropolitan Opera in November 1970

As Klytämnestra at the Paris Opera in January 1987

As Klytämnestra at the Metropolitan Opera in December 1984

As Ortrud in the Wieland Wagner production of *Lohengrin* at the Vienna State Opera in May 1965

FAYER

FAYER

As the Dyer's Wife in *Die Frau ohne Schatten* at the Vienna State Opera in June 1964

COLETTE MASSON

As the Dyer's Wife at the Paris Opera in October 1972

As the Dyer's Wife at the Metropolitan Opera in October 1966

LOUIS MELANÇON

With mother in Salzburg in 1962   Rehearsing with Erik Werba about 1980

Backstage at the Lyric Opera of Chicago with son Wolfi and Elisabeth Schwarzkopf before a performance of *Così fan tutte* in November 1961

From the first moment, I loved everything at the new Met. The dressing rooms are very pleasant, with carpeting and a sofa, and even a piano and private shower and toilet. Although I usually prefer to put on my own make-up, because having someone fiddling around with my face before a performance makes me nervous, I've always liked being made up at the Met because the make-up master, as the make-up artist is officially called, really is a master. My round face, small eyes and nose, and round cheeks soon became a longer face with big eyes and a longer nose and thinner cheeks to make me a much more interesting-looking Kundry, Amneris, or Dyer's Wife. Also, because of the gigantic size of the Met auditorium, singers really have to be made up properly, or a large part of the audience farther back in the house can't see their faces. At many opera houses in Germany, make-up is often taboo in modern staging, especially in the theater. Ironically, actresses don't put on make-up until they become themselves again. But at the Met the make-up master often took more than an hour to give me a different face for each of my roles. I never loved my face, and I always wanted to be prettier, paler, and more interesting, but nature had different plans. I console myself with the idea that the shape of my face, my bone structure, and the placement of my sinuses gave me the right resonance for my voice. If I had a different face, I would probably have a different timbre.

At the Met the dressers and hair stylists are also always right there when you need them, but watch out if there is someone who doesn't know the drill. Unlike in Vienna, there aren't two or three equally skilled people who can take over when necessary. But the tailors, shoemakers, and wigmakers are first-class at the Met, and extremely helpful and fast when something needs to be changed quickly. However, I found one thing quite awful at the Met, and that was the rehearsal rooms. I don't remember even one with a window. It's true that there is "fresh" air circulating all the time, and, probably because of that, better air than the air on the street, but I find the idea unbearable that the poor coaches work the whole day only in artificial light and filtered air. And it's the same for the conductors, orchestra, stage directors, and singers, because the orchestral rehearsal rooms and the rehearsal stages are all located three floors underground.

If you enter the house through the aforementioned Servants' Entrance (Excuse me: Artists' Entrance), you first reach a kind of limbo through which you can't pass unless you are known or announced. There was a murder in the building once, just as there was at the Vienna State Opera, and that's why security is so strict. When Renata Tebaldi's popularity at the Met was at its height, a security guard didn't recognize the great Italian prima donna, and he asked her who she was. "I am Renata Tebaldi," she said, and he replied, "How do you spell it?"! This is a big difference between New York and Vienna. In Vienna, everyone knows you if you are a Kammersänger.

And at the Met, no one is addressed as Kammersänger or with any other title. Everyone is simply Chris, Ted, Nat, Jess, and even the all-powerful Met Artistic Director James Levine is just Jimmy. No one ever addressed Rudolf Bing as Sir after he was given the title, but everyone did call him Mr. Bing because he looked very distinguished, like the British subject he was, and this had an awe-inspiring effect. "Jimmy" walks around the house very casually dressed, always with a towel over his shoulder, because he doesn't just sit in an office all day, but he conducts and plays the piano at rehearsals. He was influenced by what could be called the Austro-Hungarian School of music-making since he was George Szell's assistant for a long time when Szell led the Cleveland Orchestra. Once I sang the *Kindertotenlieder* with Szell, when Jimmy was his assistant and also the coach who accompanied me at our rehearsal. In those days, Jimmy was still very young, but even then I thought he played very beautifully.

Except for the luxurious dressing rooms and the very elegant offices, everything backstage at the Met is rather ugly, but practical. For example, there's a long corridor on the way to the dressing rooms, admittedly with a red carpet, that is lined with gray lockers where we singers can safely put away our bags and coats. The large garbage cans from the old Met seem to have been brought along to the new house, and they stand everywhere. There are also many machines where you can buy coffee (although it doesn't seem right to call such a thing coffee), soft drinks, sandwiches, and candy.

The setup backstage is excellent, really quite breathtaking. There are huge additional stages at the sides and back of the main stage, and also a stage underneath where whole sets can be built and moved into place. Everything rolls and lowers automatically, which can have quite a frightening effect, and many monitors are used to control the technical goings-on. The Met stage-hands, who come from many different races, treat everyone in a friendly and helpful way. They also often stand and listen to the performances until they are chased away. Backstage, one hears many languages, but you hear mostly Spanish and Italian, and in the administrative offices, all languages are spoken. Almost everyone backstage, whether lighting technician, stage manager, or chorusmaster, also speaks both English and German.

There are numerous opera lovers in New York, and the Standing Room is full of experts. The performances start relatively late (mostly at 8 p.m.), because many in the audience work and must travel a long way. Consequently, performances seldom finish before 11, and Wagner and Strauss operas often last until after midnight. Then many people have to travel home by car, subway, or train, which often takes more than an hour. Only a few can afford apartments close by in Manhattan.

If the opera lasts until after midnight, the orchestra and stage personnel must be paid overtime. How often I remember a worried manager coming backstage with a watch in his hand during the second intermission of *Rosenkavalier*, *Frau ohne Schatten*, or *Götterdämmerung*, and saying to the conductor, "Please, please, conduct a little bit faster!" Since the newspapers usually published their reviews the very next day, the critics were already back in their editorial offices during the final trio of *Rosenkavalier*, and I often wondered how they found out how the piece ended!

The New York audience is capable of great enthusiasm when celebrating their favorites. On special occasions, the management also honors singers, and I was praised with speeches in front of the curtain and given silver plates and flowers and a shower of confetti for my twenty-fifth and thirtieth anniversary years at the Met as well as for my farewell performance as Fricka in *Die Walküre*. Once I sang the role of Dido in *Les Troyens* on my birthday March 16, and at my solo curtain call, someone in the audience suddenly started to sing "Happy Birthday." Immediately everyone joined in and sang a birthday serenade. Europeans might consider all this a bit kitschy, but it's really a great pleasure for a singer. Of course, one shouldn't take it too seriously, as with everything else in the theater.

Colleagues at the Met are especially nice. They send each other good luck telegrams or flowers at a premiere, and at the Met I've never seen a colleague "totally unintentionally" leave bad reviews lying around for someone else to find. Perhaps it has something to do with the hugeness of the city and the large size of the house. Perhaps it makes individuals more generous and the feeling of camaraderie stronger. Also the management sends not only the usual flowers at a premiere, but also other thoughtful things like caviar or champagne. And fans can come into the dressing room. At the Met there is a "guest list" to which the artists add the names of people who ask to come backstage. Usually fans send a note that says "Please, put me on your list." American fans are loyal for many decades and also very helpful. When you leave the theater, they carry your flowers and other presents to your car for you. And sometimes they even drive you home.

Ah! Home! For some years I had a real home in New York, an apartment on the 40th floor of a very modern apartment building near Carnegie Hall with a view of Central Park. It's nice to have a home in a foreign country, because sometimes a singer spends several consecutive months there. Not all, but many European artists have apartments in New York, since it's very difficult to live in a hotel for so long without your personal things. At least I cannot do it, because I'm a homebody.

Friendly relations with European colleagues at the Met are much stronger than they are at home. There is a kind of "blood-brother" community, and in New York singers have time to see each other socially. It was in New York that I learned what a wonderful cook Leonie Rysanek was. She gave me my first recipe for Semmelknödel, or more correctly, for a Serviettenknödel since the dough was formed in a napkin. Once, when I was completely alone in New York at Christmas time, Karl Böhm and his wife Thea invited me for Christmas Eve when they were living at the Alden Hotel near 80th Street on Central Park West. Since this was during my debut season at the old Met, I was living on the East Side, near Park Avenue and 38th Street. As I've already mentioned, I had no idea that there was a Central Park, and their neighborhood was new and strange to me. Since it was snowing heavily, I wanted to take a taxi, but there were no taxis to be found, and the only ones I did see either had lighted signs on their roofs which said "off duty," or someone else was quicker than I to wave them down. Friends had advised me to take the subway, and I decided to try it. So, for the first (and last) time, I experienced New York from below. It was an amazing experience, and, of course, I got lost. After a two-hour delay, I finally reached my destination, and found that the dear Böhms and all their guests had waited until I got there to exchange Christmas gifts.

This crazy city has become something of a second home to me, and I love it. But New York is, of course, a lot more than a city. New York is a philosophy of life. I feel rejuvenated there, the living is easy, and no one looks to see how you are dressed, or if your handbag matches your shoes. Miracles can still happen in New York, although perhaps no one goes from newsboy to millionaire these days.

But I know someone who succeeded in New York for whom I have the greatest respect. Many years ago when I sang in Jerusalem and gave a master class with the encouragement of Isaac Stern, I was tormented by a nasty neck sprain and migraine. Someone recommended a physical therapist to me named Shmuel Tatz, and he worked wonders. Already after the first treatment I felt a lot better. A few years later, Shmuel called me at my hotel in New York, and told me that he had come to the city because his wife was studying piano at the Juilliard School. They wanted to stay, so he was looking for new clients, and I was the first person he called. Of course, I was really pleased to find this extremely competent man again, and he immediately came to my hotel with his massage table folded under his arm. I recommended him to others, and slowly he built up a list of clients. At first he could only rent a tiny studio (without a window!) in the Carnegie Hall building, and he worked there all day long, in the truest sense, with only his own two hands. Always when I come to New York, the first person I visit is Shmuel, my physical therapist. In just two years, his knowhow and diligence paid off. He now has a big studio, even assistants, and he is well-established in his profession. Only in New York could this happen!

Concert Halls in Vienna and America

Musikverein and Konzerthaus

Performances at the Konzerthaus, an architectural jewel in the style of the Viennese Jugendstil, have a totally different character than those at the Musikverein. Konzerthaus performances are more avant-garde, and to me that's more interesting. I'm honestly proud to be the only woman who is an Ehrenmitglied der Konzerthausgesellschaft (Honorary Member of the Konzerthaus Association).

The Musikverein, built in 1870 in the classic style, is the home of the Vienna Philharmonic. Subscriptions for their concerts on Saturday afternoon and Sunday morning are passed from one generation to another, and it's extremely difficult to get tickets if you don't have a subscription. The Musikverein schedule isn't really optimal for singers, because everything is too close together. There are rehearsals, then sometimes a "pre-concert" on Friday afternoon, followed by Saturday afternoon and Sunday morning subscription concerts. At my last concerts with the Philharmonic in 1992, which were in honor of its 150th anniversary, I was scheduled to sing *Das Lied von der Erde* and the *Rückert Lieder* of Gustav Mahler. I had some doubts that all would go well because the voice gets congested with phlegm and crabby in general as a singer gets older. (Crabby is my word for it, because this is exactly how it feels.) But because I know that singing also has something to do with mental attitude, I did everything I could to wake up like a "Glöckerl" (little bell), and the concerts went quite well.

The acoustic in the Musikverein is highly praised, and is probably created by the many stuccos in the ceiling and on the walls, as well as by the Caryatids that "hold up" the gallery. When I arrived fresh from the bombed-out German provinces and sang there for the first time, I quietly studied the hall from the stage and found it quite hideous. Everything is gold on gold. The Viennese don't call the Musikverein the Golden Hall without good reason, and the female figures were the last straw for me. I believe I counted 59 golden breasts from the stage that day, but then I paused and said, "No, can't be. Has to be an even number. 58 or 60?" There was just too much gold for my taste, and the whole style was foreign to me. The impression from the auditorium, however, where everyone sits very close together and extremely uncomfortably, is totally different. The audience sees a stage completely filled with musicians from the orchestra in front of a platform where additional members of the audience are seated, and behind all this is the magnificent organ. Millions, no, probably more than a billion people from all over the world know this scene because the Vienna Philharmonic's annual New Year's Day concert is televised from the Musikverein. The hall is quite overwhelming, especially when one remembers the wonderful sound and thinks about the great musicians who have played and sung there, and the celebrated composers who have experienced performances of their own music at the Musikverein. The walls radiate sound and tradition.

The offices of the administration are still wonderfully old-fashioned. The rooms are large and smell of coffee, all the doors are wide open, and big writing desks are everywhere, with piles of paper on them. Many plants and flowers make these offices feel cozy. But the best and dearest piece of "furniture" is a woman in her late eighties named Frau Direktor Margarethe Gruder-Guntram. She is the soul of the organization, and she is lovingly inherited by all Generalsekretärs in charge of the Gesellschaft der Musikfreunde (nickname: Musikverein), the Society of the Friends of Music. The Frau Direktor is the first to arrive in the morning and the last to leave in the evening. The Musikverein is her real home, and she is backstage at every concert. We all love her.

The Musikverein is more authentic than the State Opera, because the State Opera was rebuilt in a slightly more modern style after it was destroyed during the Second World War, while the Musikverein was completely restored. Also, the audience at the Musikverein is different from the one at the State Opera, and you can see the difference in the balls each one sponsors at Faschingszeit, carnival time, which is celebrated annually just before the religious observance of Lent. At the State Opera, the ball is big and lavish, while at the Musikverein it's more refined. At the Musikverein, the Vienna Philharmonic (after all, it's *their* ball) always opens the festivities with a famous conductor at the podium.

My farewell lieder recitals in Vienna in April 1994 took place at the Musikverein. At the first, I sang Schubert's *Die Winterreise*, and at the second, a program of songs by Beethoven, Mahler, Schubert, and Wolf. It was a melancholy evening for me, because so many memories are tied to this hall, where I sang concerts with the three "great ones" (Böhm, Karajan, Bernstein), and also with James Levine, Riccardo Muti, Lorin Maazel, Claudio Abbado, and Vaclav Neumann to name only a few, and innumerable lieder recitals, first with Erik Werba, and later with Charles Spencer.

Writing about the Musikverein reminds me that the Vienna Philharmonic, the orchestra that I love the most, gave me a special honor on my 25th anniversary as a singer. I received their "Silver Rose," and I cherish it very much. I am also proud to be the only female musician given the title of Honorary Member of the Vienna Philharmonic. It's one of the honors I value most.

The combination of the hall where the walls seem to breathe music, the Philharmonic orchestra itself, and the special Musikverein audience, comes together to make me finally forget my obsession with knowing whether there are 58 or 60 golden breasts in the Großer Musikvereinsaal. I am filled with joy and pride, and also with gratitude, when I think that I was able to contribute to the music-making of the Vienna Philharmonic in the Musikverein. I am also delighted that the atmosphere in that hall lives on.

Avery Fisher Hall and Carnegie Hall

Avery Fisher Hall is the home of the New York Philharmonic, whose music director for many years was Leonard Bernstein. When alterations were made to the hall because of problems with the original acoustics, Karl Böhm was asked to help judge the results. As usual with such acoustical tests, a gun was to be fired in the renovated hall. But Böhm asked, "Why? What symphony has a gun shot in it?"

Avery Fisher Hall is very large and rectangular, with a huge ground-level seating area and only relatively small balconies on the three sides of the auditorium facing the orchestra. And today, despite gun shot tests and other measures, the hall still has "dead spots" where the sound isn't good. I sang many lieder recitals in this hall, but I never felt it was ideal because the hall is so very large and part of the audience has to sit very far away from the performers, especially in the small balconies at the back. In such a hall, a singer is tempted to sing louder than normal, or to put only dramatic songs on the program. Paradoxically, quieter, more intimate songs, in which singers must focus their voices throughout, carry much more clearly and achieve a much better effect than more dramatic songs where singers can use a big voice to try to fill the hall with loud sound.

The famous "Young People's Concerts," in which Leonard Bernstein explained music to children, took place in Avery Fisher Hall (then called Philharmonic Hall). With Walter Berry, I had the pleasure of taking part in one of these programs called "A Toast to Vienna in $^3/_4$ Time," in which Bernstein explained this type of rhythm to the audience, and Walter and I sang a few Mahler songs. It was incredible to experience how well Bernstein communicated with his young audience. And of course, many adults came to these concerts also, so that they could become familiar with music in a simple and very enjoyable way.

The most traditional concert hall in America, which is greatly respected by all artists, is Carnegie Hall in New York. Many people in Europe think that this hall was built by some rich American just so he could make his name eternal. But the real story of Andrew Carnegie is quite different. He was born in 1835 in a poor Scottish village in a period of economic depression which forced the family to emigrate to America in 1848. Carnegie's father was a weaver in America, and his mother also had to work hard. Young Andrew, who was clever and energetic, first worked in a cotton mill, and then delivered telegrams, became a railroad employee, and finally a manager. He achieved riches and fame because he was the first to recognize the advantages of using steel instead of iron in American industry. At the age of 65, he sold his businesses for $400 million dollars, and dedicated the last 18 years of his life to doing charitable work. During his lifetime, Carnegie gave away over $350 million, and because of his example, many wealthy Americans became philanthropists. Carnegie Hall, which opened in 1891, is one of the fruits of his generosity.

Carnegie Hall has a dream acoustic. It's really surprising that, more than a hundred years ago, without modern technology and measurement tools, the builders of this hall could achieve such an unsurpassed sound quality. But perhaps it isn't so surprising, since the builders of antique open-air theaters, such as the one at Epidauros, were able to achieve a great acoustic 2400 years ago! When I sang in Carnegie Hall, I always felt that I was singing in a kind of musical Valhalla, because all the greatest international singers, soloists, orchestras, and conductors have appeared there, and still do. Important popular musicians like Ella Fitzgerald also sang in Carnegie Hall, and many great events took place there, such as the memorial concert for Leonard Bernstein shortly after his death. I once attended a large charity gala at Carnegie Hall for AIDS patients. The performers—Kurt Masur, James Levine, Jessye Norman, Midori—and all the orchestra players, appeared without a fee, and more than a million dollars was raised, as the chairman of the event proudly announced at the end of the concert, while mentioning some of the most recent casualties of this terrible illness.

In this beautiful concert hall I gave my farewell lieder recital in America in 1993, with James Levine at the piano, and this was a great honor for me. I thought about how proud America can be for taking in so many Europeans, and how this spirit enriched American culture. Because of Nazi rule, many eminent Jewish scientists, academics, and artists left Europe and came to live in the USA, including famous conductors such as Bruno Walter, George Szell, Erich Kleiber, and Josef Krips. Fritz Reiner conducted in Chicago, and the San Francisco Opera was managed for many years by Kurt Herbert Adler. These men brought the European musical tradition to Americans.

When I sang in a concert performance of *Rosenkavalier* under Eugene Ormandy and heard the first measures played by the Philadelphia Orchestra, I could hardly believe my ears because the sound was so much like that of the Vienna Philharmonic. I had the same experience in Israel when I sang in a performance of Gustav Mahler's *Das Lied von der Erde* with the Israel Philharmonic under Leonard Bernstein. There it was—the same Vienna-like sound.

America welcomed Europe's artists with open arms as they fled the Nazis, and American audiences knew Gustav Mahler's music much earlier than the audiences in Germany or Austria. And it was the same with the music of Arnold Schönberg and Alban Berg and many others. Many great American orchestras were built by European artists who were exiled through the cruel stupidity of the Nazi government. And skilled teachers fled also, helping great music schools to develop in America as well as in England. The way vocal technique is taught in America is very effective, and I don't know of any incorrectly educated American singers.

With this solid technical foundation, American singers could appropriate the European tradition. I believe Old Europe must make an effort to avoid losing its standing because of a certain arrogance which says, "*We* have the heritage, and *we* know how it should be done." American singers have an incredible will and diligence, which many European singers don't have, and some also have the good fortune to receive substantial private support. As was apparent at the AIDS benefit concert, Americans can't count on their government for help and must manage to do things on their own.

The world has gotten smaller, and beautiful voices and talented singers can be found everywhere. I'm very happy that today people from all races are hired at opera houses, if they're qualified. It wasn't always like that. When Sir Rudolf Bing invited the famous American alto Marian Anderson to sing at the Met, there was a scandal because she was black. Also Leontyne Price had difficulties at the Met when she first sang there. Some subscribers threatened to cancel their subscriptions! Even in the sixties, Reri Grist, the delightful dark-skinned soprano, wasn't allowed to show her own hair, which was tightly curled, in pictures for the Salzburg Festival program. Even though she was already a well-established star in Salzburg, she had to wear a wig or a hat in photos. And I think this was the case not only in Salzburg, but in other European countries too.

Those times are over, thank God! But I must admit that sometimes we could even laugh about it a little bit. When Leontyne Price sang Pamina in Mozart's *Zauberflöte* in Vienna, Walter Berry was singing Papageno. In the scene where he looks at a portrait to see if it's really Pamina, Papageno is supposed to say "Lips: red; Hair: black; Nose: white…," but Walter said, "Lips: red; Hair: black; Nose: …also black," and everyone enjoyed his little joke.

Memories of Salzburg

The Salzburg Festival, like Bayreuth, is a "Valhalla" for singers, and performing there is something we singers dream about. I can still remember my father once traveling to Salzburg before the war to see a performance. For him, it was a great experience, one he described in glowing terms. It was the most important event of the year, and much too expensive for my mother to accompany him. The cost of two train tickets from Aachen to Salzburg and back, plus two tickets to a performance along with hotel and meals, would break their budget, which was based on provincial opera house wages. Back then, there were no "Neckermann macht's möglich" tours ("Neckermann makes it possible"—Neckermann was famous for making things affordable in Germany), which today include transportation and hotel and tickets to an opera performance. Now tourists sometimes don't even know the name of the opera that they are attending in Salzburg, and often don't understand anything about it. Once when I sang Cherubino in Salzburg and Walter Berry was in the audience, he sat next to a very nice young American soldier. Suddenly the soldier turned to him and said with a very broad American accent, "I can't help thinking this Tcherobine character looks like a girl!"

On the one hand, it's good that a new audience is introduced to opera through these group tours, and hopefully the tourists will understand something about what they see and hear. On the other hand, it's sad for singers to know that they're singing in front of a totally ignorant audience. And here is one of the big differences between Salzburg and Bayreuth. At Bayreuth, the audience is full of Wagner lovers and Wagner experts. Who else would sit on those hard benches for five hours? Not long ago, a TV reporter had two tickets for a performance of *Un Ballo in Maschera* with Domingo at the Salzburg Festival, and he offered the tickets, along with a free helicopter ride to Salzburg and back, in exchange for tickets on the same day in Bayreuth. But he could find no one in Bayreuth who would accept his offer, even though he was giving them the opportunity to hear a great singer like Domingo. The Bayreuth audience is Wagner-obsessed, which is the opposite of the situation in Salzburg where the repertory is so varied that no regular audience attends particular performances. Instead, the audience comes to Salzburg to see and hear the great star singers and conductors.

Another difference between Bayreuth and Salzburg is the way the audience dresses. In Bayreuth you seldom see women dressed as if they were models in a fashion show, while in Salzburg there is almost a competition to see who will wear the most beautiful gown. The Salzburg newspapers even print pictures of the gowns, along with the names of the happy wearers. I must admit that for a few years I was intent on attending a special opening in Salzburg in the newest gown from the Viennese fashion house of Adlmüller, and I bought a ticket to a glittery Karajan premiere only just to be in the audience. It was an epicurean pleasure to be dressed up among people who are equally dressed up, especially at a time when no one dresses anymore. The audience was full of royalty, politicians, and successful business people, with Karajan loyalists in the less expensive seats. Most of the audience arrived in big limousines, some in Rolls-Royces and others "just" in Mercedes, while the citizens of Salzburg and the tourists stood in large groups across the street from the Festival Hall, watching the wealthy, beautifully dressed people get out of their cars. The crowning glory of all this was Karajan's third wife Eliette, who would rush into the auditorium after everyone else was seated and the lights were starting to dim. She was always accompanied by a splendid-looking man, and she was always dressed in the latest fashion from the house of Dior with magnificent jewelry and her long blond Lorelei-like hair. Certainly, all this was worth the price of admission!

One has doubts about this kind of audience's appreciation for music. However, those who returned year after year to Salzburg seemed to develop into real music lovers, and certainly no longer came only for the social events. Perhaps this was because the music was always beyond reproach in Karajan productions, while the scenery and costumes and other parts of the production might easily be considered overdone.

Only Bernstein was acclaimed to the same degree as Karajan. At first, all Karajan's Salzburg performances took place in the Felsenreitschule, a building that was part of a riding school until 1960 when the new festival halls were completed. Karajan always conducted in the larger one, and seldom, if ever, in the smaller one. On the extremely wide stage in the large Festival Hall, Karajan, with the support of his stage designer Günther Schneider-Siemssen, could really go all out. They exploited all the modern visual and acoustical resources available to them at the time. Karajan's production of *Boris Godunov* by Modest Mussorgsky was more Russian than Russia, with bells that pealed so loudly that they seemed to be suspended above the middle of the auditorium.

The audience celebrated Karajan and itself, and the productions were not only great artistic achievements, but also lavish spectacles, with only the most famous singers on stage. Afterwards everyone reconvened at the restaurant in the Goldener Hirsch, where you could see famous people sitting on the very uncomfortable but "typically Salzburg" wooden chairs. Surely the evening's performance was soon forgotten as the champagne flowed. High society gathered, but no one ever saw Karajan there. He was a very shy man, and, when he was younger, he even had difficulty speaking a whole sentence smoothly. Also, he always had a lot of work to do the next day, and many people today seem to forget what a very hard worker he was.

A Karl Böhm premiere was not at all as lavish, and the audience was completely different, full of Mozart and Richard Strauss lovers. Böhm mainly conducted in the small Festival Hall, where the ambiance is much less festive. There one can't be seen as easily, since the foyer is much smaller, and that is probably why the ladies' evening gowns were considerably simpler, and few famous people attended. But for Mozart operas, the small Festival Hall is an ideal setting, as good as the Landestheater or the Residenzhof. Critics characterized these performances under Böhm as modest, but the most wonderful music was made there, in part because Böhm received so much less media coverage than his famous colleague. Böhm was always the servant of art

For many decades, Karajan and Böhm were a constant presence at the Festival, and I had the good fortune to appear with both of them. I first sang the Composer and later Ariadne in *Ariadne auf Naxos*, and I also sang Cherubino, Dorabella, Iphigénie, the Marschallin, the Dyer's Wife, and Leonore in *Fidelio* under Karl Böhm, in addition to many concerts. Under Karajan I sang more concerts than operas. I sang the Verdi *Requiem*, Mahler's *Das Lied von der Erde*, Beethoven's *Missa Solemnis*, and Bach's *St. Matthew Passion*. In opera, I sang Brangäne, Fricka in *Die Walküre*, and Waltraute in *Götterdämmerung* at the Easter Festival, and Eboli and Octavian during the summer.

When I sang in Salzburg for the first time, I decided to rent an apartment. After all, I had to be there for about two months, and a hotel would have been much too expensive. Besides, I didn't want to spend such a long time living in only one room. Luckily, many Salzburg residents rent their apartments or houses during the summer, and go to quieter places to avoid all the tourists. In the summer of 1955, I lived with my mother, as always, just a ten-minute walk from the festival halls. That was very important to me back then because I didn't own a car, and taking a taxi would have been too expensive. Also, the walk was good for me because all the tension I began to feel while warming up at our apartment would ease a bit, and I'd arrive more relaxed at the rehearsal or performance.

Later, with my husband Walter Berry and our whole household, I rented a large house outside of Salzburg. In the fifties and sixties, Salzburg was quite different from the way it was during Karajan's later years. The town was not yet overrun with tourists, and you could still walk comfortably through the Getreidegasse, one of the main streets in the old part of Salzburg, and you could park cars everywhere. No one complained about the hordes of tourists; little did we know how crowded it would be thirty years later. The large Festival Hall was only in the planning stages, and I sang in the small Festival Hall and the Felsenreitschule, which back then was still uncovered, which made it an especially beautiful place to sing. The large live tree at the left side of the stage was visible under an open sky, and this tree, the rock face backdrop, and the rest of the natural surroundings were part of the playing area. Salzburg residents stood up on the Mönchsberg, a high hill partially surrounding the old part of Salzburg, and looked down on the performance. The audience could see the moon and stars—if they weren't caught in the famous Salzburg rain, which happened much too often. All of this was part of the old magic of the summer festival.

The original offices of the Festival management were in the small Festival Hall in comfortable, tiny rooms. Most of the workers shared offices, and only the President, Baron Heinrich Puthon, and the Festival manager, Dr. Tassilo Nekola, had private offices. All the offices smelled of coffee, and the atmosphere was one of friendliness and trust. Dr. Nekola once told me that Dimitri Mitropoulos, who was one of the leading conductors of his time, always signed a blank contract for Salzburg and never discussed his fee. We singers had small dressing rooms which we had to share now and then with colleagues. It's true that in many theaters it goes without saying that several actors or singers have to share a dressing room, and if you are young and only singing a small role, this doesn't bother you very much. But if you are singing a demanding role and want to get ready in a peaceful and relaxed atmosphere, it's very unpleasant to have to share a dressing room with others, not to mention a common toilet.

Old theaters always smelled very nicely of make-up, just as hospitals always used to smell of chloroform. The special make-up odor stayed in the walls and carpets, giving the theaters a unique atmosphere. Today, in the age of deodorizing sprays and Mr. Clean, the wonderful old theater smells are gone, since deodorizers not only destroy all natural odors but themselves are much more pungent than powder or make-up. Only at La Scala in Milan and Covent Garden in London do these unmistakable old theater smells still exist today.

When the large Festival Hall was completed, everything became very elegant. Linoleum sparkled everywhere, and each dressing room even had a piano. An enormous number of administrative offices were included, and the "Beamtenlaufbahn" was full of long corridors lined with office doors. Karajan had a wing of his own to handle the administration of the summer and Easter festivals, and in his corridor there was a red carpet. But the smell of make-up was completely gone! Certainly the new building reflected its era, which was far more impersonal than the previous one, but I still look back on the "old days" with melancholy and nostalgia.

I had the great honor of singing the first notes at the opening celebration of the large Festival Hall on July 26, 1960. Karajan conducted the Gloria from Mozart's "Great" *Mass in C Minor* with the Vienna Philharmonic. The first thing I sang was the "Laudamus te," which I love, and later I sang a duet with the wonderful soprano, Leontyne Price, whom we called the "Black Orchid."

The idea that Leontyne Price and I should sing at the opening was a sudden inspiration of Karajan's, and the question that worried me most was (as usual) what was I going to wear? Since it was a morning concert, I couldn't wear a long evening gown, so I decided on a "cocktail dress," which was a popular thing for a woman to wear back then. I had to make a quick trip to Munich to pick one up.

At the celebration itself, the speeches seemed endless. We singers sat and waited and waited, and we were very bored, as was the Philharmonic and Karajan also. Our "chief" slumped quite casually in his chair, until it was finally time for a typically Karajanesque entry for the orchestra. It's difficult to describe, but he stood up from his relaxed position, and with one sweeping gesture—raising his arms across his body at the same time as he rose from his chair—he gave a precise downbeat to the orchestra. Two different moods, complete casualness and concentrated precision, were seamlessly connected in that one gesture. Among all of us musicians there were secret winks of approval—at last!

Along with mass tourism in Salzburg also came the "selling" of performing artists. Alongside lace panties, bras, and Mozartkugeln (a special candy with Mozart's picture on the wrapper), among carpets, antiques, and cars—from every shop window you can see the publicity photos of various recording artists smiling at you. Even taxis display these images. But you don't see any artists walking through the streets of Salzburg anymore, and they haven't done so for a long time. In the past, artists would meet in the coffeehouses, but today they flee into the countryside and live near the various lakes, trying to enjoy a kind of working vacation. The Salzkammergut would be a wonderful place to have a vacation, if it weren't for the famous (or should I say infamous) Salzburg rain, which can pour continuously for days. I have a rule of thumb for Salzburg weather: "If you can't see the fortress, it's raining. If you can, it will rain soon." My son Wolfgang was born in March 1959, and that summer the whole family, along with Wolfi's nanny, came to Salzburg for the festival. It rained continuously. The Salzach, the river that flows through the center of Salzburg, overflowed its banks, and many bridges were washed away. On the shore, you could only see the tops of streetlights rising out of the water. Outside the Hotel Steinlechner, I waded through knee-deep water in the streets, while stranded cars stood everywhere. And our dear nanny was very angry. "If only I had stayed in Vienna with the baby," she would say, "then I would be able to go out for walks." The weather in Vienna was, of course, wonderful at that time.

For how many years did I spend my two "vacation" months of July and August, when the Vienna State Opera is closed, in cold weather and rain! Several singers, especially foreign ones, refused to come to Salzburg because of the terrible weather. Georges Simoneau, for example, had a sensational success as Ottavio in *Don Giovanni*, but he flatly refused to come back to Salzburg a second time. However, when the sun does shine in Salzburg, the city is a miracle of beauty. And whenever I see the city of Salzburg in the sun, I'm overwhelmed.

We always worked hard in Salzburg. Rehearsals and more rehearsals, even when we'd already performed a work together many times with the same con-ductor. Not even Sunday was a day of rest. For us Salzburg was like a vacation only when we had a few minutes between rehearsals and performances to look at the wonderful scenery.

Unfortunately for me, a warm Alpine wind often blows in Salzburg, and this wind has always affected me badly because I'm very sensitive to weather. It doesn't only give me migraines, but it also makes me nervous. I would wake up in the morning restless and jumpy with butterflies in my stomach for no obvious reason. These butterflies were not helpful at all when I was singing! So I took various pills, which relieved my symptoms somewhat, but also made my throat dry, which was a real nuisance.

Salzburg and its festivals always were special, and will remain so. After the very opulent Karajan years, the new festival managers Dr. Franz Willnauer and Dr. Gérard Mortier are seeking a fundamental change in the kinds of perfor-mances given in Salzburg. They want to make the festivals more contemporary, without star cults and with cheaper seats, so that younger audiences would attend. I myself always think of Salzburg as a Mozart city, which should con-centrate on performances of his music. This would fit so nicely into my person-al performance scheme. Salzburg would play Mozart, Verona Verdi, Pesaro Rossini, Bayreuth Wagner, and Munich Strauss. Then all the festivals would have their own special character, and be assured of a first-class audience which would be especially interested in the kind of music performed in each city.

From 1955 until my farewell on August 9, 1993, I spent many summers in Salzburg singing in operas, oratorios, and orchestral concerts, and giving lieder recitals. Despite rain and alpine winds, I have many beautiful memories of performances in Salzburg that can truly be called "festival" level. And these performances took place thanks to the great conductors Karl Böhm and Herbert von Karajan, who for decades made sure that Salzburg performances were of the highest artistic quality.

At one performance in Salzburg in the late fifties, I remember experienc-ing a special moment when I thought fleetingly of Goethe's words "Vervweile doch, du bist so schön" (Please linger, you are so beautiful), and every fiber of my being was filled with an indescribable happiness. I was singing Dorabella in Mozart's *Così fan tutte* at the Residenzhof, with Karl Böhm conducting the Vienna Philharmonic. It was a rare high summer evening when the weather was clear, and Irmgard Seefried, who was singing my sister Fiordiligi, and I had just made our first appearance and had begun the duet "O guarda sorella" where we sing of our love while looking at pictures of our future husbands in lockets around our necks. We were wearing delightful rococo-costumes by

Caspar Neher, and our heads were crowned with tiny hats, full of flowers and bows, with long silk ribbons that gently fluttered in the evening breeze. From the stage, which was on the grounds of the Archbishop's residence, I could see the lighted towers of the Cathedral across the river, all greenish gold. The breathtaking beauty of the city of Salzburg and the wonderful sound of the Vienna Philharmonic playing Mozart's music bought me one of those rare moments that one would gladly cling to forever. In that gentle breeze, I felt as if God's breath had touched me.

America in the Open Air

There are many very famous open-air festivals, especially in America, that seem to work very well. Some of these are Tanglewood, near Boston, and Ravinia, near Chicago, and concerts are also given at the beautiful Hollywood Bowl in Los Angeles. Both Tanglewood and Ravinia have music pavilions, where the orchestra and part of the audience sits under a roof. Behind the seated audience, there is a large grassy field where people bring their own blankets and chairs, and the area becomes a big public gathering place. Some just lie on the grass, others bring elaborate picnics, and some young women even nurse their babies. And all of these people are able to hear a first-class concert under the stars.

The oldest and most famous festival is Tanglewood, which was founded by the conductor Serge Koussevitzky in 1938, and which also has a prestigious summer music school, the Berkshire Music Center, begun under the direction of Koussevitzky in 1940. Experts are sent to all countries of the world to search for young talent, especially for conducting talent, and the best are given the opportunity to study at Tanglewood with a first-class faculty. Leonard Bernstein studied conducting at Tanglewood in 1940, and later taught there. Today Seiji Ozawa, the music director of the Boston Symphony, is in charge of Tanglewood and its music school.

Bernstein brought the spirit of Tanglewood to Europe and Asia. With Justus Frantz, he founded the Schleswig-Holstein Music Festival, where he taught and made music with a student orchestra. Now, every year, a new youth orchestra is organized there and gives concerts. For Asian musicians, Bernstein founded a summer festival in Sapporo, Japan.

In 1970 I made a tour of open-air concerts in America. Since I stayed mainly in hotels that had swimming pools, I always called this my "Swimming Pool Tour." Such tours are quite strenuous, not only because of the routine of flying, unpacking, rehearsing, singing at the concert, repacking (without forgetting anything!), and flying on to the next city, but also because of the invitations to receptions. I attended these receptions now and then, but I usually preferred not to go because I didn't know anyone, and the small talk was totally pointless. But one thing I do remember from this tour was a student with long hair tied in a pigtail at the back, which was still quite unusual in those days. He drove me to rehearsal, sat in the audience, and listened. Then, while driving me back to the hotel, he said, "You don't have to take drugs in your profession. You get high when you make music!"

I also remember another strange experience in America. When I was singing in *Rosenkavalier* in San Francisco, I got a phone call from a fan who wanted to invite me to dinner. Because I was completely alone, I accepted. It turned out that my fan was a very good-looking young man. He told me that he had all my records and was very happy to take me out. We got into his car, and I expected that we would drive to a restaurant. Wrong! We stopped in front of a pretty residential house, and he invited me to come in. I hesitated at first, because I'd seen so many detective stories on TV. No one at the hotel had any idea where I had gone, and now, looking back, I'm amazed at how reckless I was. But then I thought to myself, how nice this young man was, and surely nothing would happen, so I entered the house and was greeted by a group of young men who seemed to be living in a kind of commune.

In the middle of the living room there was something that looked like a big black bed, which they insisted I try because it was the latest thing, a water bed. The mattress was filled with a liquid that adapted perfectly to one's body shape. They started to smoke, but I declined with thanks—it smelled a bit sweet in the room already—and they played the newest recording of Joan Baez for me. It was really quite cozy, and all of the young men were opera fans. Then they invited me to have dinner at a big table in the kitchen, which was very prettily set. Two or three of them cooked, completely vegetarian, and the food was very tasty. With the meal, they served a good Californian wine, and everything was very charming.

But after the meal I didn't want to stay any longer. I was happy that everything had gone well up to that point, so I excused myself, saying that I had to save my voice for the next performance. My fan drove me back to the hotel, and finally the whole spooky evening was over. Not until I was lying safely in my bed did I allow my imagination to paint a picture of all the horrible things that could have happened, and no one would have known where I was!

Near San Francisco, I also sang at the Concord Pavilion, another huge American venue for open-air concerts. This was in September 1987 on a tour with Leonard Bernstein and the Vienna Philharmonic during which I sang the Lamentation from the "Jeremiah," Bernstein's first symphony. But I must admit that Tanglewood is the American festival that is closest to my heart, because of its beautiful natural setting, its long tradition, and because of the love Leonard Bernstein had for this festival. The youth orchestras I heard there always astonished me because they were so fabulous technically, even though they came together from so many different countries and only for a short time. And everyone always spoke English! They studied with the experienced orchestral players of the Boston Symphony individually until the first rehearsal, when the conductor took over. The young players reacted with great enthusiasm, and they really came together beautifully to make music. It was wonderful to see with what trust and dedication they followed Ozawa's or Bernstein's direction.

From Milan to Tokyo

I've sung in many opera houses and concert halls throughout the world, and the two that impressed me most were the old opera houses Teatro alla Scala in Milan and Teatro Colón in Buenos Aires. Both houses have a wonderful acoustic, and the Teatro Colón is said to have the best acoustic of any opera house in the world. I appeared there twice in the late sixties during what was called the "German Season," and I sang many roles: Cherubino, Ortrud, the Composer in *Ariadne auf Naxos*, Octavian, and the *Wozzeck* Marie. With my then-husband Walter Berry, I used the long trip there by boat as a vacation, and it was very restful. I remember one Viennese passenger who said, when we were out in the middle of the ocean, far away from any landmarks, "Wos! Do samma erst?" (What! We are only this far?) Walter and I flew back, but the trip was still very, very long because in those days many planes still had propellers.

In South America, everything was improvised. Nothing was ever ready for the dress rehearsals, neither costumes nor wigs, nor stage sets. Then, as if pixies had been at work overnight—a miracle—everything was there at the premiere! But I freely admit that I sang in cities like Buenos Aires only for the money.

In southern Argentina we were astonished to find houses and whole villages that looked Bavarian. Many German immigrants had settled there, as well as in Buenos Aires. Not only Jewish people who had fled Germany lived in the surrounding countryside, but also former high Nazi officials who were in hiding. But I didn't find that the South American countries were as influenced by European culture as the North American ones were.

Before the days of intercontinental flights, when travel was mainly by boat, singers liked to stop off in the Canary Islands because in Las Palmas, the capital city, there is an elegant, wood-paneled opera house. Since the days of Enrico Caruso, many great singers have made guest appearances there before taking the next boat and continuing their journeys either to Europe or America.

All the opera houses in northern Italy, such as the Teatro Communale in Bologna, Teatro dell'opera in Rome, Teatro Regio in Turin, Teatro Fenice in Venice, Teatro all Scala in Milan, and Teatro Communale in Florence are wonderful old-style buildings. I was invited to sing lieder in all these theaters and many others in Italy in an effort to bring the tradition of German art song to an Italian audience. But this was very difficult, unless I was singing in places where lieder and chamber music had been performed for many years and an audience had developed for it, such as in Rome, Turin, and Milan, and at the festivals of Monfalcone and Stresa.

Singing lieder in Italy can be very frustrating. For example, I once sang *Winterreise* at the Teatro Communale in Ferrare. No one in the management had made the effort to print a translation of the words in the program, or even just a short synopsis of them. The poor audience had to sit in the dark while I sang this very sad song cycle for almost an hour and a half, and they didn't understand a word or have any idea of what it was all about. They were condemned to persevere until the bitter end without the delight of hearing a single high note. And they weren't allowed to applaud between the individual songs either. I was frustrated, and, although the orchestra seats were relatively full, the boxes were totally empty. Later I learned the reason for this: the boxes are sold by subscription for the entire season to a number of opera-loving families who go only to opera and never to concerts, and the boxes can't be resold. The Italian audience enjoys Italian opera, but who among them would consider going to something as seemingly boring as a German lieder recital? In cities where a sincere effort has been made over many years to develop a concert audience with more varied tastes (and it has been a difficult struggle), there is now an enthusiastic audience. The unique musical missionary work of Erik Werba can be seen in Italy today because many of his former students, who didn't become practicing singers themselves, head Italian concert associations and are passing on the love for German song that they received from him.

Dr. Werba's work seems to have had a truly international influence. Once, after a recital in Seoul, I was amazed to meet many German-speaking Koreans who had studied with him in Vienna. Koreans, by the way, have especially beautiful voices, probably because of the resonance created by the bone structure in their faces, which usually have wide cheekbones and small noses.

Nowadays there are wonderful, modern concert halls, which seat several thousand people, in most international cities from Helsinki to Tokyo, and they are all built in a similar style. These halls, especially the Megaron in Athens, are extremely elegant, and built on a large scale, and they prove that a functional building can also be beautiful.

In Japan I sang in many halls. In 1963 I opened the new Theater Nissei in Tokyo, singing Leonore in *Fidelio* as a guest artist with the Deutsche Oper Berlin. I didn't return until 27 years later for a series of concerts. At first I hesitated to come because it was a big risk to try a comeback after so long. A whole new generation would hear me for the first time. At a press conference before the concerts, I saw many reporters who hadn't even been born when I sang in Tokyo in 1963. But the audiences at the concerts were very enthusiastic, as they are in all cosmopolitan cities, and in Japan the people in the audience even climb onto the stage. I always left the concert halls after taking many bows and receiving many gifts. The Japanese buy many, many records, and they wait patiently for hours in the hotel lobby to have them signed. Also in Japan I heard many beautiful voices—strangely enough, hardly any tenors, but many very good mezzo-sopranos. Almost all of the singers had studied with Erik Werba in Vienna!

I feel at home wherever music is made. Even though Tokyo seems strange because of all the incomprehensible (to me!) signs, I immediately feel comfortable when I go to an orchestral rehearsal, and we all make music together, regardless of the color of our skins, yellow, red, black, or white. The music always connects us! A concert hall resembles a church in that everyone there is united with the same thoughts and feelings, in the church through a common belief and in the concert hall through music. Nothing disturbs the harmony of souls.

But one thing that always did disturb me was having to sing in a multipurpose hall. There the musical vibrations were disrupted for me by the lingering echoes of business and political meetings. I have also taken part in concerts in huge sport arenas—unfortunately! A truly harmonious musical mood can never be created in such a place. With "serious" music, we don't only recreate the musical notes, but also the spirit of these pieces, and big halls are really not suitable for lieder recitals at all. The problem, of course, is money: small halls, small income; big halls, big income. In London there is a small hall, like the Brahms-Saal and the Mozart-Saal at the Konzerthaus in Vienna, called Wigmore Hall. All these are ideal for lieder recitals. Wigmore Hall seats about 800 people; I sang my very first London recital there in 1957 and my last one in 1993. In between, I tried the newly built Barbican Center, where there is a bigger hall, but it is prosaic and gray, and it didn't give me any real joy to sing there, even though I received a much higher fee. If a singer sings in football stadiums or other very big places with microphones, amplifiers, and loudspeakers, I think it's better to tell the audience that they might just as well stay home and put on a CD or a tape.

I've quickly forgotten many of the modern halls that I've sung in because they look too much alike and lack a special musical soul. The walls of these halls must soak up the sound of the music played in them for many years before they acquire their own tradition. When I and the other musicians and the audience come into an empty hall, we must feel that "Here music is made." All the new modern opera houses and concert halls must acquire a kind of musical patina from long use, so that they don't only shine on the outside, but radiate from within themselves the true soul of music.

Another Costume, Another Role

Carmen

I'm personally the exact opposite of Carmen, but it's one of the roles I've sung most often. Since I'm so different from Carmen, it took me many years to develop an approach that worked for me.

I first learned the role of Carmen immediately after the war with my mother. In addition to teaching me how to sing the music, she also tried to show me how to act the role. Looking back, it all seems quite funny, although we were very serious about it at the time. My mother danced for me and taught me how to play the castanets (very badly). These castanets, by the way, were the same ones that had survived the bombing of our house in Giessen by being hidden in the little trunk in the basement. My mother showed me how to swing my hips and make a sexy face, and I conscientiously imitated her, with the result that nobody asked me to play the role of Carmen for many years.

When I was first starting out in Frankfurt, I sang Mercédès, and, of course, my voice cracked on the high A in the trio during the fortunetelling scene. When Georg Solti was getting ready to take over as opera director there in the 1951/52 season, he asked me to sing the title role in a performance he was conducting. I gladly accepted the offer, and sang the role, but only once. In reviewing the performance, one critic wrote that "if a singer has enough experience to sing Carmen, she usually isn't young enough to do it, and Miss Ludwig is still very young." Who could blame him? During the first act, the flower that I was supposed to throw to Don José slipped down into my blouse, and I couldn't find it, no matter how hard I tried. But it didn't make any difference anyway since my Don José, the great heldentenor Wolfgang Windgassen, had already rushed off stage because he needed a drink.

Afterwards, I studied Carmen with Harro Dicks in Darmstadt, and he tried in vain to transform me into a femme fatale in the contemporary style. He told me to make my first entrance eating a banana, which was supposed to drive the men crazy, and I had no idea why at the time. Then, in the fourth act, I simply couldn't work myself up into a rage against Don José because for me he wasn't a man, but only a tenor. So the production in Darmstadt didn't work out either.

Next I found myself in the second cast of the 1956/57 production of *Carmen* in Vienna, originally designed for the American singer Jean Madeira, who had a great success in it. Madeira had a splendid, dark contralto voice, and looked fantastic. She was very tall, and she had experience with things like net stockings, and, most amazing of all, she could lift her skirt with her teeth! She really looked fabulous; she looked like what we used to call a "pin up girl" in the 1950s. Since I was in the second cast, I had to go on with almost no rehearsal. I'd been promised one stage rehearsal, so I put on my costume and make up for the first time at the celebrated Vienna State Opera, and was disappointed when my scenes were run through quickly and carelessly with only a small, white spotlight. At the performances themselves, my make-up was totally overdone, and, dressed in Madeira's net stockings, I tried to raise my skirt with my teeth. Of course, I failed dismally. Karl Löbl's review in the *Vienna Express* was headlined "An Obstinate Child's Gypsy Wedding." I was totally frustrated, and believed I had no future as Carmen.

Finally, I was contacted by Otto Schenk, who was getting ready to stage a new production of *Carmen* in Vienna. I told him all about my unfortunate experiences with Carmen, and asked him what he had in mind for his new production and what the sets and costumes would be like. I told him, "I'm not small and dainty, and I have round cheeks and a short nose" in order to explain to him that he had to make allowances for my appearance, or I wouldn't be able to make the character believable. We came to an agreement, and, for the first time, I met in Otti, as we called him, a director who could help me create the kind of Carmen that would work for me. I didn't do anything phony. I didn't wiggle my hips and try to look like a seductive vamp. And, for once, my costume didn't look as though it came out of a Spanish travel brochure. I played Carmen as a young woman of the people, a poor factory worker, who lives thoughtlessly and only follows her appetites. I made her shameless, fearless, amoral, and lusty. She had to be genuinely dramatic in the "card aria" in the third act, and bitterly cold when her passion for Don José dies in the last act.

At the podium Lorin Maazel conducted with spirit, and this was also the first time I sang *Carmen* in French. The costumes were in the style of the 1920s, only subtly Spanish, and so I felt comfortable. But later when I performed as a guest artist in another production outside of Vienna, I was lost again. Vocally, I loved the part. Making a voice sound sexy is a lot of fun, regardless of the language. I sang the Habañera and Seguidilla as *chansons*, but I think the most beautiful aria is the one in the fortunetelling scene in the third act. My mother always had the interpretation of Leo Blech, the famous *Carmen* conductor from Berlin, in her ears, and she considered it very important that I begin the "card aria" with an almost whispered pianissimo and return with the smoothest legato possible to that same pianissimo effect at the end of a phrase. It's the vocal high point of the opera for me, because I could color my voice very darkly and make a very dramatic impression on the audience because of the movement from the softest pianissimo to fortissimo. This is also the moment in the opera where Carmen's character changes. Her fatalistic belief in the cards gives her foreknowledge of her impending death, and yet, in spite of this knowledge, she fearlessly leads her life right to the end as the spirit moves her.

I must also add one other special association the last act of *Carmen* has for me. At the rehearsals for a London production, Jon Vickers, the Don José, flew into such a dramatic rage that he actually drew blood when he stabbed me, even though the knife was only a stage prop. I still bear the scar to this day.

The Marschallin

The Marschallin in *Der Rosenkavalier* by Richard Strauss is especially dear to me because of the text by Hugo von Hofmannsthal, and I have made her womanly philosophy my own. She says, for example:

> Die Zeit, die ist ein sondebar Ding.
> Wenn man so hinlebt, ist sie rein gar nichts.
> Aber dann auf einmal, da spürt man nichts als sie.

[Time is a strange thing.
As one lives from day to day, time means nothing at all.
But then suddenly, one is aware of nothing else.]

When I was young, I didn't even wear a watch, and later, when I had to pay more attention to the time, I only kept a watch in my pocket. The thought of wearing the passing time on my wrist seemed unbearable to me. I always wanted to live—so my mother said—in the present, but actually there is no such thing. Such an unruly sense of time makes it difficult for me today, looking back, to put old photos and past experiences in chronological order.

When I first sang the Marschallin, I was forty years old, exactly the time when people start looking back over their lives. And so it happened with me. It was as if I myself were speaking the Marschallin's words when she, still a young woman in her thirties, already sees herself as the "old princess, Resi," and says:

Wie kann denn das geschehen?
Wie macht denn das der liebe Gott?
Wo ich doch immer die gleiche bin.
Un wenn er's schon so machen muß,
warum laßt er mich denn zuschaun dabei mit gar so klarem Sinn!

[How can it happen?
How does the dear God do it?
I always stay the same, after all.
And if He has to do it like this,
Why does He let me watch it happen with such clear senses!]

So felt I. And as my thoughts mingled with hers, I took up her philosophy as my own, especially these two thoughts:

Jedes Ding hat seine Zeit.
[Everything has its time.]

and

Leicht muß man sein,
mit leichtem Herz und leichten Händen
halten und nehmen, halten und lassen.

[Light must one be,
With light heart and light hands
Hold and take, hold and let go.]

Today, as I write these words, I know that in December 1994 I shall end my professional life as a singer, and I'm thinking, like the Marschallin, that I must let this artificial life go with a light heart and light hands. Just as the Marschallin examines her face in the mirror, so I examine my profession. The Marschallin says,

> Mann is dazu da, daß man's ertragt.
> [One is here to endure it.]

And in another place,

> In dem Wie, da liegt der ganze Unterschied.
> [In the how lies the whole difference.]

The Marschallin sings these phrases in her monologue in the first act, and I interpreted them as I would a Schubert song. With the orchestral accompaniment, it's possible to make the text very clearly understood, and to express every subtle nuance of resignation and sorrow with vocal color.

There are two kinds of Marschallin voices. Each type changes the character of the Marschallin somewhat, and my mezzo voice is the darker of the two types. Which you prefer is a matter of taste. On the one hand, there are Marschallins like Elisabeth Schwarzkopf or Lisa Della Casa, and, on the other, Marschallins like Regine Crespin, Sena Jurinac, and me. The silvery, light voice of the Schwarzkopf type of Marschallin makes the character sound more distinguished and aristocratic. The darker voices make her sound more womanly, even motherly.

The beginning of the trio near the end of the third act, "Hab mir's gelobt, Ihn lieb zu haben," was always a problem for my mezzo voice because it lies very high and should be sung pianissimo. Only soprano voices can really do that. So I always began very gently, but with a heavier sound. On the other hand, the Marschallin's first act monologue lay wonderfully in my middle register, and it is glorious for a darker voice to sing.

The Marschallin's autumnal resignation, her "light" farewell to Octavian, and her wise withdrawal from the passing scene, all these I have taken to heart. At the close of my years as a singer, I'll follow the Marschallin's example, and let things go as lightly as she does.

Trouser Roles

I generally never liked playing "trouser roles." I certainly never liked acting the role of the seventeen year and two month old and still-wet-behind-the-ears playboy Octavian in *Der Rosenkavalier*. He understands absolutely nothing about the wise things the Marschallin says to him, which, I suppose, is the privilege of youth. And I never liked singing him either. He has a few beautiful phrases, but nothing really easy because he's suddenly always hitting high notes without any preparation. I also didn't care to play him because I always had to be so careful about how much I ate, as I also did when playing Cherubino in Mozart's *Le Nozze di Figaro*. Boys must always be thin and, for obvious reasons, I couldn't show any of my feminine attributes. I had to wear a Brustleiberl in Vienna and a Busenquetsche (literally, bosom crusher) in Berlin, within which one can scarcely breathe. Legs tensed, knees straight! I had to get used to hugging under the arms as men do rather than around the neck. I had to totally forget my femininity, and that was impossible for me. In America, I was always considered too round and feminine for Octavian. In Europe, it's understood that the charm of the role is directly related to the fact that Octavian is played by a woman.

Once, I attended a reading of the text of *Rosenkavalier* without accompaniment. It was intriguing to see the character of Ochs von Lerchenau clearly, without the music, even though in the opera his part is largely *Sprechgesang* (literally, spoken-sung). It was also wonderful to hear the text in the duets and trios spoken separately so it could be clearly understood, since you really can't make out the words when everybody is singing together during the opera. Octavian was played by a young man, and, surprisingly, it was not at all interesting. Part of the appeal of the opera lies in the spicy situation in which the two lovers are both played by women. In European countries, this is sometimes too well understood, and when I sang the role, I received letters fairly often from lesbians who thought I was one of them.

And *Rosenkavalier* can be risky for other reasons. In the third act when Octavian is disguised as Mariandl, Ochs invites "her" to drink some wine to which Mariandl responds, "Nein, nein, nein, nein! Ich trink' kein Wein." This doesn't suit me at all because I really like a good glass of Austrian wine.

So, when I first played the role, I always drank the "wine" anyway, as a joke, when Ochs wasn't looking. Eventually this got me in trouble because I drank a glass of real wine on an empty stomach by mistake, and became so genuinely tipsy that I suddenly wasn't sure which line I had to sing. To help myself keep the lines straight, I discreetly sang everyone else's lines. Once and never again! It was only in Vienna that I was given real wine. In other opera houses we were usually served apple juice or some other sweet stuff, which I hated. One always has to be careful on the stage, where almost anything can happen.

I didn't like Cherubino in Le Nozze di Figaro either. The only trouser role I really liked was the Composer in Ariadne auf Naxos by Richard Strauss, because he is so innocent, so possessed by his music, and so naïve in his first meeting with a woman. And, best of all, the music is wonderful to sing.

Speaking of Mozart reminds me of the role of Dorabella in Così fan tutte, which was fun when I was younger but not later on. I never really liked singing all the recitatives and the big ensembles. Only the duets with my sister, Fiordiligi, were magical, as was the trio "Soave il vento" with Fiordiligi and Don Alfonso. Actually, Dorabella was very well suited to me when I was younger. The role is funny, coquettish, carefree, and not difficult to sing, but perhaps it's precisely because there are no hurdles to jump that I lost interest in the role.

Fidelio was my "problem" child, a role I loved very much. Because it's a true soprano part, it really lay much too high for me, and I sang it with a lot of calculation and a lot of technique. I planned in advance exactly how I would sing each section—some parts as a lyric soprano, some as a dramatic soprano, and almost never as a mezzo. Right up through the big "Abscheulicher" aria in the first act, I was always a bundle of nerves because the high B at the end is difficult, even for sopranos. Imagine how difficult it was for me! I knew exactly where I could save my voice, which phrases to pass over lightly, and where to breathe and take breaks in order to sing the high note. But even with all my calculations, hitting the note was still always a matter of luck. If a conductor slowed down the tempo just slightly, he could make me miss it. Otto Klemperer, with whom I recorded the opera, kept ideal tempi for me. Later on, I only sang the role with Karajan and Böhm, except once when I sang it with a different conductor in Berlin, and I had great difficulties. But after the "Abscheulicher" aria was over, I could relax, and the critics wrote that I was looser in the second act. Such comments were made about other singers too, and I always wondered why critics didn't understand that we singers are deathly afraid of that big aria.

Leonore/Fidelio is a glorious role, and also the theme of the opera is wonderful too. Leonore doesn't just want to free her husband. She wants justice to triumph, but in a warmly human way, not at all like the fanatical pursuit of justice in *Elektra*. Because Fidelio was my problem child, I had the greatest satisfaction in singing it—when the performance went well and I hit the high B.

Klytämnestra

Klytämnestra (in *Elektra* by Richard Strauss) is an anxious person who cannot sleep because she is guilty of the murder of her husband, King Agamemnon. For me, her daughter Elektra is truly impossible to live with, because Elektra wants absolute justice. She wants revenge for the death of her father, and incites first her sister Chrysothemis (without success) and then her brother Orest (with success) to murder their mother. How much heavier does the murder of the mother weigh than the murder of the husband! For me, Klytämnestra had some justification for her actions, while Elektra has none. Agamemnon sacrificed Klytämnestra's other daughter, Iphigenie, to the gods so they would give him favorable winds for his return from Troy. But truth to tell, he sacrificed Iphigenie for men's favorite "sport," namely war, which, besides, kept him away from home for years. Klytämnestra searches in vain for help from her daughter, and her frustration eventually changes to hatred. Above all things I tried to make the audience feel sorry for Klytämnestra, and understand the mother-daughter conflict.

I tell you my ideas about Klytämnestra to explain why I never portrayed her as an evil old witch. Inwardly she is a wreck, but outwardly she doesn't need to be. I never liked to use too much make-up when singing the role, because it distorts Klytämnestra's face and makes it look old and ugly. I also tried to add to the vocal expression of the character with my whole body by using fidgety hand movements, nervous starts, and sudden head movements.

Klytämnestra is a wonderful part to sing and act. Because it would be a shame if the audience didn't understand Hofmannsthal's marvelous text, absolute clarity in singing her words is essential. Of course, the emphasis is on the singing, and Richard Strauss has created superb, psychologically true music for her, where beautifully sung phrases alternate with partially sung, partially spoken ones. This picture of a neurotic is so brilliantly done by Hofmannsthal and Strauss that even listeners at a concert performance, without costume, wig and stage make-up, see the character of Klytämnestra clearly before them.

The Dyer's Wife

The Dyer's Wife in *Die Frau ohne Schatten* by Richard Strauss is a wonderful character who can be played very effectively on stage. She is a woman full of inner turmoil, and it's possible to show her development from a dissatisfied wife to a loving one as she gradually realizes her husband's inner goodness. Since this is again a soprano role and I was singing it, Karl Böhm had to make cuts in the score for me, and he did a very good job. Nevertheless, I was very nervous. Strauss, like Wagner, is generally not too difficult to sing, since both composers emphasize the text and its interpretation more than pure bel canto style. Since a beautiful sound is less important than the meaning of the words, a singer can occasionally shorten a tone or start a tone a bit late, if it has to be held a long time. And singing in German allows you to "spit" quite a few of the consonants. This "spitting" is one of the little tricks we singers hand down from generation to generation, but never reveal to outsiders.

I sang the Dyer's Wife for the first time in 1964 at the Vienna State Opera with Karajan. Later, I sang it in New York during the opening weeks of the new Metropolitan Opera at the Lincoln Center in 1966. The performance was a sensational success, and the Dyer's Wife was my breakthrough role at the Met.

I sang the Dyer's Wife for only a decade because, in spite of Karl Böhm's cuts, the part was still too high for me. I was completely burned out the day after a performance, both psychologically and physically, and I needed time to recover. I was also exhausted vocally. Luckily, I was wise enough not to sing the role too often, especially since I knew that there was no other female singer (no understudy or "cover") at the Met who could stand in for me if I caught a cold or had some other emergency. Later, I always insisted that there be another singer ready and waiting to sing the role for me, so that I wouldn't be under so much stress.

The later years of singing this role were also difficult because Barak, my husband in the opera, was always played by Walter Berry, who was also my husband in real life—and we were getting a divorce. Imagine my emotional turmoil. On the stage, I was playing a woman who sees that she has misjudged her husband when she recognizes his goodness and simplicity and after she resists the temptation of selling her "shadow" (symbolic of her ability to have children) for a beautiful young lover and other material things. In real life, I knew reconciliation was impossible because we had simply grown apart. It was surely a difficult time for both of us, and I simply couldn't handle the psychological strain. So I sang the Dyer's Wife for the last time at the Salzburg Festival with Karl Böhm in 1974.

Ortrud

I sang Ortrud in Wagner's *Lohengrin* for the first time at the Deutsche Oper Berlin when it reopened after the war in 1961. Wieland Wagner directed, and Heinrich Hollreiser conducted. Since I was well established in the opera business by then and very busy, I didn't have time to study the part with a coach. Instead I studied it "dry" (without accompaniment) at home, which really meant in various hotel rooms. Since my mother usually accompanied me on my trips so she could take care of my son Wolfgang who also came along whenever possible, I really learned the role with her. I thought at first that Ortrud was really magnificently angry, and consistent in her character. It was through my mother, who had sung the part when she was young, that I got to know the many facets of this proud and evil woman.

In the first act, it's tempting just to "stand around" because Ortrud sings nothing except a few lines in ensembles at the end of the act. But actually the first act is very important because it's where Ortrud's character and beliefs must be made clear to the audience. Her facial expression and body language must be that of a strong personality, who dominates her husband Telramund, and who obviously despises the new Christian society which has come to power. To help get these ideas across, Wieland Wagner gave me a scepter to hold as a symbol of Ortrud's belief in the old gods. I could gaze at it intently and use it in many other ways to express Ortrud's strength and determination.

At the beginning of the second act, Ortrud dominates. In the first scene, she is embittered, despising Telramund and concocting an evil plan in the darkness. Here the Ortrud voice alternates between whispering and mockery. Afterwards, when Elsa appears on her balcony and Ortrud calls her name several times, the cries must sound like the cries of a suffering animal. The following scene with Elsa must be sung with the smoothest of Italian-style legato and with great beauty, to captivate Elsa and lull her into cooperating.

Once she has achieved her goal, Ortrud can unleash her desire for vengeance in her call to the old gods. Here I think that a singer shouldn't spare her voice, but pull out all the stops. Hollreiser gave me wonderful support here by sharply tightening the tempo. The effect was twofold. The section was simply easier to sing, and the contrast with the previous legato singing was very dramatic, resulting in the audience breaking out in cheers afterwards. I must admit that this was a moment where I really enjoyed my own screams, and my whole body trembled with the pleasure and intensity of them. Ortrud's pretense of humility follows and creates another contrast, and a singer also needs to show the wounded pride that always lurks underneath.

Finally, as the scene concludes, Ortrud comes to dominate Elsa, sounding regal and haughty. All these different emotions, and the contrast between full-out and beautifully controlled legato singing, creates one of the most dramatic scenes in opera. At times, the line is very high for a mezzo-soprano, so the role is sometimes sung by dramatic sopranos. The important thing is to sing most of Ortrud's music beautifully, so that the audience respects and understands her, and perhaps even feels sorry for her.

Ortrud returns at the very end of the opera to wildly scream out her scorn for Lohengrin and all that he represents. But these screams must be sung very carefully for the simple reason that Ortrud hasn't been on the stage or sung a note for more than an hour. So it's critical for the singer to warm up beforehand in her dressing room to make sure that blood is flowing well through the vocal cords.

A second problem for those of us mezzos who sing the role is that these final screams lie very high for us, and we have to sing as if we were rather high sopranos. The technique I used I call "register singing." When I stayed in my upper register and used a facial position that showed a lot of teeth, which, coincidentally, is great for making Ortrud look as if she is gloating during her short-lived moment of triumph, I could sing the high tessitura lightly, and avoid, as is sometimes done, transposing all the notes lower, which is much less effective.

In my opinion, Ortrud is by far the most interesting role in *Lohengrin*, and I sang her with passion. Strangely, I never found the role difficult.

Kundry

Kundry in *Parsifal* is one of my favorite characters, partly because of the many changes she undergoes during the opera. In the first act, she is a haunted creature, searching for balm for the wounds of Amfortas, which she herself had caused unknowingly. In the second act, she is entirely transformed, and the act begins with the famous Kundry screams, as her "master" Klingsor again takes possession of her. These screams are not at all easy to do. They can sound quite unnatural, and if they don't sound vocally "true," they lose the effect that Wagner meant for them to have on the audience. And if one lets loose too forcefully, these screams can seriously damage the vocal cords.

As Kundry is awakened, she changes into a beautiful, seductive woman, and this side of the character is wonderful both to sing and to act. I did the role for the first time in Vienna under Karajan, who both directed and conducted. Unfortunately, Karajan wanted three different women for the three different Kundrys. For the first act and for the screams at the beginning of the second, he chose Elisabeth Höngen. I was to be the "beautiful" Kundry for the rest of the second act, and, in the third act, he wanted the actress Judith Holzmeister for the "penitent" Kundry. This could be done because Kundry has only two words in the third act, which an actress could easily whisper. But Karajan only managed to realize his vision partially, and Elisabeth Höngen played Kundry in the third act. Because I had no understanding of the complexities of Kundry's character at the time, I was more or less just a body in the second act.

Later, when Karajan left Vienna, I finally got to sing the whole role, and I slowly grew into the character and got a feeling for the different facets of Kundry, and the secret of her origins. Who is Kundry really? Parsifal's mother? The spirit of Mary Magdalene, a seductress in search of redemption? Acting Kundry is wonderful, and singing the role also. When Parsifal sings "Du weinest—sieh! Es lacht die Aue," I was so moved that I always started to cry, especially when Jon Vickers was my Parsifal. Vickers was always completely believable onstage in whatever role he was playing. He had a way of singing in between the notes, which was far more expressive than merely singing the music as written, and he could really express the meaning of the music. The last time I sang in *Parsifal* with him was at the Met, with James Levine conducting, and I remember how Levine conjured up a pianissimo-carpet for me during Kundry's narrative "Ich sah das Kind." And I'll never forget Vickers' cry of "Amfortas" after Kundry's kiss, as Parsifal suddenly realizes what is happening to him. At that moment, the anguish in Vickers' voice was far more powerful and moving than any beautiful singing could ever be.

Wagner's Ring:
Fricka and Waltraute

Unfortunately I'm not a soprano, and couldn't sing Brünnhilde in Wagner's *Der Ring des Nibelungen*—to my eternal sorrow! So I made do with both Frickas and Waltraute.

I have very little to say about the *Rheingold* Fricka. For me, she is boring because she has almost nothing to sing, and she just stands around a lot. But the *Walküre* Fricka is something else entirely. I love the argument she has with her husband Wotan, which Wagner has written with such psychological truth. As a childless wife, she is, of course, infuriated that her husband has put so many bastards into the world. Partly she pretends and partly she is really indignant that incestuous love is going on between his twin children Siegmund and Sieglinde. With all the means that a woman possesses—but always as a woman and not as a fury—Fricka demands her rights! She should be played and sung confidently, always with great noble gestures, and never as a quarrelsome housewife. She is definitely the stronger personality, but, in spite of that, I always tried to put a certain sorrow in her exit, sorrow about having triumphed over her husband. Once, in Chicago more than 30 years ago, so much was cut out of this scene that almost nothing remained. This is not a good solution. I always made an effort to sing Fricka's words very clearly, because everyone in the audience must understand all the words or they will get bored. By the way, my most wonderful, unsurpassed Wotan-husband was Hans Hotter.

In *Götterdämmerung*, Waltraute, like the *Walküre* Fricka, has only one scene, but what a scene! It is the turning point of the whole Ring. If only Brünnhilde could be made to understand the curse on the ring and refuse it! I always sang the scene as the literal expression of the relationship between two sisters, but I also felt an almost missionary zeal to express Wagner's ideas about greed and its terrible destructive power.

Waltraute's narrative is wonderful to sing, and a good conductor gives the singer time and keeps the orchestra very quiet, as the tessitura is very low. Above all else, again the highest principle is: sing the words as clearly as possible! And also sing beautifully, because great sorrow should be heard in the sound of Waltraute's voice—the sorrow of Wotan's fate—because by this point in the story, he knows about the curse, and yet cannot convince mankind to give up its lust for the gold.

Venus and Brangäne

The *Tannhäuser* Venus was very difficult for me, because in Vienna we sang the Paris version and the part of Venus is longer than in the Dresden version. My knees always trembled! Unfortunately, "Geliebter, komm" is not the whole part. When Venus asks Tannhäuser to stay with her, the musical line is awkward (especially for a mezzo), and slowly spirals up higher. And I didn't like playing the role of Venus anyway because her character doesn't develop.

Unfortunately I couldn't sing Isolde in *Tristan und Isolde*, and I didn't like Brangäne. I considered her very stupid, and, because of that, dangerous. Why does she give the love potion instead of the death potion, as she is ordered to? Why does she warn the lovers so late in the second act and only rush in when King Mark is already coming to discover them? In the last act she also comes too late to tell Isolde that Mark forgives her, but by then Isolde is already in a trance, and ready to sing her Liebestod. No, I didn't like singing this character! Wieland Wagner almost changed my mind by telling me that Brangäne was an instrument of fate, but it still was a frustrating part for me to sing.

Of course, the music for the night watch is wonderful. Paradoxically, Wagner expresses this high state of agitation with notes that are held a very long time. When a singer has a conductor who "bathes" in the music and takes this section too slowly, she feels that she is in serious danger of running out of breath. I went to Karl Böhm once and asked him to help me by using a tempo that would flow a little faster and be slow but not too slow. He replied: "But Christa, then it would be a waltz! It's in three-quarter time!"

Verdi Roles

Lady Macbeth was a role I enjoyed singing, although I think that the opera is in need of an additional scene, because the transition to her insanity is too sudden.

Karl Böhm asked me if I wanted to sing Lady Macbeth with him, and in Vienna there was a score from the time when Elisabeth Höngen sang the role as a mezzo-soprano, containing suggestions for singing some notes lower. I agreed with pleasure, took the score, and flew to my engagement in New York, intending to learn the part there. Soon I realized what I had gotten myself into! I bought two recordings, one with Leonie Rysanek and one with

Maria Callas. Rysanek was *the* Lady, and made her great breakthrough at the Met with the role when Callas canceled. It was simply terrific how dramatically she sang the part, but her approach wouldn't work for me at all. Perhaps I could sing it more like Callas? What to do?

Zinka Milanov, whose art I deeply loved, lived near the apartment where I was staying in Manhattan. Because I knew that she taught, I asked her if we could work on Lady Macbeth together. In the forties, Zinka was the great Italian prima donna at the Met, and from her recordings I knew her wonderful timbre, technique, and musical instinct, all of which captivated me. But because I had also heard many stories about how viciously she talked about younger sopranos, I went to study with her a bit hesitantly. She lived rather modestly on West 72nd Street in a tiny apartment where the living room was dominated by a huge painting of Zinka as Tosca. She was quite a stately lady, who said about herself in a very jolly way, "I always sang like an angel!" She welcomed me very kindly, offered me coffee, and told me immediately that she had heard me at the Met. She said I was pushing my voice too much, and would have to be careful to always *sing* and never go beyond my vocal possibilities.

We first did a few exercises, and she wanted me to sing on "mo," which suited me very well, since my mother always had me sing on "yo." After this first hurdle was jumped, we went on to the position of the voice and mouth placement, and the ones she advised were exactly those which I had already learned. We then proceeded to "the Lady," which I had learned only musically, but not how to manage technically. Zinka taught me a "bel canto" Lady, one where I would always sing and never force, and this approach helped me with the characterization. I could better express the flattery she uses to persuade her husband, her feelings of guilt, and her frail psyche. It then made more sense that she would go mad from thinking about the murders she had encouraged her husband to commit. Also, by singing Lady Macbeth bel canto, I didn't need to lower any notes, except—and this was unfortunately a sore point—the last pianissimo high D flat in her "Una macchia" aria. Though I sang many high notes as Lady Macbeth, and in the big ensemble a high D flat, I couldn't manage it in that aria and certainly not pianissimo! For this reason I always declined offers to sing Lady Macbeth in Italy, as I was too afraid that the audience would wait with great expectation for this high note.

The lower parts in the Verdi operas, such as Eboli and Amneris, I sang at the start of my days in Vienna. Azucena in *Il Trovatore* and Mistress Quickly in *Falstaff*, I sang relatively late, also in Vienna. One exception was Ulrica in *Un Ballo in Maschera*, which I sang first at age 18 in Frankfurt (but only once!).

Azucena was on a special occasion: the return of Herbert von Karajan to the Vienna State Opera in 1977 after a 13-year absence. Luciano Pavarotti, with his unbelievable real high C in the "Stretta," and the wonderful Leontyne Price, one of the most exciting voices I know, sang at the same performance. But I never had a heavy Italian sound in my voice, so I felt a bit out of place.

I had a lot of problems turning myself into Mistress Quickly in *Falstaff*, especially in the Vienna performance staged by Filippo Sanjust. He wanted me to be a traditional Italian Quickly, and he had me wear what was, for me, an impossible costume. I had little glasses on my nose and a basket in my hand. He wanted to disguise me, but it didn't work. I wasn't short and fat, but the tallest lady in the ensemble, and I towered above all the others. And I didn't have a full heavy alto voice with organ-like tones for the famous "Reverenza" either. I knew that there was no point in pretending vocally and physically, and singers must tailor the roles they sing to their own possibilities. But with an Italian directing me in an Italian role, I didn't dare question anything.

At the Salzburg Festival production in 1981 and 1982, where *Falstaff* was under the complete artistic control (staging and conducting) of Herbert von Karajan, the realization of Quickly suited me better, thank God. Karajan didn't want to disguise my idiosyncrasies. Instead, he used my comic talents to make me part of the circle of "Merry Wives" who were poking fun at Falstaff, and Quickly didn't stand out as the comic old woman.

In the "Reverenza" to Sir John Falstaff (a part which Giuseppe Taddei portrayed with unsurpassed roguish humor), I played without comic exaggeration, and I was much funnier than I had been in Vienna, because I didn't try so hard to be funny!

This 1982 production of *Falstaff* was the last production I did with Karajan. He wasn't very well physically; he was in constant pain and walked with difficulty. Most of the time he held onto a chair onstage during "position" rehearsals. Although we all worked in harmony, sometimes he seemed to me like a ruler from another time. From the first rehearsal onward, we often wore our costumes, and the stage was already completely decorated. Because he played a tape recording, which we had made earlier for a recording, we didn't have to sing. We only pretended to do so. He would push us back and forth like chess pieces—what a wonderful toy! Musically, he followed the example of Toscanini, and he said that he always played Toscanini's recording for himself to listen to the tempi. Even though Quickly's character doesn't really suit me, I particularly love this opera. I always look forward to the scene where Falstaff meets Ford. When Falstaff leaves to make himself beautiful, the gay music suddenly changes to express the unhappiness of the jealous Ford. There and elsewhere, Karajan found the right balance between strict timing and witty playfulness in his production.

French Roles

Aside from *Carmen*, which some say is not a typical French opera anyway, I always had reservations about singing French music because I feel that there's a strong tie between the elegance of the French language and the perfume of French music, and the style is best suited to singers who are steeped in French language and culture. In addition to Carmen, I sang three other French roles: Dido in *Les Troyens* by Hector Berlioz, Charlotte in *Werther* by Jules Massenet, and the Prioress in *Les Dialogues des Carmélites* by François Poulenc. Although Dido has some beautiful music to sing, and is, for this reason, greatly coveted by many mezzos, I was rather cool about the role because I felt indifferent to a lot of Berlioz's music.

Charlotte wasn't really my cup of tea either. She constantly asks Werther something in one sentence, and he answers her with a wonderful aria. Toward the end of the opera, the role gets a bit better for the mezzo, and she has a very beautiful letter scene and aria, which begins "Les larmes qu'on ne pleure pas…." But the aria is still too short! Yet *Werther* has other, happier associations for me, because at the rehearsals for the Metropolitan Opera production, I met my second husband, Paul-Emile Deiber, who was the stage director.

In *Les Dialogues des Carmélites*, I sang the old Prioress, and I also worked on this part with my husband Paul-Emile, but for a production in Nice. By then we'd been married a few years, and my command of the French language was a bit better.

The old Prioress is a wonderful role, with only two scenes, but both are very impressive. In the first she talks seriously with the young sister Blanche and reveals her thoughts about what it really means to enter a religious order. In the second scene, she lies on her deathbed and questions her faith, the only thing which has given her life meaning, because her belief in God is no comfort as death approaches. It's shattering. Poulenc's music is wonderful to sing, and the whole opera is very beautiful. Unfortunately, the opera is performed much too seldom, because it doesn't appeal to a large audience.

Another old character I sang was the Countess in Tchaikovsky's *Pique Dame*. Although you can win the greatest success of the evening with her death scene, which is wonderful to act, I didn't like the role very much because there's simply too little to sing in it.

The Moderns

I haven't sung much modern opera, but in my early years in Darmstadt, I sang in both *Antigone* and *Judith* by Arthur Honegger.

I remember one "modern" staging of *Antigone*. The choir was static and wore masks, and I as Antigone had a very short and very stiff black 1950s "wind-safe" hairstyle and chalk-white make up. Because of my round face, the scenery builder Dominik Hartmann was prompted to say, "Antigone with a pug face. Why not?" The stage director Harro Dicks found my voice too beautiful, and he told me to travel by train from Frankfurt (where I lived) to Darmstadt in a third-class smoking compartment, so that my voice would sound scratchy by the time I arrived. This guaranteed that my farewell to the citizens of Thebes wouldn't sound too fresh and youthful!

Der Besuch der alten Dame by Gottfried von Einem is based on the play by Friedrich Dürrenmatt, and Claire Zachanassian is a fabulous role. Who wouldn't want to play her? When von Einem was composing the opera, he asked me what would be my best vocal register, and I answered an Amneris one, which means a lot of middle voice with some high notes. But then he sent me the first proof copies, and I was horrified. It was much too high for me, and there was a lot of text. In this high register, it would be impossible for me to pronounce the words clearly, and we started to recompose the part in a register which would suit my voice better. Here is a letter he wrote to me at the time:

9/3/70

Dear,

I received your wishes for changes. Va bene! In you we've lost a composer. Maybe it will turn out that when you have the part "Intus" [in you], you could take something of the original setting back again. Let me know your wishes for scenes 7, 9 and 10 as soon as you have them. No. 7 is already in your possession. The 9th scene you should be receiving shortly, provided that you mailed the postcard with my writing, which I sent to you at the Goldener Hirsch, to London. You aren't in the second act.

From tomorrow I will be with Mr. Dürrenmatt at Neuchatel, Pertuit du Sault 34, and from the 18th of September I am for five days, and from the 9th of October also for a longer time, in Vienna.

With many sincere regards always

Yours
Gottfried von Einem
(Torturer of Ladies)

The notes we "re-composed" are only available in my own score and in the coach's copy. I know that other mezzo-sopranos in later productions in other opera houses had quite a lot of difficulty singing the part in the original register. The main thing is, of course, to make sure that the audience understands the text which Gottfried von Einem took from Friedrich Dürrenmatt's play. Clara's character is what I call "thin-skinned"—sensitive and neurotic—and I liked playing her very much. Her disappointment with Alfred, the love of her youth, can only be avenged by organizing his death, even though she loves him beyond death. I know that it's possible to find different meanings in this piece, but I think the story of Claire Zachanassian should be played concretely and simply. Although the production was a great success at its premiere and at all subsequent performances, audience attendance eventually went down, and, unfortunately, *Der Besuch der alten Dame* is seldom played these days.

I always liked to sing Gottfried von Einem's music, because he loved the human voice and so provided wonderful opportunities for coloring the voice with sensitivity. Aside from "the old lady," I've sung many of his songs, and I especially loved singing the cycle *Bald sing' ich das Schweigen* based on poems by his wife Lotte Ingrisch. Von Einem had a gift for putting the most beautiful lyricism next to exciting, powerful, jackhammer-like music. These contrasts were wonderfully effective, and they were what I liked especially in his music.

In the sixties in Paris I sang the opera *Duke Bluebeard's Castle* by Béla Bartók in the original Hungarian with Georg Solti. The text under the notes was in very small type, and I already needed glasses back then, but couldn't bring myself to use them, because glasses create a certain wall between the singer and the audience. After the concert, Solti said to me: "Now and then it was really very good Hungarian, but sometimes it was like Chinese."

One can recognize Bartók's musical language immediately. It's not like the moderns nowadays, where one can't identify the composer, and Bartók is already a classic for us. I sang *Bluebeard's Castle* later in Buenos Aires, and I loved the piece very much because it is beautifully written for the voice. I've also sung Bartók songs, and his music is the basis for works like the ones Gyorgy Ligeti composes nowadays.

In the years after the war, modern music was strongly encouraged. Rolf Liebermann, as Director of the Classical Music Department at Hamburg Radio, presented a lot of modern music, and I was often invited to sing. I interpreted *Memento: Epitaffio per Federico García Lorca* by Luigi Nono at its first performance in Hamburg in February 1953, with Bruno Maderna. The piece was based on the poem *Epitaph* by Federico García Lorca. I couldn't actually sing this piece, but rather I recited it, since it had a "singing line" in the style of Alban Berg's opera *Wozzeck*. I had to "speak" in a certain tone pitch, and give a specific length to the vowels.

I called Luigi Nono Francis of Assisi, because he looked the way one imagines this saint: slim and tall, with burning black eyes. Unfortunately, I didn't recognize any melody in *Memento*, and Nono was quite upset about that. But for me this was an ultramodern kind of music, and I couldn't do anything with it back then. But not long ago I received a tape with this piece on it, and suddenly it didn't sound so modern to me anymore. That's how our taste and ears and our openness to modern music have changed in 40 years.

Surviving Rehearsals
and
Stage Directors

My Love-Hate Relationship with Wieland Wagner

When I worked with Wieland Wagner for the first time on the *Aida* which opened the Deutsche Oper Berlin season in the fall of 1961, he controlled the entire production. He designed the sets and costumes, and he directed the singers. I was totally against his method of direction, which was to try various poses in front of a huge mirror in the ballet rehearsal room to see which ones were the most effective. During the rehearsals, he and I developed a kind of love-hate relationship. He didn't like me, and I didn't like him, but we both respected each other. Perhaps I totally misunderstood his approach, but I simply couldn't accept his saying things like: "Here Verdi was wrong. This shouldn't be sung *dolce cantabile*, as is written in the score, but with a harsh expression!"

Wieland Wagner was a real revolutionary, and he showed great foresight in his productions. He was the first to clear the stage of unnecessary decoration and old-fashioned junk, and he achieved new, powerful effects through the use of lighting and color and "Spannungsdreiecke" (tension triangles) in which the singers stood together and held individual poses. Karl Böhm said that Wieland Wagner had "views, visions." But I painfully missed the small, psychologically true gestures that a director like Günther Rennert used in his productions.

In addition, Wieland Wagner had some odd ideas about how to express psychological states through costume. In the second act of *Tristan und Isolde*, for example, he had Isolde wear a costume with exceptionally large breasts to show her desire for love. Siegmund in *Die Walküre* had to wear an especially long, narrow leather apron, which suggested a phallus, to show his sexual desire. I thought Wagner underestimated the intelligence of the audience with such things, and I told him so. He took no notice, and said that in the theater there is only one king. That's how our love-hate developed. Yet, despite all my resistance, I was very impressed by his finished productions, and he came to recognize the artistic possibilities in me. Our correspondence, which began when he engaged me for Bayreuth, reflects these themes.

Wieland Wagner was already fatally ill when our correspondence began, but I didn't know that, so in order to cheer him up, I sent him a note and a photograph of myself as Brangäne, holding two flasks and seeming to ask which potion should it be—love or death? Here is his reply:

> 7/13/1966
> at present in the
> University Clinic, Munich

Dear Miss Ludwig,

I am sorry that, due to adverse circumstances, I am unable to rehearse Brangäne with you in Bayreuth. My views about Brangäne differ quite a bit from earlier Brangäne portrayals, and therefore I would like, in a few sentences, to try to tell you at least a few things about the Brangäne of this production. In the past, Brangäne was always something like an old servant with a few Azucena-like tendencies, because of the fact that the alto, most of the time, was older than Isolde, and because of the penetrating alto sound that was usual in those days. In Richard Wagner's letter to Schröder-Devrient in Karlsruhe, he says he wanted Isolde to be like a child who plays with the swords, but to have a dark timbre, and Brangäne to be young and have a bright timbre, and this is why she has a high tessitura in the first and third acts. Brangäne doesn't give Isolde the potion by her own choice, but because of and in agreement with "the mother," a magical, mythical character. Brangäne refers explicitly to the orders of "the mother," who wants to secure the love of the aging Mark for her daughter with drugs (the lady undoubtedly expects, allow me to say it, cold feelings or impotence, as one says today, on his part!), and Brangäne only sees at the end why she is condemned to give the potion to Isolde (and also Tristan), and that's why she breaks down completely during the argument with Isolde. At first she believes she is doing a good deed, and only falls apart internally when she sees the consequences of her deeds so clearly in front of her (the collapse of Tristan and Isolde). From then on she carries the weight of her own destiny and feels guilty and responsible for something, for which she isn't responsible at all, poor girl.

In the second act she is almost ruined by her fate. She has become "far-sighted." She senses the coming disaster. She already smells, so to speak, the deaths of which she thinks she is guilty. She wants to warn

Isolde, and not at any price does she want to be a party to the final adultery. She accuses herself of the supposed guilt, as in Greek tragedy.

In between the second and the third acts, she bravely does that which also could have brought about her own death: she admits her alleged guilt to Mark, and hopes in the third act (human blindness) to have turned everything around for the better.

I am totally against Brangäne stealing the show from Isolde during the Liebestod, by touching and supporting, etc. Because of this, Brangäne stays broken down at the side of Mark, or symbolically, dying happens alone, and having a supportive friend takes away from the mystery of the death of these two lovers.

I think that we have understood each other, and I now sincerely wish you good rehearsals and much success in Bayreuth.

With friendly regards, also to Mr. Berry, I remain

Yours
Wieland Wagner

I replied shortly after I received his letter:

7/16/1966

Dear Mr. Wagner,

Many thanks for your kind letter. First, I would like to tell you how sorry I am not to see you here, and wish you the best for a speedy recovery.

I would have liked very much to work on Brangäne with you, but it wasn't to be, and Peter Lehmann is doing his best, and I also believe that he is working according to your wishes.

Judging from your letter, I never had anything in mind for Brangäne other than what you describe, and I am happy that we are in complete agreement.

Today is the third recording session. I have listened to some of the other two acts, and think that it is going to be a beautiful recording. I admit that I was terribly nervous because singing here has finally become a reality for me after 15 years, and that makes me feel it is doubly sad that you are not here. I'm coming for the performance on the second of August, and I would like it to have a thorough discussion-rehearsal with you on the morning of the third.

Very kind regards, also from my husband,

Sincerely yours,
Christa Ludwig

P.S. One entrance is terribly unclear to me. I mean in the third act I arrive on the same ship as Mark. However, I enter the stage from the other side. Even though it's opera, this seems very illogical. Maybe you could change it in such a way that I come from the same side as Mark. Please think about it. The costume with the tails on top looked awful, as if I was in the ninth month, fat and shapeless. The tails at the back look better.

My note precipitated a long reply:

> 7/18/1966
> at present
> University clinic Munich

Dear, dear Miss Ludwig,

My sincere thanks for your kind words, which made me really happy. You are absolutely right, you definitely arrive on the same ship as Mark, because the old coach's witticism about "a third ship" can, without doubt, be counted as one of the really bad jokes in this profession. As I assume that the castle courtyard is circular and that Marke, the superfluous helmsman, and Melot come from the right side as seen from the auditorium, I wanted to give Brangäne the more important entrance above the whole stage, especially because she does change her mood (joy, naïveté, happiness, as well as an understanding of the catastrophe) during her appearance and simply needs more room for this than the other, unimportant men. The small piece of illogic, which you, with your thoroughly Viennese-School-of-Staging-without-doubt-sharpened mind, have discovered, highlights Brangäne's character and is logically understandable in that Brangäne searches for a road away from the always dour fighting, probably assault-ladder-installing and gate-storming, silly men, in order to proclaim in a timely manner and before anyone else, the new happiness and the imminent honeymoon. Brangäne, in my opinion, has earned this special entrance, because her confession to Mark and her acceptance of guilt towards him (which, without doubt, took place between the second and third acts) also deserves recognition in this scene. If you find this appearance troubling, however, I don't mind if—I almost wrote for God's sake—go the short road from the right. You are only less prominent.

Your letter, by the way, just comes at the right time. I have thought a lot about you (I do have a lot of time for that now). We didn't understand each other either in *Aida* or in *Lohengrin*. Our mutual understanding first got better in the coffeeshop at the Hotel Sacher. Until then you were the only artist I didn't get on with. I get on a lot better with women than with men, because women are more intuitive and artistic, and I want to be completely open with you today. I always had the impression that you lacked any understanding of staging style and that you never understood why exactly, in static pieces like *Lohengrin*, one should also play statically. Further, I always had the impression that you have a tendency towards exhibitionism (Ortrud's curse). I make a clear distinction between exhibitionism on stage and the role-before-the-self I strive for. However, in reality this has to happen in artistic form and takes us back to the singer (in that sense I am a total opponent of Felsenstein, who wrecks the personality of the singer, in order to force his own ideas on the singer). I am, however, also an enemy of the "personal." Every character in the opera demands an artistic heightening, not only in opera, but also, above all, in theater. It was, without doubt, not just your fault that we never agreed. I take the theater much too seriously than to be a friend of the uncommitted Viennese Kammersängerei, and the view that life isn't serious and art is cheerful. To me it is the other way around. Along with your many famous Viennese female colleagues, I have always thought of you as a typical Viennese Kammersänger—pose, stand at the footlights, encourage applause at any price through playing to the gallery and the "Merker"-community.[1] Since our long conversation at the Sacher, I knew that the divide between us should be filled in. I hope you have deduced that from my request that you take over Brangäne this year. If you promise to go through thick and thin with me, as Frau Mödl, Frau Varnay, Anja Silja, and Birgit Nilsson have, I promise to view you not only as a phenomenal singer, but also as a spirited actress, and may I already ask you now, to take over Brangäne in the four *Tristan* performances and Kundry in all of the *Parsifal* performances (probably four) next year? As a real novelty we will also rework the first and third acts (but please don't tell our honored Karajan anything about this treason!). The second act is very difficult, and we want to play it totally newly adjusted for you.

Please consider this request completely private and confidential, as it contains a lot of combustible material. Please show absolute discretion with all colleagues, all Viennese acquaintances, and even the *Express*, until after the Festival. For specific reasons I have to reserve the public announcement for myself.

Unfortunately, the Bayreuth Festival is not blessed with a lot of money, as you know, and for the past fifteen years we have only been playing because generally everyone earns their money somewhere else. Despite that I promise I will do everything humanly possible to protect you from hunger and thirst. I know too well that we all need money, but as the proverb says so beautifully, one can't find money in the pocket of a naked man.

---

[1] Merker is the nickname for *Mitteilungsblatt des Vereines Opernfreunde*, a privately printed newspaper by and for the standees at the Vienna State Opera, which contains frank reviews of opera performances in Vienna and elsewhere. Since 1989 the paper has been called *Der neue Merker*.

Please take the completely unusual honesty with which I am writing to you as it is meant: as a recognition of your true artistry. The *Tristan* tapes, which I have heard now in the hospital, are outstanding. The nervousness, about which you wrote, did not inhibit you, and it works very well for Brangäne, even dramatically.

With warm wishes and the request that you clearly mark the time required in your calendar of important dates beginning on June 15th next year (of course, not continuously), despite the daily temptations which come up, I remain

Always yours
Wieland Wagner

This time I replied with a very long letter:

7/23/1966

Dear Mr. Wagner,

Where do I start? Probably first, that I am happy about your openness, which I missed until now. I always say that people come together through talking, and right now I should not be writing to you, but speaking with you, because only too often misunderstandings come from a poor choice of words—not only on the stage.

Wasn't it your absolute opinion that in the theater there is only one king, and everyone else has to be subordinate to him? Do you recall our first meeting at *Aida* in Berlin? I arrived with a thoroughly worked-through Amneris, and without explanation, all emotions were taken away from me. I was totally lost.

Bear in mind that I come from Mozart and above all from lieder singing, where every word, every musical phrase has its spiritual and emotional resonance. Playing on the surface, I mean, gesture without meaning, is unknown to me. I know that you say now that this is out of the question, but static acting probably requires much more personality than I possessed–or possess?

A typical example of the static type is for me Varnay. She creates an aura without action, which is unique (Oh God, I hope I don't explain this badly).[2] I understood your style of staging very well, but to be very honest, I was completely against it, especially with *Aida*, and what a pity that was the first time we worked together.

I believe it would be hard for me to resign myself to the idea that Italian and German opera can be played in the same style and possibly even in similar costumes. I shape the character from the musical phrase. I am, after all, a singer. But music alone is not enough for me in the the-

---

[2] Today Miss Ludwig likens Varnay's ability to express emotion without moving a muscle to a photograph, and her own, more animated style, to a motion picture.

ater. Because our first meeting was in *Aida*, the divide between us was almost insurmountable. And then at *Lohengrin* in Berlin, you were uninterested. There I had no idea what to do and "played" statically, which wasn't and isn't good for me (but I may not always feel this way because one, thank God, changes all the time). Then came *Tristan* in Berlin—Brangäne shouldn't have any arms according to your direction. Again I was terribly inhibited, and wished you were on a desert island.

I think so much about my roles that I simply cannot toss away my opinions. I need a conductor and a director with whom I can talk and who possibly can be convinced or can convince me. The director and conductor should take a singer's type and current possibilities into consideration. Do you know what I mean? For example, because of my voice, I have to play Fidelio differently than I originally felt was right, in order to do Beethoven justice. But now I stand completely behind my concept and because of that, I can break through to the audience, I mean to the human beings there. In my opinion, the most important thing for a singer is not to reach out to the audience as a whole, but to create a spiritual contact from individual to individual across the footlights. To achieve this connection seems to me to be my real task.

One only becomes an exhibitionist if one plays something in a way that one isn't convinced is right and that one doesn't feel. Then one just "acts." You are an enemy of personal things on stage—me too. But only by sublimating one's very personal experiences, and bringing them into a part, can one enrich it artistically, and through that, come back to oneself. But for that, patience is needed on the director's part—pardon—and a little psychology—again pardon!

How many singers are there who just say: "Yes, just as you like"? I simply cannot do such a thing because I see that attitude as a lack of interest. Therefore, I was not fighting against you, but fighting for the ground underneath my feet. I once asked one of your singers: "Why do you do everything so unquestioningly?" and the reply was, "Why fight? I couldn't care less, and Bayreuth is simply Bayreuth!" (You will never learn the name of this singer. My lips are sealed.) I do care, and when I must not only understand, but also assimilate very new ideas and a style which is fundamentally strange to me, then I need time. And, still, I am of the opinion that music comes first. When the score says "dolce," I cannot chop up the phrase for expressive purposes, or sing it hard.

All this sounds as though I will probably make you thoroughly angry, but I only want you to know the background of my passive—no, really active—opposition. Only for my own soul must I write these things down. Better, of course, would be talk and reply.

I am only beginning to understand life, music, expressiveness, truth, and what it is to be mature, and I am eager to reach the core, but only through real understanding and not through just assuming foreign ideas. Have I expressed myself correctly?

It's really difficult.

For example, until now I have only sung Kundry, I know that, and I am dying to work on the role with you. It would be really wonderful, if you would make this effort. Hopefully, I haven't totally scared you off with this letter. I would prefer not to sing Brangäne next year. I think she doesn't suit me.

Of course, I want to earn money, but not through singing "it doesn't matter what or where," but through a few first-rate achievements. Everything has its price, but, despite that, I know exactly when, where, and how much I want to sing.

In the summer of 1967, I really didn't want to accept anything, so I could work on some of my forbidden dreams (Isolde, the *Siegfried* Brünnhilde, Elektra), to see if it is possible or not for me to sing them, but Kundry is, of course, a wonderful idea.

The 15th of June is difficult because of my Viennese contract, and the already fixed festival concerts. What can we do about that? In 1968, I am unfortunately already engaged in Salzburg.

Sincere thanks for the detailed drawing. I will be entering from the left (as seen from the auditorium).

I was happy to hear here in Salzburg that you are feeling a lot better. Be a good patient, so that you will soon be able to leave the clinic.

Sincerely yours,
Christa Ludwig

My final letter was in September:

50 Shelley Lane
Great Neck, N.Y. 11023
September 13, 1966

Dear Mr. Wagner,

I heard with great sadness here in New York, that you are not able to come for *Lohengrin*, which Walter and I are sorry about. Especially I wanted to discuss several things with you, but in the first place I, of course, wish you good health.

Director Hilbert (of the Vienna State Opera) is coming here for the opening of the new Met, and I will discuss the matter of leave from my contract, for June of 1967, directly with him. I will tell you the result of this conversation immediately.

I would be grateful if you could let me know the dates for my performances. Unfortunately, we still don't know yet when exactly there will be a ship going to Montreal, but maybe we could agree for the time being that my last performance in Bayreuth should take place around the 18th or 20th of August.

Tonight is the final dress rehearsal for the opening of the new Met, a monster show called *Antony and Cleopatra* with camels and goats on stage. Obviously, because of the many camels, our premiere of *Frau ohne Schatten* was postponed. Moreover, numerous technical difficulties surfaced such as the complete failure of the revolving stage, etc., as is mostly the case in new houses.

Again wishing you a very speedy and good recovery, I remain with kind wishes, and giving you the best regards from my husband,

Yours,
Christa Ludwig

Wieland Wagner's death later in 1966, the same year our correspondence took place, was a shock to everyone, and perhaps it's a law of fate that revolutionaries must die young.

·

It's Wonderful to Die on Stage

It's wonderful to die on stage. You can be stabbed like Carmen, or assassinated like Rodrigo in Verdi's *Don Carlos*, or commit suicide like Cio-Cio San in *Madama Butterfly*. Some singers don't even know what they're dying of on stage. Gilda in *Rigoletto* has a particularly nice death. Put in a sack, already half-dead, she still gets to sing movingly and for quite a long time. Since we've seen a lot ways to die in American films, we try to copy these things on the operatic stage. How does one fall differently if one is stabbed from the back or from the front? It's a lot of fun for us singers to learn these things. And, strangely, you can fall down full-length on the stage without hurting yourself, or fall out of a chair without breaking an arm. But just don't try these things at home—no way! But as soon as you stand on a rehearsal stage or the main stage, you can fall without hesitation, even down staircases! If in real life I had a painful hip or an injured knee, I didn't feel a thing onstage. I skipped and jumped and danced and fell without pain. But as soon as I left the stage, just one step off the stage, the pain would begin again. What was this? A victory of mind over matter? It couldn't be autosuggestion because I didn't tell myself that I didn't have pain. It's the mystery of theater. Onstage I'm someone else, and that person has no pain.

Before slipping into "strange" characters and/or uncovering hidden facets of themselves, singers need to discuss their characters with the stage director. He (or she) hopefully understands psychology, because we singers have to lay bare our inner selves, and the director has to help us to overcome our inhibitions. However, some stage directors are more like photographers and are only concerned with making beautiful pictures and trying out poses to see what looks best. Since even as a beginner I always asked the stage director why and how come, I once got the answer, "Don't think. That's what *I* am here for!" What I thought of that, I'm sure you can imagine.

Stage directors have different approaches. Wieland Wagner, for example, concentrated on big gestures, while Günther Rennert cared more about small details. With Rennert, I did Mozart operas, Rossini's *La Cenerentola*, Gluck's *Iphigénie en Aulide*, and Monteverdi's *L'Incoronzione di Poppea*, and also Beethoven's *Fidelio*. When we singers worked with him on Mozart operas, he was very precise about the Italian text, and paid so much attention to it that we understood every word perfectly, and every head movement and every step was fixed exactly. And he never wanted ensemble changes. If, for example, one of the singers who was in the original cast of his very charming Vienna production of *La Cenerentola* died, it was agreed that the performance would be canceled and the production would never be played again. We worked so well together as a team in Rennert's productions that we could close our eyes and know exactly where everyone else was standing on the stage. Nothing was accidental, although it seemed to the audience that all our movements were easy and elegant, and everything was very charming.

Iphigénie en Aulide, which was performed at the Felsenreitschule during the 1962 and 1963 Salzburg Festivals, was a masterly achievement in the particular style that Rennert had in mind. All our movements were supposed to be in slow motion, and no matter how slowly I moved my arm, I always heard, "Too fast!"

At the Vienna State Opera, Rennert suffered from the apparent inattention of the chorus. While he gave his instructions, the members continued talking among themselves in a lively fashion. After asking indignantly if they had heard anything he said at all, the chorus did exactly what he wanted! That is Vienna's secret. Often uninterested and distracted at rehearsals, but, in spite of that, completely focused when it counts.

It's difficult for a stranger to understand the way rehearsals take place in Vienna. Once, at a rehearsal for a revival of Gottfried von Einem's opera *Der Besuch der alten Dame*, when Eberhard Wächter sang Alfred and I sang Claire, Eberhard and I were having a conversation about personal things quite openly during the rehearsal. When our director "Otti" Schenk said that it would be better if we rehearsed properly, Eberhard said, "But Otti, you have to understand. We haven't seen each other for an eternity, and we have so much to talk about!"

By the way, Otto Schenk once said that he didn't need to say anything to me because I did everything the way he wanted intuitively. I, on the other hand, would say that rehearsing with him was incredibly easy because he always showed me every step and every movement. That's what I call a good collaboration!

If a director is interesting, a singer is like wax in his hands, but, alas, if a director (or conductor) is slow or uncertain, immediately the interest of the singer dies, and the stage directions become arbitrary. Some stage directors act out every step and every movement. This is very comforting for the singer, but this kind of directing would be rejected outright by an actor. Singers often don't know what to do with their hands, and this is why Wieland Wagner usually gave us something to hold.

It's difficult for singers to agree with the ideas of different conductors, but it's even more difficult to adjust to different stage directors. A lot of understanding is needed on both sides. Also, a director needs to know purely technical things, like what effect a movement will have in the auditorium, which body position conveys which mood, and what reactions it will elicit in a large house, even in the seats from which one can't see the facial expressions of the singers. Once I sang the old Countess in Tchaikovsky's *Pique Dame* at the Vienna State Opera. This opera has a wonderful scene in which the Countess, sitting in a chair and remembering old times, falls asleep. She is awakened by Herman who threatens to shoot her if she won't tell him her gambling secret, and then she dies. Because of my husband Paul-Emile's experiences as both an actor and stage director, he was able to sit in the audience during the final rehearsal and afterwards show me movements and positions in the chair that would allow me to bring the personality of the Countess "over the footlights" more effectively.

The basis of effective acting is observation. One has to watch people closely, and for a long time. How do frightened people behave, how do self-assured ones? How do they hold their feet and hands? How does a farmer, a factory worker, a government official, or a king speak? What do they do with their bodies, how do they sit down, walk? How do they close a door? How do they behave when they get bad news? How long does it take them to understand what's happened? How do they react to injustice? All of these things a singer has to observe carefully and study, in order to use them on the stage.

However, complete naturalness won't work in opera since sung speech is in itself unnatural, and long cantilenas, too. Because of this, a director who stages an opera has to be musical, must be able to read the score, and shouldn't just stand up holding only the libretto, not knowing when a large or small section of music arrives that allows a singer to "play" without having to sing. Unfortunately, today there are "modern" stage directors who don't even like music, and they create productions which really work against the music in the score.

Stage actors study and rehearse about the same amount of time as singers, but singers have things much harder. They must master the "impossible art form" in which a word, even a syllable, is sometimes drawn out over many bars of music, and words have to be "interpreted" in trills and coloratura. Coloratura singing usually expresses highly intensified feelings—quarreling or great joy, sorrowful sobbing, or intense anger. Sometimes coloratura singers can seem neurotic, and such music is usually written for young characters (Amina in *La Sonnambula*, for example). Mothers or older women are almost never coloraturas. When coloratura singing is only the product of a "skilled throat" and the voice is treated like an instrument, no deeper meaning is expressed. But good conductors and stage directors can give meaning and life to all the ornamental singing that coloraturas do.

Please Don't Kiss!

Rehearsals are a wonderful experience, especially when a singer prepares a role for the first time and comes to understand a character by working with a good stage director. What a joy it is to take on a different personality and to interpret a character unlike your own. A singer just has to be careful not to "take it home"! Rehearsals can replace visits to a psychotherapist because they allow singers to act out the many personalities that may be hidden inside themselves. In private life, one can't show all these faces, but on the stage, you may—and you must!

A woman can understand the joys of playing a role, even if she isn't an actress, and some even do "play a role" in real life. Think of the possibilities—a queen, beautiful and exotic, like Dido in Henry Purcell's *Dido and Aeneas*, or Amneris in Verdi's *Aida*, a passionate lover who becomes a woman scorned in a jealous rage. Or should it be a witch, a fortuneteller like Ulrica in Verdi's *Un Ballo in Maschera*, or a sex symbol like Carmen? Or someone a bit mannish, in a trouser role? Bloodthirsty like Lady Macbeth, or driven mad by love like Lucia di Lammermoor? A singer can really indulge herself on stage, and, what's more, she gets to wear a costume, make-up, and wig.

In Europe, rehearsals usually take place between ten in the morning and 1 in the afternoon, and then again from five to eight in the evening. At the Metropolitan Opera in New York, we usually rehearsed from 10 or 11 in the morning until six in the evening, with a one-hour break for lunch. In Buenos Aires, rehearsals didn't start until around two in the afternoon, and lasted until five, and then started again after dinner, continuing until late into the night. Also, performances start late in South America, and I was always horrified, on checking the time backstage while singing Ortrud there, to realize that my last "screams" would take place well past midnight!

From the first "position" rehearsal until the premiere, there are at least four to six weeks of rehearsal, and the exact length depends on the stage director and the opera. When a stage director is "given his head," as Felsenstein was in Berlin, rehearsals can last for months! Because of this long rehearsal period, singers in a new production naturally become a close-knit group even when they don't know each other at all beforehand, and it is difficult for a newcomer to fit into such a homogeneous ensemble later. For example, when I first came to Vienna in 1955, I met many of the great stars of that time at rehearsals, such as Hilde Güden, Lisa Della Casa, and Irmgard Seefried, and I felt totally out of place. These three elegant, well-groomed ladies competed with each other to see who had the finest fur or the most expensive ring, or who was dressed the most stylishly. Only Sena Jurinac was an exception. She was always natural and simple, but an equally wonderful artist. Hilde Güden even rehearsed *Così fan tutte* a few times in a delightful white fur hat—perhaps her hair wasn't at its best—until the director Günther Rennert said, "Please take that thing off your head!"

The first weeks of rehearsal are totally carefree because you don't have to worry about your voice yet. You can often "mark" (sing quietly in "half-voice") an octave lower, and you still have time to get over the effects of a head cold before the premiere. In spite of this, I was always angry with colleagues who came to rehearsals like germ factories, and who didn't try to avoid infecting others.

Above all things, singers have to discuss the difficult places in their roles openly and honestly with the conductor as well as the stage director, so singers know exactly how to use their bodies in those places. They need to be able to interpret the part believably, without being obstructed from singing the difficult passages beautifully. For example, singers have to be careful not to walk too quickly before singing a difficult passage, so that they aren't out of breath. And they have to avoid contorting their bodies in ways that would make it impossible to support the breath properly for a particular tone or series of notes. Many singers say yes and amen to everything, do everything at rehearsals the director wants them to—until the first rehearsals with the orchestra, where they have to sing and act at the same time. Then all the stage movements are forgotten, and they just stand and sing.

I myself was always inclined to overact. I moved much too much, made too many big arm movements, reacted too much, and did too many dance-like movements. Rennert often said to me: "Please stop using your acting talent so much! Too much movement causes confusion, and none of the movements has any weight or importance any more." Economy is far more effective. Stage movement, like musical interpretation, has to be filled with a deeper meaning that goes beyond the actual movements themselves. Otherwise the movements remain superficial, and it is this kind of movement one sees all too often on opera stages. Ideally, there must be a complete synthesis of movement, musical interpretation, and pure singing, and heaven knows, that is not easy! But when a singer masters all three, like Maria Callas did, then a kind of miracle occurs. I don't know if I've ever succeeded with this synthesis, but perhaps I might have with Dorabella in *Così fan tutte* or the Dyer's Wife in *Die Frau ohne Schatten*. I leave it to the audience to judge.

After the "position" rehearsals, the conductor appears, and the greater he is, the later he comes. Sometimes there are still a few position rehearsals, which can be very important, depending on who is conducting. Once I was in a Rennert production of *Le Nozze di Figaro*, which was moved from the Salzburg Festival to the Vienna State Opera, where Karajan took over the conducting from Karl Böhm. Karajan didn't agree with the placement of any of the singers, and he came onstage and changed almost everything. And what did Rennert do? To our great astonishment, he did nothing, perhaps because he knew that Karajan would get his way in the end. So, as the wiser person, he gave in.

When the first orchestral rehearsals begin, the stage director no longer plays a leading role because suddenly only music, voice, orchestra, and conductor are important. Everything that has been rehearsed with the stage director for weeks is forgotten. Singers are only careful to stay on good terms with the conductor, and sing as beautifully as possible. During the week before the premiere, there are major rehearsals with sets, lighting, costume, and make-up. These rehearsals seem endless, but suddenly all the movements worked out with the stage director come back. When you are completely exhausted from many weeks of physical and psychological exertion, then comes—no, not the premiere yet—the dress rehearsal, which is a run-through that's just like a performance. Often this rehearsal is public, and the auditorium is full of people.

And then, a day or two later, the premiere finally comes. Most of the time you arrive in the dressing room totally exhausted. The fear of getting a cold and not being able to sing, which would make all the weeks of work a waste of time, is over. You've done it! A tired face looks back at you from the mirror, but a little make-up gives it life. But don't think that you'll have peace and quiet until the performance begins! Oh, no! The management, colleagues, the stage manager, the production assistant, the stage director, the conductor—have I forgotten anyone?—everyone comes to your dressing room to wish "toi, toi, toi." They all mean well, but it's just that you don't get any peace. When Heinz Rühmann played Frosch at the Vienna State Opera's traditional New Year's Eve performance of *Die Fledermaus*, he put a "Please do not disturb" sign on his dressing room door. At the Met in New York, I hung out a sign once that said "Please don't kiss!" because everybody there, and I mean everybody, kisses.

Although rehearsals tired me very much when I was older, especially the rehearsals in the last week before a premiere, I still attended them. However, there are a few stars whom the opera houses allow to arrive just before the dress rehearsal, or even the premiere. They don't need a long series of rehearsals, and some rehearsals are terribly boring for a singer who has sung a role many times. With horror I still remember the hours of useless standing around I did at rehearsals in non-German speaking countries for the second and third acts of *Rosenkavalier*, until the singers in the chorus finally learned when and how to react because they didn't understand a word of what was being sung on the stage. A Greek colleague in New York, who was singing Valzacchi, gave me a gift to calm me, an Oriental string of beads called Komboli, which Greek men finger. Using them made me very calm, but watching me made the stage director very nervous. Perhaps more singers should use this technique to make things move along a little faster.

The Greatest Artists Are
Always Searching

Every generation experiences artworks with different eyes and ears. But whether or not there is progress, I can't tell. Certainly if we think differently, we feel differently. When working on a Mozart opera, we always ask questions, like how did people behave when they wore crinolines and white wigs? Were their movements natural or affected? Or we ask how would German gods or creatures in Greek mythology behave? Stage directors and designers try to bring Iphigenie, Orest, Titus, or Wotan closer to contemporary audiences by having the characters wear modern clothing or smoke cigarettes. But I'm not sure that this contributes to the "development" of opera, the "impossible art form," which is so often declared dead. Can we reach young audiences better if the characters wear contemporary clothes instead of period costumes, which don't mean much to us nowadays?

I myself am definitely in favor of freedom of interpretation, provided the interpretation is within the bounds of good taste, the music-making does justice to the composer, and the staging doesn't distract from the music. It's true that today the expression "good taste" seems to suggest dullness because everything has to be garish and over the top. And I've personally had enough of operatic characters in old soldier's uniforms. I've been in two different stagings of *Elektra* in this style already! Do the prisoners in *Fidelio* always have to be in a concentration camp and the guards SS people? We've seen this for over 30 years now! But isn't it odd that only in theater and opera do we have this kind of interpretive freedom? No one would consider laying a hand on a great painting or statue. But, of course, freedom of interpretation keeps opera houses and theaters from turning into museums.

Suppose that the big state theaters in places like Vienna, Munich, Dresden, and Milan always provided first-rate "classic" productions of the operas that had their roots in those cities. By renovating (not changing) these traditional productions every few years, it would always be possible to see high quality authentic stagings of the great operas. Perhaps then tradition would not be a curse, but rather a spirit of great things upon which new great things could be built. Audiences wouldn't only see Marschallins in pants suits, hockey-playing Cherubinos, and Despinas that tend bar.

Other theaters could do productions that are more experimental where stage directors and designers use modern technology with artistic imagination, but without letting the new technology dominate. Unfortunately, lack of talent too often hides behind the label "modern." Such "modern" productions really have only one purpose: to make a name for the stage director and designer. The story of the emperor's new clothes reappears in another disguise. Everyone is afraid to speak the truth because no one wants to seem old-fashioned or, even worse, old. Theater and opera directors all want to be young and chic and progressive, so Gretchen fondles her jewelry while standing naked in front of a mirror, and uses a sewing machine. Such are our contemporary "achievements" in staging, and there are many other examples where things go too far in the name of freedom. Such productions are neither in good taste (those awful words again!), nor are they faithful to the style of the music. Composers have always tried to adjust their music to the themes and countries in which their works are set, and I can understand playing operas in the century in which the composer actually lived. But Handel's *Xerxes* in blue jeans?

For me, the lives and fates of opera characters should be tied to the music, and trigger feelings that give the people in the audience something that they can carry over into their daily lives. I believe that a talented interpreter not only has the right, but the duty to always examine and create a piece of theater art anew. It's easier for actors than for singers, because they can speak faster or slower or pause where they wish, unless they are speaking in verse, where the form is more rigid and more music-like. They can discuss rhythm with the director, as well as when and where to speak faster and then louder, or when to whisper, totally according to their taste and "feel" for the text. Singers, however, are tied by the note values in the music. Everything is predetermined, written out beforehand, as either loud or soft, fast or slow, legato or staccato, and the accentuation of the words is set by the height or depth of the note values. Singers have to find their own interpretations within these golden bonds, which come through individual timbres, the unique sound of each voice, and distinctive interpretations. All these things make one singer stand out from the rest because, as Goethe says, individuality of expression is the beginning and end of all art.

Today, in the age of recordings, many want to learn the easy way, by listening to important recordings and trying to copy them. I knew a very talented young conductor in Vienna, who said to me before the performance of a Mozart opera he was taking over: "Don't worry. I conduct exactly like Karl

Böhm!" Sadly, he never found himself, and he was, like many others, a fire in straw, with a fast but short success. Such a shame! Surely one should have great models to study, as Lotte Lehmann was for Elisabeth Schwarzkopf, and Rosa Ponselle for Callas. The famous conductor Serge Koussevitzky helped form Leonard Bernstein, who, in turn, was an excellent teacher of a whole new generation of conductors. My great operatic models were always Maria Callas for expression and Zinka Milanov for pure, beautiful sound, and, for singing lieder, Irmgard Seefried and Elisabeth Schwarzkopf. At my first lieder recitals I'm certain I was a mixture of them both. I tried to copy the simplicity of Seefried, and, at the same time, the refinement of Schwarzkopf, and also her ability to captivate an audience. Schwarzkopf seemed to me like the Pied Piper of Hamelin. She bewitched all listeners not only through her art of interpretation and singing, but also through the way she performed and bowed, and how she seemed to greet every single person in the audience, always the grande dame—this also is a great art!

In other fields I have experienced two additional "pied pipers." One was Margo Fonteyn, who was grace personified and had incredibly strong artistic expressiveness, despite her advanced age (for a dancer). The second was Marlene Dietrich. I think she was about seventy (or maybe older) when I first experienced her art. She was a dream figure in a dream dress, which was also lit up briefly once from the back, so one could see a hint of her famous legs. I remember how she very elegantly picked up the flowers which were thrown to her, how she held her arms and hands, how she understood how to hide the telltale signs of aging—but, of course, all that would be nothing without her immense art of interpretation. I'll never forget how she sang her famous song "Sag mir, wo die Blumen sind" (Tell Me Where the Flowers Are). People in the audience were so deeply moved, they cried.

I needed many years to find my own style and separate myself from the great models and the golden ties of my teachers: first, from what I learned from my mother, and later, from what I learned from Erik Werba and Walter Legge. For many years Legge was the leading EMI record producer, and he is still unsurpassed. Gifted with a sensitive ear, he was a devoted fan of beautiful voices; he could spur people on to the greatest achievements by always saying "You can do it even better!" Legge shaped his wife Elisabeth Schwarzkopf into the important artist she became after the Second World War.

After recording sessions, Legge would often play old recordings of long-dead singers late into the night for us young singers at his beautiful London home. And it wasn't the scratchy sound of the old records that he wanted us to hear, but the interpretation. For me he played Lotte Lenya singing songs by

Kurt Weill and Bertolt Brecht, and said, "Christa, you must sing your lieder with this kind of expression."

Back then I slowly began to understand, but understanding is a long way from doing. Patiently Legge recorded my first lieder record with me, and recording a single song sometimes took as long as three hours before he was finally satisfied that the word "sun" really sounded sunny and the word "rain" had the feeling of a rainy day. But in this way, with patience and a lot of time on both sides, he made the most beautiful recordings of Callas, Victoria de Los Angeles, Elisabeth Schwarzkopf, Dietrich Fischer-Dieskau, Nicolai Gedda, and Hans Hotter. Today the recording of Beethoven's *Fidelio* that he produced, with Otto Klemperer conducting, is still a best-seller—after more than 30 years! With Walter Legge, quality always took priority. He also had very definite opinions about tempi and the interpretation of the songs of Hugo Wolf, which my other mentor, Dr. Erik Werba, didn't share at all. Between those two poles, I had to find myself!

Herbert von Karajan's opinion that there is no absolutely right tempo applies also to lieder interpretation, because every day our pulse is a little different, and, because of that, also our way of thinking and moving. To this singers have to add differences in breathing based on the condition of their vocal cords, which are not totally healthy every day. But these things are of purely technical importance. Then comes how the singer interprets a song, the text and the music, in order to reach the listeners. And this changes from year to year also. The body changes, and likewise the vocal cords, and one understands more.

I believe it was Fischer-Dieskau who said that a singer should "sing words and speak music." However, to reach this level, singers have to be allowed a certain freedom of interpretation, which will also be noticeable in tempo and dynamics. Many critics find fault with such freedom, but to that I can only say a professor teaches and an artist searches, and the greatest artists are always searching. And then they die before they find the philosopher's stone. But that is exactly what's exciting about interpretation. The audience listens to the same songs, operas or symphonies, even the same interpreters, but the interpretation is always a little different because the search continues. Of course, the emphasis on interpretation shouldn't go so far that on concert posters the name Karajan is written large, and Beethoven small. Or in opera announcements, the stage director's name or a singer like Domingo, when he is singing a role like Otello, shouldn't be written very much larger than those of the other singers (and the composer).

The question of tempo is important. I have met contemporary composers and sung their works, and all of them agreed to tempo shifts if it helped the expression. They would even change the metronome numbers that they had originally written. Have composers changed so much? I don't think so. An obvious example is the recent discovery that Beethoven's tempi are supposed to be faster than the ones we've known and loved for decades. This is really an insignificant thing! Hasn't Furtwängler given us great Beethoven interpretations in the "wrong" tempo? Our listening habits, concert halls, and instruments are always changing. The use of a pitch that is higher by almost half a tone has altered what we hear, maybe even falsified it. This is a worldwide development, in which the big symphony orchestras in Europe and America have all played a substantial part.

The famous high F in the Queen of the Night's aria "Der Hölle Rache" in *Zauberflöte* was not sung as high in absolute pitch frequency in Mozart's time as it is today. Would it be so bad then if a singer like Joan Sutherland dared to sing it a half tone lower? The pitch of the Vienna Philharmonic, which, of course, is also the pitch used at the Vienna State Opera, is problematic for many singers, especially for tenors who have to sing their arias about a half tone higher than originally written. Also Birgit Nilsson told me how nervous she is before the Brünnhilde in Wagner's *Siegfried*, because she doesn't sing until the last act, and the whole part lies very high with a few high C's, which, however, are almost C-sharps nowadays, another half tone higher.

Also, this higher pitch doesn't help singers technically. When changing registers from one tone to the next, singers sometimes have to "cover." Let's say that in one of his operas Verdi gave a baritone a high note, with which he has to express a certain outburst of emotion. In Verdi's time, the baritone could sing this tone "open," and the note would have the desired effect. Nowadays, since the note is higher, the baritone has to "cover" it in order not to damage himself vocally, and the effect of the note is lost, because covering causes the note to sound much softer. All over the world concert halls are getting bigger, and our ears have gotten used to the higher sound of many orchestras, especially because the strings sound much more brilliant. Singers and their interpretations have to adapt to these changed circumstances, inadvertently and unintentionally.

Today there is a new flowering of interest in Baroque music, performed on "original instruments." But, of course, these instruments are only reproductions that are based on the originals. Often Baroque operas are not presented in a suitable setting, such as the wonderful old castle theater at Drottningholm in Sweden where the original acoustic still exists, but in large opera houses. The interpreters try to sing everything in the "authentic" style, which results in the listener being unable to recognize who is singing or who is conducting on many recordings. The personal touch is missing. It was through the freedom to add ornamentation, which was mostly not written down by the composer but fell under general rules, that the listener in Baroque times recognized the individuality of the performers. Jazz improvisation is similar. In Baroque music, a performer may vary repeats or "compose" additional transitions and trills, completely according to his or her imagination and feeling for the music, but always faithful to the style. However, some musicians nervously decline to improvise and hide behind the notion of faithfulness to the original work, but they are really only afraid to make a mistake.

In an article that Joachim Kaiser wrote after the death of Vladimir Horowitz, he said that "The Titans are dying out." To me, there are no more Titans, only successors to Titans. And successors to successors. We now hear the third generation following Toscanini or de Sabata, and they are in their sixties, and the conductors in their forties are further removed from the Titans yet. They no longer have the essential connection with the great ones, even though they get a lot of publicity and make a lot of recordings. When I recorded *Fidelio* with Klemperer, which was the first time I worked with him, I immediately knew that he was unique. He never seemed to do anything special. He just conducted, and the result was always absolutely right. Arthur Nikisch, Bruno Walter, Wilhelm Furtwängler, Erich Kleiber, Leo Blech, and Otto Klemperer were the greatest music directors in Berlin's history. Yet Klemperer became a really great conductor only after his illness, and Böhm only became a master in old age.

I myself don't believe that the general public has any real discernment. Only the initiated can distinguish the difference between good and exceptional. Critics speak today of "new ears," as if a beautiful sound is no longer the same beautiful sound that it used to be. For me, the history of performance, and the challenge of it, is to constantly explore and re-explore both the spiritual and intellectual content of the music. Conductors like Bruno Walter and Otto Klemperer understood this, but I don't think many of today's conductors do.

In times where personalities are thinly sown, we have first class, yes excellent, musical practitioners, who lack intuition, imagination, and a feeling for composers, who, even though they lived in the past, can speak to us about today. Courage is needed to reveal one's own feelings in interpretation and not tell the audience with raised forefinger: "The composer wanted it like this, and no other way." But at the same time we singers must never forget that we are only the servants of the great minds who created all the wonderful pieces of music we enjoy today.

Conducting
Styles

Karl Böhm

From my earliest days in Vienna, Karl Böhm was my mentor. One reason for our rapport may have been the happy coincidence that his son Karl Heinz and I were born on the same day. Böhm was very proud of Karl Heinz, and always spoke of him as "My son, the movie actor."

In Karl Böhm I found a true father. For me he was like the spiritual father the philosopher Rudolf Steiner says many people find around the age of 30. Böhm guided me past many obstacles, and showed me the way out of the provinces and into the great world. He gave me the base on which to build an international career.

Böhm had very definite ideas about how things should be performed. For example, he felt the recitatives of Mozart had to be shaped more by tempo than by psychology. He also believed that all notes and rests should be held for their exact duration, as they had been written. And he knew how a Mozart aria must always end: an imperceptible *ritardando* should be the cue that unleashes the applause. He was a master of "pulse," of exactness, and he knew how to bring music to a climax and achieve the maximum effect. It wasn't surprising that Herbert von Karajan, with a touch of sarcasm, gave Böhm the most precise watch available as a 75th birthday gift.

Böhm could be very unpleasant, especially to new young singers. During my early years in Vienna, they were all afraid of him, and those of us who had been around awhile knew that, when newcomers had barely stuck their noses out on the stage, a grumpy "too late" would come from the conductor's podium. So, for example, in the second act Susanna-Cherubino duet—quickly the door would open, and before we could do the same with our mouths, he'd already be shouting "too late!" We actually had to learn to sing a little before the beat to make the entrance work to his satisfaction. And Böhm was very quick-tempered. When the orchestra made a mistake, he often walked off the podium in mock disgust saying, "I'm leaving!" but he always came back. Sometimes our wonderful coach, Herr Pilz, would spot a wrong note in the printed score. Later Böhm would suddenly stop a rehearsal to say he heard this same false note. . . . What an ear!

Böhm was one of the rare conductors who understood the voice. First of all, he had a talent for it, and, second, he was married to a singer, Thea Lienhard. He knew what could be expected from a particular voice, he knew at what age and stage of development a singer could sing a certain role, and he knew when a singer would be ready for a role, even if she wasn't ready yet. At our first meeting in Frankfurt, he told me that he intended to put on *Wozzeck* at the State Opera, and he wanted to try out a very young singer named Walter Berry in the title role. He considered this decision very carefully, because he knew the welfare of a singer who was barely 26 years old was at stake. Walter's timbre and his voice type were exactly right, but the part could damage his voice. In the end, Walter sang Wozzeck then and later with great success. Because he had a strong instrument and such good technique, he didn't hurt himself, and he was the best Wozzeck for many years. By keeping the right tempo and pausing whenever a singer needed it, Böhm, the conductor, never overtaxed anyone. And somehow Böhm also knew, even before I met this young singer, that Walter Berry would be my first husband.

When I told Karl Böhm that Herbert von Karajan wanted me to sing Isolde with him, he raged, "This is criminal!" Then, after a short pause to think things over, he continued, "But with *me* you could sing it." When Karajan suggested I sing the Nurse in *Die Frau ohne Schatten* under his baton, Böhm said, "You could more easily sing the Empress than the Nurse." The role I did eventually sing with both Karajan and Böhm was the Dyer's Wife. Böhm made wonderful cuts, which allowed me to sing what was really a soprano part during the opening weeks at the new Metropolitan Opera House in New York, and the whole production was an enormous success. He knew exactly where the climaxes were, and how to pace things so as not to wear me out before them. He helped me keep the tempo, and he highlighted the best qualities of my voice whenever possible. But I could never really recognize his beat. Because his gestures were so economical and small, I never knew what he meant, and I had to depend solely on my ears. Since I was a precise singer who stayed on pitch and with the beat and observed all the note values and rests, I was in nearly all the productions that he conducted. His wife, Thea, liked me too, and it made me very proud to be close personal friends with both of them.

Although he was a clever and sensitive man, Böhm made one big mistake.

While he was director of the Vienna State Opera, he had a sensational success at the Met and spent a lot of time in New York. This was fine according to his contract in Vienna, but the Viennese took careful note of his absences, especially because everyone knew that Herbert von Karajan was just waiting for his chance to take over as director at the first sign of weakness. Returning from New York one day, Böhm was met by a group of scandal-hungry reporters at the Vienna Airport, and he somehow let them goad him into saying that he wouldn't sacrifice his American career for the sake of the Vienna State Opera. The uproar was terrible! The papers were full of indignation.

Just at this time, I was scheduled to sing Octavian under Böhm at the State Opera, and it was a performance I'll never forget. I was already on stage, lying in bed with the Marschallin and waiting for the opera to begin, when suddenly there was pandemonium in the audience. Böhm had entered the orchestra pit and was moving towards the podium. Loud boos and cat calls echoed throughout the house. It was incredible. Very likely, this orgy of abuse began in the much-feared standing room area. My knees shook, and I could scarcely sing, but Böhm paid no attention to the crowd. When he made his way to the podium before both the second and the third acts, he was booed vehemently each time. But at the end of the performance, when he came out for his curtain call, he was greeted with warmth and enthusiasm. As opera director he was jeered, but as musician and conductor he was cheered.

Herbert von Karajan

Early in 1956, Karl Böhm was driven from his post as director of the Vienna State Opera, like so many before and after him. Thank God, he continued to conduct there when Herbert von Karajan moved in as "artistic director." Karajan had a remarkably strong personality which was almost palpable. "The Chief," as he was called, brought an elegant but casual modern style to the venerable old opera house. Here was an opera director who didn't wear a tie but sported jeans, a comfortable black pullover (cashmere, of course), casual shoes, and a very fashionable haircut. Gray, with a hint of blue, his hair was cut short and swept up very dramatically.

A new era began when he arrived, and the entire opera house staff suddenly became more chic and modern, since everyone wanted to ape "The Chief." Karajan was seldom alone. Instead, he was constantly surrounded by a retinue which prepared his path by keeping a lookout for his arrival and then passing the words "The Chief, The Chief" from mouth to mouth. When Karajan was in the house, rehearsals were more diligent. If "The Chief" dropped by during a performance, everyone worked harder. He had so much charisma that I was always very calm when I was on a plane with him. No plane carrying Karajan would dare to crash!

Karajan conducted often, making even standard repertory performances seem special. He was away often too, certainly no less than Böhm, but when Karajan was in Vienna, everyone knew it. During these years he courted and married his third wife, the beautiful young French girl Eliette Mouret, and the papers loved every minute of it. At the annual opera ball, the elegant couple would stand at the front staircase greeting the guests, and Eliette, a former model, was always dressed in the latest fashion. The papers reported that her long blond hair was dried only by the sun, and the precious gems she wore made her the envy of every woman. Tongues clicked at the concert hall when Anita Gütermann, the second Frau von Karajan, sat in a box across from the third Frau von Karajan. I knew Karajan's first wife Elmy Holgerloef in Aachen, where she was the municipal theater's picture perfect operetta diva. My God, Karajan was very handsome, and this made him the dream man in many women's hearts. And with Karajan came his charming and equally elegant aide-de-camp André von Mattoni. As confidential secretary, Mattoni held all the strings and made sure that "The Chief's" halo was always shining brightly.

Stage direction became Karajan's great passion. Perhaps it's just human nature to always want what one doesn't have. Pianists yearn to conduct, as do composers, violinists, cellists, and even singers. Thank God not many singers want to stage the productions they're in! Although Karajan's favorite toy was stage direction, he hadn't learned the craft, so he needed an insane number of rehearsals just for the lighting. People joked about his "black spotlights" because his productions were always very dark. He loved the singers' voices, but not their figures. He often said to us, "I wish you were all made of glass!"

At that time, women wore their hair long and blond like Eliette, and on stage everything was very elegant. Wags whispered maliciously that the fabric for the costumes at the State Opera was equally suitable for a dinner at St. Moritz, where "The Chief" had an elegant home. For Karajan's *Carmen* production in Salzburg, the gypsy costumes and the soldiers' shiny boots all looked brand-new. It wasn't a remarkable production, although Karajan worked well with the singers. He liked to act out the scenes for us, and, psychologically, everything he said was absolutely right. The problem was he didn't know enough about stagecraft to translate his ideas into physical gestures and movements that would allow us to communicate his ideas about the characters to the audience. He lacked a knowledge of rudimentary techniques like the "dramatic triangle," which can be used very effectively to help singers create tension on the stage. Over the years, he gained a lot of experience, but his first productions simply lacked technical skill. But one good result of Karajan's "black spotlight" was that it forced the audience to concentrate more intently on the music, making the Vienna Philharmonic the true stars of Karajan's productions with orchestral playing that is still unsurpassed.

Karajan's celebrated baton technique allowed him to achieve his musical goals. With 120 musicians playing as one, he could evoke such a soft pianissimo that the dynamic movement from soft to loud was a truly thrilling experience. To us singers, he was a hero because he wove a glorious carpet of sound upon which we could confidently lay our voices. Karajan knew exactly where the trouble spots were for singers because he had been chorusmaster in Ulm before he took up his post at Aachen, where at 27 he became the youngest general music director in all of Germany. Like Karl Böhm, he had experience that made him enormously helpful to singers. He knew the right tempo and the right volume to use, and he knew exactly where a singer had to hold back to be able to sing a climax or a particularly difficult phrase later on. With Karajan, the orchestral players were taught to listen to the sounds of the voices on the stage, and the singers were taught to listen to the individual "voices" in the orchestra, and to subtly imitate them. In this way, the orchestra and the singers could make music together as one, creating a beautifully homogeneous sound.

Karajan's rehearsals were extremely concentrated. Even though he sometimes rehearsed only the most important parts of the opera, each singer knew exactly what sound to use to express his or her character's personality. I remember a spot rehearsal in Vienna for the *Tannhäuser* Venus which I was singing in the later "Paris" version, which is much longer and more difficult than the original "Dresden" one. When Venus begs Tannhäuser to stay in the Venusberg with the words beginning with "Wie hätt' ich das erworben," the musical line is very uncomfortable for a mezzo-soprano. Aware of this, Karajan said to me, "You must sing this passage as you would a Hugo Wolf song, quietly, and with a feeling of looking inward. Don't be afraid, I am accompanying you." And how he did accompany me, even with a full orchestra. He drew the text from my lips, breathed with me, made the orchestra understand that it must listen for me, and laid one of his famous pianissimo carpets under my voice. He wove a similar carpet for me during Kundry's narrative "Ich sah das Kind an seiner Mutter Brust." Once he came to my dressing room before a performance of that role and made a cross on my forehead, saying, "I am with you!"

Many years later on his 80th birthday, I wrote him a thank you note, and he replied with this letter:

> Frau Kammersängerin Christa Ludwig
> Vienna State Opera

Dear Christa,

Your especially dear letter touched me deeply, and I must say you are truly the only one who wrote such a thing to me. In return, I must say that you are also the only one who made the transition from an Austrian singer to a singer renowned throughout the world, which alone justified the investment that I made on behalf of the Vienna State Opera in the exchange agreement between Vienna and Milan. I must admit that you were a very good listener, for you learned everything necessary to be perfect interpreter in the bel canto style. With the experience that contract gave you, you developed yourself and became a thoroughly cosmopolitan artist at a very young age.

Thank you for everything that you have given the world. I am glad to hear that you busy yourself with the development of younger artists, and if you need anything, "Du weißt, wo Du mich finden kannst" [You know where you can find me] (Parsifal).

Heartfelt greetings,
Yours
Herbert von Karajan
Salzburg, February 2, 1988

Karajan was the conductor whom many singers loved, and I think it was the soprano Mirella Freni who said (and not without good reason), "With him, I would even sing Sarastro." Singers could give their best performances with Karajan because he had a well known "feel" for each singer's current vocal condition. He adjusted himself accordingly, and cloaked the singer, when necessary, so that vocal difficulties couldn't be heard. Usually, he surrounded himself with the same singers, as most conductors do, and each came to know the other's strengths and weaknesses. We grew as an ensemble at a time when the opera ensembles of great houses were fast becoming a thing of the past. In spite of this ensemble spirit, he always tried out new young singers, spurring them on to great accomplishments by pushing them to the limits of their abilities, and sometimes beyond.

Because Karajan encouraged singers to give everything, many considered him a "voice-killer." I don't agree with this at all because of my own experiences with him. In the 1960s, my voice moved continually higher, and Karajan believed that I could sing dramatic soprano roles with him because I occasionally sang excerpts, such as Brünnhilde's final narrative in *Götterdämmerung*, Isolde's Liebestod, and the Elektra Orestes duet from the Richard Strauss opera, on records or in concert. He also believed that I could sing the roles of Ariadne and the Dyer's Wife (with judicious cuts). For his Easter Festival in Salzburg, he invited me to sing the *Siegfried* Brünnhilde from Wagner's Ring Cycle, which I started studying during one of my winter engagements in New York. This Brünnhilde is the shortest of the four Brünnhildes in Wagner's Ring, but it has the highest tessitura, and I noticed that I grew very tired while studying, and took many breaks to gulp water because my throat was so dry. These were signs that the role was much too high for me, and I told him so. He didn't have much time to find a replacement, and the whole experience was very unpleasant.

Here are two letters I wrote to Karajan around this time:

August 1968

Dear Herr von Karajan,

I would like to send these lines as a follow up to my telephone conversation today with Herr von Mattoni.

You know that we enjoy the greatest artistic satisfaction when we make music with you, but in prominent roles. The St. Matthew Passion, which you originally promised us at the 1968 Easter Festival, was to have been our most important engagement. Then the Passion was canceled, and the whole situation changed. Here in New York, perhaps because of the size of the house, Walter's voice has developed, so that it would be a step backward for him to sing Donner in 1968. In addition, his upcoming engagement as Wotan makes it really impossible for him to do Donner. Also, in the future, I would prefer to sing dramatic soprano roles, and not be interrupted on that path by singing parts like Fricka in Das Rheingold.

This sudden development into a dramatic soprano certainly could not have been foreseen by either of us, but you led the way years ago with roles like the Dyer's Wife/Barak, Fidelio/Pizarro, Brünnhilde/Wotan. It would be a shame not to pursue this path further. Because of this, we are interested in the Marschallin and Ochs you offered us.

We have always brought our problems to you openly and honestly, and have done so again this time. We are certain that you understand our situation and will resolve our difficulties with a spirit of generosity.

With sincere greetings and best wishes to you,

Yours,
Christa Ludwig
Walter Berry

And a few weeks later:

September 4, 1968

Dear Herr von Karajan,

Back in Vienna, despite your good advice, I thought some more about my dramatic soprano plans, which have created problems for me. You were extremely generous to postpone the recording sessions [for *Siegfried*] until October, but, in spite of that, I have now definitely decided to neither record nor perform this role because my voice is exhausted for a whole day after a run through of Brünnhilde. How can I possibly sing this role daily in such circumstances?

I am very unhappy about this decision, most of all because I would have so enjoyed working with you. It is also extremely unpleasant for me to repay all your kindness by creating difficulties for you, and I regret this beyond measure. I hope very much to be permitted to work with you in my original voice type and do roles such as the alto part in the *St. Matthew Passion*.

I have gone back and forth in my resolve, but I believe this is the correct decision.

Yours,
Christa Ludwig

But Karajan didn't give up. He asked me to sing Isolde with him.

In studying Isolde, it was obvious that the music lay better for my voice than did Brünnhilde's music. One day in New York, I sang the entire role for my mother, Zinka Milanov, and a friend, Dr. Lilly Engler, a psychiatrist who was born in Vienna and who understood singing (and singers). For a genera-tion, Milanov had been the most important soprano in the Italian repertoire, and she sang many times with Toscanini. Since she lived very close to my apartment in New York, I went to her for advice, and I also studied the role of Lady Macbeth with her. With these three women as my audience, I sang all of Isolde without any breaks, and when I finished, the opinion was unanimous: "You sing it very beautifully, but why sing this part when you are such a good Brangäne? Is it just to satisfy your personal ambition? You would risk your voice." And Milanov added, "Remember that you'll soon have the problems that come with menopause." At that time, I was too young to know about these difficulties, and my mother hadn't sung long enough to feel menopause's effects. But I soon found out what Milanov meant.

So I accepted the judgment of these three ladies, put Isolde aside, and again declined Karajan's invitation. I shared all my thoughts with him. He was very kind and understanding, even though he had no idea where he was going to find a replacement. He told me the parable of the cat and the dog. The dog was commanded to jump, and he jumped. The cat thought seriously about whether or not she was capable of jumping, and she never jumped. "So," he continued, "if you think you can't do it, you can't. Just sing Brangäne." It wasn't true that Karajan ruined voices, held grudges, and refused to engage singers who turned him down. I firmly believe that the circum-stances surrounding these incidents have to be considered. When I had a vocal disaster while singing Eboli with Karajan, I left Salzburg immediately and refused to sing any of the other performances. Karajan never held this against me, and I sang with him many times afterwards.

Critics have already written about Karajan's musical talent, and I leave that subject to the experts. What I can discuss is his ability to bring people together to create a wonderful musical experience, and his sensitivity to soft, subtle sound, the opposite of the "Anything you can sing, I can sing louder" approach that Anna Russell comically describes in her commentary on Wagner's Ring. With his approach, Karajan produced, not one, but three or four generations of singers. His primary focus was to instruct the orchestral players to listen to the sound of the singers, as I've said. He also insisted that the transition between individual chords be seamless, except for the places where pauses were written into the score by the composer. These breaks had to be respected. To make music through the bar lines, to sing whole phrases through to the end, and never to force are things that I try to teach my own students. For me, this is not only the way to make music, but also the way to look at life. Karajan was a highly gifted musician, and he was the kind of conductor whose sound you could recognize on the radio, even if you tuned in late and didn't hear the announcer say who was conducting. This was also true of Bernstein.

Embodying Voltaire's idea that it's not enough just to be an artist, Karajan became an excellent businessman too. He was always interested in the latest technology, and he was the first to make opera videos. Certainly he led an enviable life. He had villas and automobiles, an airplane and a yacht. He attached a beautiful wife like a rose to his lapel and had two talented children, but, above all else, he had power. He was a tireless worker who promoted himself as father figure, which was something that went over very well with the Germans. "The Chief" became "The Master," and the faithful André von Mattoni was always present to polish Karajan's escutcheon. But when Mattoni grew old and sick, Karajan took good care of him. Karajan was faithful to his friends, and as clear as glass in his decision-making. It's also true that the great man wasn't easy to get along with, as many in his circle had to learn. But one thing is certain. The sound of the Berlin Philharmonic flowered superbly under his direction.

Our relationship was always warm and very jolly. When I said to him once that singing was hard work and a lot of trouble, he coolly responded, "If it's so difficult, why do you do it?" Perhaps we had the kind of relationship we did because he knew my parents when he was first starting out in Aachen. There he conducted many performances of operas like *Fidelio* with my mother singing the title role and my father as stage director. And, in a way, he continued with me what he had begun with my mother thirty years before. In Aachen, he would come to dinner now and then because my father was Viennese, and we cooked in the Austrian style. When I was about seven, I remember I had to put on my best dress one day, offer my hand to Karajan, curtsy, and then disappear. I was extremely embarrassed. God, how I hated doing it! And because of this experience, I never forced my own son to do such a thing.

Karajan often spoke to me about my mother's outstanding musicality. He said that he could have sent her to the train station during rehearsal, and she would have come back on the correct beat. My mother also told me stories about the 27-year-old Karajan who was usually directing operas and concert works for the first time as the youthful general music director in Aachen. At that time, he was a very dynamic, effusive personality, whose emphatic gestures while conducting made a great show for the audience. When the Berlin Philharmonic came to Hanover with Karajan in 1954, my mother said to me that we absolutely had to see this extraordinary display. So we went, but, behold, Herr von Karajan didn't overreact anymore. Much calmer and no longer in need of grand gestures, he now had an overwhelming radiance. It was difficult to tell where these waves came from, but they seemed concentrated in his body and to radiate from him as he conducted with his back turned towards us. He had a magic that everyone talked about, a great charisma, but he no longer had his youthful, stormy, exaggerated style of conducting.

Lorin Maazel

Although I was too young to remember much of the youthful conducting style of the young Karajan in Aachen, I did experience a similar stormy style in the performances of the young Lorin Maazel. I met Maazel during the 1955/56 season in Rome, when he conducted Gustav Mahler's Symphony No. 2, and I sang the solo part. He was then director of the Italian Radio Orchestra, and he was being hailed as the new Toscanini. I was 27, and he was about 25, even younger than Karajan was during his early days in Aachen, and far more excitable. He was so effusive that people laughed at him in public. The Mahler Second is very difficult for everyone in the orchestra, and the task of conducting such a complex work at age 25 and the stress of giving all the right cues made him even more effusive.

In 1957, Egon Seefehlner, who was then director of the concert halls in Vienna, engaged Maazel to conduct the Mahler Second, and again I sang and again experienced how people made rude comments and laughed. During one climax, where Maazel's conducting grew ever more intense, there was a drum-beat, and the timpanist, inspired to equally high drama, began to fall backward on his stool off the riser just as he was about to make his entrance. At the very last moment, just as he was falling over, he managed to reach his drum and deliver his beat, and this made everyone laugh. Yet everyone knew by this time what an enormously talented musician Maazel was.

The 1993 Salzburg Festival was probably the last time I sang with Maazel. By then his movements were calmer and clearer. It was interesting for me to have followed his development over the years and have to have been a part of it.

I have an indelible memory of his Berlin *Fidelio* of June 1966. Maazel suddenly called me in Vienna and explained that he had suffered a terrible mishap at the Deutsche Oper Berlin. In the last act, the words "Wer ein holdes Weib errungen, mische seinen Jubel ein" are first sung by Florestan alone, and then by the whole chorus. Maazel always conducted without a score because he had a prodigious memory, but usually conductors don't do this at the opera because so many things are happening simultaneously on the stage, in the orchestra, and with the chorus that the interaction can easily go wrong. And that was exactly what had happened in Berlin. Hans Beirer, who sang Florestan, made a mistake, the orchestra was right, but the whole chorus made the same mistake as Beirer. The orchestra and the singers went in separate directions, and Maazel had to stop the performance. The audience was furious and booed.

Maazel felt that the next time he conducted *Fidelio* in Berlin, it had to be special, and he asked me if I would sing the title role and Walter Berry the Pizarro. I had a performance a day or two before in Vienna, and hesitated because I thought to myself, how can I sing my problem child Fidelio so soon after a performance in Vienna? But I decided to do it out of loyalty, and I flew to Maazel's next *Fidelio* in Berlin. I was greeted with applause as soon as I appeared on the stage. Everything went wonderfully, and Maazel had an enormous success.

Here's a contemporary account of these events, which gives a different perspective:

Fidelio—or, All's Well that Ends Well

From our Berlin Opera (War) correspondent, Peter Csobádi

As the A-tone died away recently in the orchestra at the Deutsche Oper Berlin, and Lorin Maazel walked to the conductor's podium, the air was electric. The cognoscenti in the audience awaited a scandal, prepared to do battle.

It all began with a saber blow during a *Fidelio* performance a few weeks previous (reported in the *Kurier*), which exactly corresponded with a guest appearance by Birgit Nilsson. The boos, a spontaneous reaction from a disappointed audience, were intended for Lorin Maazel and Hans Beirer. Which of the two deserved to receive them, i.e., which was most at fault, is hard to say.

Principal soloist, Hans Beirer, set things straight a few days later with an explanation to the German press, in which he declared he was not the culprit but rather it was the conductor, who had given no cue or, at least, no clear cue.

General Director Gustav Rudolf Sellner, in his own press conference, took the blame in a manly way by blaming a spotlight which had been installed at his order and which had blinded Florestan.

Then *Bild* (Berlin) caused a sensation with the headline "Never Again under Maazel," which was supposedly a direct quote from an interview with the celebrated soprano Birgit Nilsson. Since such words from the intrigue-filled world of international musical life are not made public every day, a Vienna paper picked up the story from *Bild*, whereupon Miss Nilsson telegraphed the following to General Director Sellner (Berlin) from the Hotel Europa (Vienna):

> Am shocked by the Bild article since I was not interviewed at all [Stop] Have also not said that I never wanted to sing with Maazel again [Stop] Your opera and public are singular, and I hope I can sing with you again soon [Stop]

Although this telegram was made public by the management of the opera, the text did little to counteract the publicity. *Bild* quoted the last two sentences and added to them a critique that appeared in the Vienna paper on February 15 (an annihilating one). In addition, the article bore the title (across four columns) "Opera Conductor Pays To Polish His Reputation." Well-placed, it appeared on the day of another *Fidelio* performance under Maazel and included the following announcement:

> He will stand at the podium this evening, as announced, for a gala *Fidelio* performance. Reaching deep into the pocket of his general manager, Maazel pulled out Christa Ludwig and Walter Berry. The married couple demanded $2000 to sing— per throat!

Horribile dictu, an opera director who has sunk so low that he invites a premier cast to his house.

These are the conditions which caused the air to be electric as the A-tone in the orchestra ebbed, and the conductor made his way to the podium.

The expectations of impending scandal were disappointed. The outcome of this most recent *Fidelio* performance was reported, not in *Bild*, but in *Welt*, and the headline read "Impressive Artistic Achievement." To reinvite the cast from the premiere was really worth it. Christa Ludwig (Leonore), James King (Florestan), Walter Berry (Pizarro), Peter Lagger (who replaced Josef Greindl as Roco), Lisa Otto and Donald Grobe (Marzelline and Jacquino), as well as Barry McDaniel (First

Prisoner) sang and acted with intensity, and Lorin Maazel conducted with an exactness and verve that was simply a triumph.

The next day Lorin Maazel left Berlin for Rome to conduct a recording of the opera, *Tosca*, with Birgit Nilsson in the title role.

(*Kurier*, Vienna, June 30, 1966)

Leonard Bernstein

At a time when artists felt more and more that it was their duty to become involved in politics, Leonard Bernstein took up the liberal cause. He didn't shut himself up in an ivory tower, but instead threw himself into life. There was a terrible outcry when Bernstein invited the Black Panthers to his home, and later there was ample evidence of Bernstein's political activity on television. He bravely protested against the Vietnam War and against any of the political positions in Washington he disagreed with. He felt it was his responsibility to continually fight for human rights, AIDS relief, nuclear disarmament, and world peace. He used his fame as a musician to makes his views public.

Singers are generally not interested in politics. Our dream world on the stage and the rough-and-tumble world of politics are opposites. I myself belong to no political party, although I am against everything that is false and malicious. I support equal rights under the law for everyone, regardless of which country they are born in, or what color their skin is. Certainly I am naïve because I live in the world of art, but I cannot understand why such a primitive thing as war, and the terrible killing of innocent people that goes along with it, has not been outlawed. Where is the influence of all the religions that teach "Thou shalt not kill"?

I was in New York during George Bush's campaign for president of the United States when a long article by Bernstein about the meaning of the word "liberal" appeared in the *New York Times*. He wrote it, he said, because the liberals in the Democratic Party in America had been portrayed as communists by

Bush supporters. Bernstein's liberal politics was rooted in his deep feeling for humanity. He loved people and all their differences. This is why the theme of his *Mass* is love among all peoples, which refers back to "Alle Menschen wer-den Brüder" (All men shall be brothers) in Schiller's "Ode to Joy" at the end of Beethoven's Ninth Symphony. This was the theme of his whole life.

Beethoven's *Missa Solemnis* was one of the many works that I really came to understand only by working with Bernstein. At first this mass is very diffi-cult for both the performers and the audience to grasp. When Bernstein con-ducted it at the Vienna State Opera, his father had just died, and he seemed to work through his grief in his interpretation. And Bernstein, who was Jewish, conducted this Christian mass far more passionately and with a deeper religious feeling than many Christian conductors.

Bernstein told me once that he would have liked to have been a rabbi because he enjoyed teaching so much. He always taught naturally, as if he weren't teaching at all, yet one always learned a lot. This was the opposite of his conducting style, where he used gestures to illustrate the feeling in the music. He was often teased about his "choreography" while conducting, but he was not putting on a show for the audience. He danced in rehearsal just as much as he did at a performance.

Bernstein always lived for people and with people, and he loved this kind of life. He used to say that he never dined or went to the movies alone. After a concert, he seemed to receive the entire world in his dressing room, and he spoke with everyone. This took a long time, and afterwards, he was invited out. I always fled from such invitations, and he always said, "Christa, you're so pragmatic." But what would he have said if I came to rehearsal hoarse or can-celed my next performance with him because of a night "on the town"? Even though I wasn't a prima donna, my vocal cords were always peevish, and they demanded that I pack them safely in cotton wool, so to speak, when I wasn't singing. They wanted nothing to do with smoking, loud talking, or excessive drinking late at night.

In 1966, Bernstein saw me in *Die Frau ohne Schatten* at the Met. Later, when I went backstage and introduced myself after one of his concerts, he said, "Oh, here comes my Marschallin." I said, "No, I always sing Octavian." But after hearing me as the Dyer's Wife, he was absolutely convinced I could sing the Marschallin. Since my mother had written "Now for Octavian and later for the Marschallin" in the *Rosenkavalier* piano vocal score that I had used when I was first starting out, I didn't hesitate long. I soon joyfully agreed to sing the Marschallin with Bernstein, especially because I never really liked playing the role of the stupid young Octavian.

When I first met Bernstein, I had no idea how much my view of life and of music would change because of him. There is an enormous difference between a brilliant musician and a genius, and Bernstein was a genius. I was raised to regard music as something sacred, but from Bernstein, I learned about its joys and pleasures. Suddenly I felt music more fully, and discovered that it had another dimension. After working with Bernstein, music was for me deeper, higher, wider. It entered deeply into every part of my being.

Although everyone was skeptical beforehand, the Vienna *Rosenkavalier* of 1968 was a gigantic success. We had a Welsh woman, Gwyneth Jones, as Octavian; an American coffee-brown woman, Reri Grist, as the sweet young Viennese girl, Sophie; and a baritone, Walter Berry (incidentally, the only real Viennese in the cast) in the bass role of Baron Ochs. I, a mezzo soprano, sang the Marschallin, a soprano role, and Bernstein, an American, conducted the most Viennese of all operas.

The stage director, Otto Schenk, taught us to play the piece in the Viennese style, and, as a conductor, our Lenny was more Viennese than the Viennese. The result was a *Rosenkavalier* that was bathed in bittersweetness and a slightly overdone autumnal mood, half-true to the Viennese soul where everything is completely half-serious. Every phrase, every nuance, every cadence, every breath was elaborated and interpreted almost too clearly. Bernstein gave himself over totally to the rapturous pleasure of the music, and the public loved him for it.

A red rose lay on the conductor's podium at every performance. Bernstein himself was showered with gifts from Viennese admirers, to the point where he seemed always to be fending off a flood of silver roses and Augarten porcelain figures of the Rosenkavalier. Me too! I still have a collection of Rosenkavalier mementos from those days. Bernstein was always a dear colleague who came to my dressing room before every performance to wish me "toi toi toi," and I knew I could relax because I was in safe hands. He didn't really understand a lot about voices because he was too much of a symphonic conductor. Yet I could always lay my vocal cards on the table with him, and tell him exactly where I needed his help during a performance.

For several years, Bernstein and Karajan were said to be at opposite ends of the musical universe. The public divided itself into two camps with gusto, making the success of each one greater. Other examples of this type of rivalry are Callas and Tebaldi, Prey and Fischer-Dieskau, Seefried and Schwarzkopf, and Domingo and Pavarotti.

Karajan always looked inward, and didn't use grand gestures. He "celebrated" the music as if each concert were a religious service. Bernstein—ten years younger, remember—seemed to approach the music with complete openness. He exhausted himself completely and sweated and hugged and kissed everyone, but his interpretations were no less exciting than Karajan's, and no less true to the music.

Bernstein is the only conductor that I know of who invited another famous colleague to conduct during one of his own concerts. I attended a performance in New York at Avery Fisher Hall where Bernstein turned his baton over to Karl Böhm who conducted a piece by Mozart. Then Bernstein returned to conduct the rest of the concert. This generosity of spirit was typical of Lenny.

I was especially grateful to sing the music of Gustav Mahler at many concerts in Europe and America with Bernstein. It was through his interpretations that I first understood how Judaism, Christianity, and also Viennese decadence are connected in this composer. I saw clearly, as if in a mirror, how the spirit of the *fin de siècle* is reflected in his music. For example, Bernstein conducted the second movement of Mahler's Second Symphony, which is marked "Andante Moderato," almost stiffly, marionette like, and I felt this was exactly the right interpretation for his view of the music. I always sensed that Bernstein's spirit was very close to Mahler's, and that both men were seeking salvation from chaos. I think that my own interpretation of Schubert's *Die Winterreise* was very much influenced by my work with Bernstein on Mahler's music.

Through Bernstein, I learned a truthfulness of interpretation which allows both the performers and the listeners to reach beyond the world of music to the realm of the spirit. Bernstein never saw the public as an anonymous crowd, but always as individual human beings. In a real sense, he constantly searched for the essence of the human spirit with the same prodigious energy with which he searched for the essence of the music he conducted. And he was almost never content with what he discovered.

In December 1989 I sang the Old Lady in a concert performance of Bernstein's *Candide* at the Royal Festival Hall in London, and Bernstein conducted. Unfortunately, the production was star crossed, thanks to the "British flu" that was raging through England at the time and infecting everyone. The first cast member to catch the disease was June Anderson, who was to sing Candide's beloved Cunegonde. We soon shared it with her. First the tenor Jerry Hadley got sick, and then me too. Bernstein also became infected. At the performances, he was feverish and sweating, and he seemed to be using his last bit of strength just to hold himself upright at the podium. He began addressing the audience, explaining the genesis of the play and telling how he and his wife Felicia had discussed some of the text. But soon he had to excuse himself because he could hardly talk because of the flu. Yet, in spite of everything, the performances were wonderful. Some critics thought that Bernstein had used familiar melodies in *Candide*, and Bernstein told us that he'd intended the piece to sound reminiscent of Offenbach, Strauss (Johann and Richard), and Lehár, among others, with even some touches of Mahler (in his lighter moods). So musically *Candide* is really a parody of old European operetta music.

Sadly, these performances in London were my last with Bernstein, and I always look back on them as the beginning of his end. Only a few months later, in March 1990, he knew he had lung cancer.

When Bernstein was dying in October, I received a telephone call from Schuyler Chapin, who was in New York while I was on tour in Seoul. He wanted to let me know about Bernstein, rather than have me hear about it through the media. Chapin and Bernstein had been close friends, and it struck me that this was a final proof of their friendship. As a remembrance of Lenny, I received a beautiful antique chain that I'd often seen him wear around his neck. For me, it's a memento that unites me with this beloved genius.

I mourn him.

Lieder

From Heart to Heart

Although the audience is an anonymous crowd, a performer can feel immediately whether the electricity is flowing between the auditorium and the stage. This is especially true at a lieder recital, where the give and take is very obvious. The affection with which an expectant audience greeted me was a wonderful feeling, and I always tried to return it through my songs. In this way, every audience was the same regardless of the city and country I was in, and regardless of whether or not the audience understood the language I was singing. The language of the lied isn't German, but the language that goes "from heart to heart," as Beethoven said, and it is understood by all. With music as the bond, all differences of race, skin color, and social class vanish. Mankind suddenly becomes a great community instead of an anonymous crowd, and this wholeness is something that political leaders vainly try to achieve. When I felt these intense moments of oneness at a recital, I bowed deeply to the belief that music really is a holy art.

Of course, when I wasn't in a German-speaking country, I, as a German lieder singer, was concerned that the audience wouldn't understand the text. The fear is always there, but I think we singers have to guard against it. We have to be careful not to exaggerate and mime a song to get the meaning across. We have to trust the audience. I myself always found the audiences in America to be very knowledgeable, and the best were in New York and in the cities where there are universities. Once I asked why it was that the audience understood so much, and I was told that the entire program had been explained and discussed beforehand, and the audience had arrived at the concert fully prepared. The Japanese are also a very knowledgeable audience, particularly in Tokyo. There, and in America, I've seen music fans with enormous collections of phonograph records, and now of CDs. I'm always amazed and very touched when young listeners come with huge stacks of records and CDs for me to autograph.

Of course, a singer has to know which type of program to give in a particular city. To my great sorrow, I've always had to be especially careful about programming the songs of Hugo Wolf, not to mention contemporary composers whose music audiences find especially difficult. For me, Hugo Wolf captures the true feelings inside the poetic texts he set, and he combines this with an acute psychological understanding of those feelings in his music. His accomplishments have become known principally through the missionary-like efforts of Elisabeth Schwarzkopf, Irmgard Seefried, and Dietrich Fischer-Dieskau. As early as the 1960s, I could give a complete Wolf recital in New York, but in German-speaking countries, it's still difficult, surprising as that may seem. Vienna, Berlin, Munich, and also Hamburg are the only cities where an audience can be found for such a recital, whereas Franz Schubert is universally welcomed by every audience. Erik Werba, my recital accompanist for many years, always said that a lieder recital must consist of three types of songs: the first to please the critics, so they can wax musicological; the second to please the audience; and the third to please the singer, so he or she can sing what they love best. For me, that's always a group of Wolf songs.

Erik Werba arranged my first recital in the Vienna Konzerthaus in 1957. He chose a wonderfully varied program, and also a white dress! Choosing a program is an art, with a little bit of sport mixed in. When I was young, I used to sing a song cycle concert, which consisted of *Zigeunerlieder* by Johannes Brahms, *Zigeunerlieder* by Antonin Dvořák, *Wesendonck Lieder* by Richard Wagner, and *Seven Early Songs* by Alban Berg. What a gigantic program! It exhausts me just to think about it now. Such a program could only be done with a fresh, young voice that doesn't tire easily. I always had to keep in mind that I had to sing for about an hour and a half all by myself in a recital, which can be quite an endurance contest. When planning a program, I also had to consider my age, and remember that I wouldn't necessarily be in tip-top voice every day. I had to make sure that I didn't burden myself with a program that was too hard, because then neither I nor the audience would have any chance of enjoying the evening.

A program must also have variety. When I was a child, I always preferred the slowest songs, which are usually very sad, because I wasn't the best pianist and I could accompany myself. I guess I developed a taste for such songs because later I often made the mistake of not having the dabs of color in a program that cheerful songs bring. I enjoyed wallowing in tragedy, and the excuse I would use was that these songs suited my voice best. But then I often heard after a recital, "Please, Christa, at least one happy song next time."

Although I sang lieder from the very beginning of my professional life, I was in no true sense a lieder singer then. Opera and lieder are two completely different types of musical expression. To me, there are singers who also sing lieder, and then there are true lieder singers, and it takes a long time to become one of the latter. If someone sings only opera for forty years, I really don't think it's possible to just say, "Now I am going to sing lieder."

When Caruso said that he would pull another voice out of his drawer for each role, he was only talking about singing Italian opera parts, so the voices in Caruso's drawer had only small differences among them. In my drawer, there were many more voices, and many of them were radically different since I sang soprano, mezzo, and contralto parts, and I also sang lieder, concerts, and opera. For me, it wasn't at all like slipping on another scarf with a slightly different pattern and color. The operatic voice is a more public voice, and closer to (God forgive me!) a scream in dramatic roles. The lieder voice is more intimate, quieter, purer, full of nuances. With only a piano for accompaniment, every vocal subtlety can be heard, and must be heard. Early in my career, Elisabeth Schwarzkopf told me that she needed two weeks after an opera evening to prepare her voice for a lieder recital. In my naïveté, I thought, "Hah! She's wrong. I definitely don't need two weeks. I can switch in a few days." But, of course, I couldn't. Every time I scheduled a recital too soon after an opera performance, I couldn't sing the songs properly. My voice was too heavy, sometimes it even sounded tired, and the subtlety of expression I needed just wouldn't come.

Erik Werba was a blessing to me. He was a professor of song interpretation at the Vienna Academy for Music, and he taught with great passion. He held master classes all over the world, and had students everywhere, including Japan, Korea, France, Germany, and Italy. He was very well-educated in the classics, very intelligent, filled with wisdom, and a tireless worker. In addition, he often played matchmaker for many of his students who weren't talented enough to have a career. "We need to produce a musically educated audience," he'd always say. He was not only a teacher, but also a true friend, and he was always looking for ways to help. For example, he put together special evenings for his students so they could practice before a live audience, and he also tutored them in private.

For Walter Berry and me, Erik Werba was like family. We shared our worries with him, and he was the godfather of our son, who was given the middle name Erik in his honor. As an accompanist, he was very reserved. He remained "only" an accompanist, and never pushed himself into the foreground. And he didn't just accompany me on the piano. He was a true touring companion. He would always cheer me up when I was nervous by saying how good my voice sounded, or how enthusiastic the audience was. In spite of his having a body like a heavyweight boxer and a bear-like awkwardness, he was a gentle person whose art as accompanist also had great tenderness. He is the one who taught me to love Hugo Wolf, and he even wrote a book about him (*Hugo Wolf oder der zärtliche Romantiker*, Vienna, 1971).

As a sideline, Werba was also one of the leading critics in Vienna. He always said that a review should be written so that the critic can read it in the presence of another and to the face of the person being criticized. He felt very strongly that the critic must never hide behind the quasi-anonymity of the press. Critics should be polite and correct, but never insulting, he insisted, and they should never ridicule the person they are critiquing.

In recent years, it has become the fashion to use great contemporary pianists as accompanists. Fischer-Dieskau, for example, likes to use Daniel Barenboim, Sviatoslav Richter, Christoph Eschenbach, or Maurizio Pollini. To me, this makes a very impressive poster, but it doesn't really add anything to Fischer-Dieskau's art since he is already a fine performer. Although a great name does increase the demand for tickets to a recital, I myself always preferred to use my regular accompanist. We knew one another well on a human level, and we also shared the same musical vibrations.

But there are always exceptions to the rule. I gave a Brahms recital with Leonard Bernstein in the 1970s and the rehearsals were very difficult because he approached the songs from the symphony side and I approached them from the lieder side. But I must say that the results were very interesting. Karajan and I also talked about doing a recital together, but the arthritis in his fingers prevented it.

James Levine is the biggest exception to every rule. He is able, almost miraculously, to be the perfect accompanist, a great opera conductor, and a fine symphony conductor, too. I think perhaps his secret—and what makes him unique—is his constant search for the right sound for Mahler and for Schubert and for Brahms. And he finds it! And also wonderful is Jimmy's enormous love for music and the human voice. I always felt that we were one musical soul at a recital, and it was a pleasure to have him accompany me at my farewell recital at Carnegie Hall in New York.

Erik Werba used to say that an accompanist must not only accompany at the piano, but also in life. The two performers must be friends, and really know each other. They must laugh together, eat together, cook together, and then make music together. Often I could tell from the first rehearsal whether or not I was on the same wavelength as an accompanist. Two performers of the same music can have totally different styles. Their background has a lot to do with it—the country in which they were born, and the teachers that influenced them. The wonderful British pianist Gerald Moore played gloriously for me, but we didn't work well together at all. He was simply too British for me, and had a certain rigidity and reserve that just wasn't compatible with my musical personality. Werba was Viennese. He played with more rubato, and the musical phrasing flowed just the way I liked it. Later I had an exceptionally fine pianist named Irwin Gage as an accompanist. Unfortunately, it sometimes seemed to me that he was playing in an entirely different style than the one that I was singing in, perhaps because our intellects and our musical sensibilities were totally different. We simply didn't fit together.

Since 1982, I've used Charles Spencer as my regular accompanist. He is British, but he lived in Vienna for a long time and went to school there. He studied both with Robert Schollum and with Geoffrey Parsons, and I think his style combines the best of both Viennese and British music-making. I didn't rehearse with him at all before our first recital of songs by Richard Strauss and Hugo Wolf, which took place at the Stuttgart Opera. I just sent him a cassette of the program with Werba at the piano, and Charles did a wonderful job of accompanying me. We also did our first *Winterreise* together without much rehearsal. It was amazing that he could be such a perfect partner at such a young age, since he was only in his mid-twenties then. We were always on the same wavelength. When we began to rehearse a new recital program, my second husband Paul-Emile Deiber and my mother would sit and critique every beat of music and discuss every word of text. For example, we talked about how the wind that is blowing through the tree must already be heard in the introduction to Schumann's *Der Nussbaum*. And how the introduction to *Die Forelle* must make the audience see the little brook hopping over its steppingstones. And how the introduction to *Winterreise* must make it obvious that the journey is already underway, and the listeners must feel the sombre mood intensely from the first note. When two musicians understand each other as Charles and I do, music-making is a great joy.

Tempi must never be a point of contention between a singer and an accompanist. In his book *Am I Too Loud?*, Gerald Moore wrote that he took the Brahms song "Vergebliches Ständchen" much slower with me than he usually did with a soprano. It is very important for an accompanist to be flexible enough to do this, because singers must find the tempo that best allows them to capture their own sense of what the music and the text mean. In addition, I didn't wake up in exactly the same frame of mind every day, or with exactly the same pulse. All of this could be heard in the way I interpreted a song on a particular day. Thank God this happens, because it made singing recitals much more interesting both for me and for the audience. Otherwise, they might just as well buy a recording and experience the way I felt on the day I made the recording, eternally the same. This is a horrible idea to someone like myself who believes wholeheartedly in spontaneity.

I've always tried to follow my intuition at a recital, and, for that reason, I'm against too many rehearsals, although some rehearsal is obviously necessary as a foundation. In this, I'm a little less German, and a little more Viennese. I always tried to do only what's in a song, and to do only what I learned from approaching the music and the text, without reading about other people's ideas, or thinking too much. Opera is totally different. If it weren't, who would feed the families of all those coaches? I once knew a leading singer at the Vienna State Opera who couldn't read a note of music. Thankfully, this doesn't happen any more, and certainly a lieder singer could never be so musically ignorant.

After working on a piece myself first, I worked on refinements with my accompanist, so that the mood of the song, whether happy or sad, was completely expressed. And I think the accompanist must give the same amount of attention to the subtleties of the song as the singer does. The different tones and modulations must flow and be expressed through almost imperceptible vocal coloration, through the tiniest hesitation on a chord, or through the exact timing of a consonant sound. This attention to detail gave me the greatest joy imaginable. Often I'd discard what yesterday seemed so right, and constantly change my approach as my understanding changed.

Finally, I always invited my mother and my husband to the last rehearsal before I actually sang a new program before the public, so they could make their complaints. Often my accompanist and I would think a song went very well, but then we would hear something from our little audience like, "Well, it was OK." OK! Just OK? Obviously, the cognoscenti hadn't felt the spark that a song needs to hold an audience and reach into its soul. Then the questions would start. "Why is there sorrow in your face, but not in your voice?" Oh, God! Was it that bad? "Why so much emotion? The secret of this song is its purity and simplicity." Every singer needs a little audience like this, made up of listeners with taste and understanding, whom they can trust completely to criticize gently but absolutely honestly. I think I had the gift for lieder singing naturally, since I enjoyed singing recitals from the earliest days of my career, but it took me a long time to refine my talent.

"Hopefully, you'll have your voice long enough to understand what the spirit of singing is all about," my mother always used to say to me. And she was right. It took me so long to mature that I was very lucky my voice lasted as long as it did. Now, after many years, I'm quite convinced that lieder singing is a thorough mix of intellect, intuition, and emotion. It's almost like the mystery of faith, and because of this, "what it's all about" is very hard to put into words. I think perhaps part of the secret is in experiencing life itself. For example, I always had a very strong reaction to Mahler's *Kindertotenlieder* from the very first time I sang those songs. At one concert in Brussels, I was so moved that I began to cry and had to leave the stage. But I wonder now how really good those performances were since I was more moved than the audience was.

But then I gave birth to my son Wolfgang, and my approach to the songs totally changed. I never again broke down at a performance. I think, looking back, that my response went from strong to deep, because I now understood what great pain I myself would have felt if I ever lost my own child. My reaction and that of the audience were suddenly reversed. In early performances like the one in Brussels, I was moved to tears, but the audience wasn't. After my son was born, I didn't cry, but the audience did. True lieder singing takes a lot of maturity, or at least it did in my case, because singers have to find the courage to express their true feelings about life through song, and not be embarrassed or ashamed. For me, it took a long time to reach that level.

Perhaps individual interpretation is the most important thing. Everyone experiences life differently, so everyone's interpretation of a song will be a little different too. And there are no laws about how songs must be done, thank God. Jon Vickers' interpretation of *Winterreise* is an example. Vickers didn't only sing Siegmund and Otello. He *became* Siegmund and Otello. So, although he had very little experience as a lieder singer, he was able to become the lost soul who journeys through that song cycle, and he was so passionate that the performance was wonderful. There are always exceptions, and one of the greatest challenges a singer faces is to know when it's right to break the rules, and when it isn't.

As it is says in Gustav Mahler's Second Symphony, "Es geht dir nichts verloren, was du gelebt, geliebt, gelitten." (Nothing is lost that you have experienced, loved, suffered.) Singers can transform all their experiences, and let them flow out through their voices. The possibilities are endless. For me I think tolerance for the differences among people, a realization that mankind and nature are one, and a respect for life are the most important things. And I also like a good joke too. All these things are found in the songs of Schubert and Brahms and Hugo Wolf, and they are all things that will please and move an audience.

"Be yourself," my mother always used to tell me. Easy to say, hard for a singer to do. You not only have to know yourself, but, perhaps even more important, you have to like yourself. An audience knows. And although I hate to admit it, vocal limitations can be a blessing. If I'd had a voice right from the beginning with which I could have sung everything from top to bottom without difficulty, I probably would have learned very little. I would have just sung without thinking. I know it's difficult to tell young singers this, because they're always ambitious and want to do everything. But trying to solve vocal problems makes you study more intensely, and that's when you can really learn something and discover your own special way of interpreting a song or an opera role.

Die Winterreise:
A Journey of the Soul

When Professor Albert Moser, the Director of the Gesellschaft der Musikfreunde (Musikverein) in Vienna, asked me to sing Schubert's *Die Winterreise* in the early eighties, I was very surprised and intended to say no. I thought that this great cycle had only been sung by men, and I especially loved it as it was sung by Hans Hotter, who opened the world of this work to me with his great dark voice. When I met Hotter by chance around the time I was making my decision, I told him about the offer from the Musikverein and asked for his opinion. After thinking for a moment, he said: "If any woman can sing *Die Winterreise*, it's you!" With that encouragement, I started to study the cycle with Erik Werba.

When working on the first songs, where the wanderer speaks about his "Liebchen," I hesitated. Clearly a woman is being spoken about. But as the cycle advances, the thoughts become less individualized, and they move into a higher, more transcendent dimension. They are the thoughts of a lonely wanderer, who is searching for a goal and who moves through many stages of life. More and more I became aware that these songs describe a state of the soul. Towards the end of the cycle particularly, no story is told chronologically, as in Robert Schumann's cycle *Frauenliebe und leben*. *Winterreise* becomes the story of a human being who suffers a great personal loss, and this human soul travels through the icy landscape of its own winter. Not only men experience such loss. For me, the most important thing is for the singer to travel together with the listeners and to lead them psychologically into the mood of Schubert's music.

At about this time, I heard a recording of *Die Winterreise* by Lotte Lehmann, and at first I was astonished when I heard the brightness of her soprano voice in the cycle. But the intensity of her interpretation quickly made me forget the soprano sound. In 1941 she sang the cycle at Carnegie Hall in New York, and she was so convincing that Olin Downes, the critic of the *New York Times* at that time, didn't even mention in his review that a woman was singing *Die Winterreise* in America for the first time. In her book *More Than Singing*, Lotte Lehmann wrote about each song in *Die Winterreise*, but she didn't mention that she had sung the cycle herself, and said nothing about her own interpretation, which is disappointing. Even though purists may object to a female voice in *Winterreise*, I think that women can sing the cycle with great empathy for the wanderer. They possess very great sensibility, born from the instinct of a mother who understands suffering and sorrow, and they are also more open to irrationality, while men are more rational and realistic. I always say that the mood of *Winterreise* is similar to the state of being that Goethe describes in one of his Mignon songs: a place beyond earthly existence where divine beings "sie fragen nicht nach Mann und Weib" (do not speak of man or woman).

A lot of things have been written about this wonderful cycle, but I think the most important thing for singers is to experience the songs for themselves, and the search for salvation the songs describe, the road we all have to travel. Singers of *Die Winterreise*, whether men or women, have to put themselves and their listeners into a state which goes far beyond music and poetry, also beyond human emotions. It's a journey of the soul, which brings us, consciously or unconsciously, a bit closer to our goal, whatever we choose to call it, and from which there is no turning back.

I sang *Die Winterreise* for the first time on November 24, 1982 in the Musikverein in Vienna, and the more I sang the cycle the more I was enriched. As I moved through the different stages of my life, I identified more and more strongly with the songs. I gave up the idea a long time ago that the Leiermann,

as a final goal, symbolizes death as the end of everything. To me he now symbolizes the eternal wheel of life, the path I followed and on which I served my
profession with my singing.

For me there is a deep and intimate connection between the lines of two
songs, the final words from the last song of *Winterreise*:

> Willst zu meinen Liedern
> deine Leier dreh'n?

> [Will you to my songs
> grind your organ?]

and the final words of one of Mahler's Rückert songs:

> Ich leb' allein in meinem Himmel,
> in meinem Lieben, in meinem Lied.

> [I live alone in my heaven,
> in my love, in my songs.]

If you know the music, you will understand.

This reminds me of what my mother always used to say about artists—
either they have "Geheimnis" (the secret) or they don't. And this "Geheimnis"
can't be described in words. Hofmannsthal has the Dyer's Wife in *Die Frau ohne
Schatten* speak about "Geheimnis," and Salome talks "vom Geheimnis des Todes
und der Liebe" (about the secret of death and love). Thank God there's still
something that's hidden from us and can't be explained! At lieder recitals, I
sometimes experienced moments when I seemed to lose contact with reality, for
example, in the Rückert song by Mahler I just mentioned, "Ich bin der Welt
abhanden gekommen," or in "Mondnacht" by Robert Schumann. Sometimes it
almost seemed to me that I was singing in a trance. I no longer searched for the
voice or the expression, but something beyond. It was as if the song was singing,
and not me. My singing was effortless. I think these might have been moments
of "Geheimnis." As long as one isn't conscious of them, it works. However, if
one becomes aware of them and tries to repeat them, then the "Geheimnis"
goes wrong, and the singing and the expression become artificial.

Your astonishment at what comes out of you is a very special experience.
You don't know what's happening to you because it comes very unexpectedly.

In this state, perhaps we should call it inspiration, the electric circuit to the audience closes, and they also feel the "Geheimnis." When it comes completely naturally from the singer, or from any type of interpreter, I'm sure that it carries over to the audience, too. I believe that audiences are very sensitive to what is real and what is fake.

There are singers who are not 100 percent perfect, but who have a certain something that makes the electric circuit with the audience close. "Geheimnis" has nothing to do with a perfect performance. It's simply "Geheimnis."

Making Music with Christa Ludwig
by Charles Spencer

"…aber wer durch das Herze singet,—er gilt mir am höchsten!"

[...but who sings from the heart,—he means most to me!]
(Friedrich Schiller)

The Beginning

Shortly after I arrived in Vienna to study piano in October 1976, I managed to get a ticket to a recital in the splendidly gilded hall of the Musikverein. I was only 21, so I didn't mind in the least having to stand at the sold-out recital to be given that evening by the famous Christa Ludwig.

As soon as Christa appeared on stage, I was enthralled. She was as charming as she was charismatic. Effortlessly, she captured my heart even before she began to sing, but when the first notes floated from her throat, I knew that my life would somehow never be the same.

That evening Christa, as was her wont, slipped up now and then on the text, and invented replacements for words which had not flown to the tip of her tongue. She even left out a verse of Schubert's "Mignon." She and her audience took it all in their stride. This was something both were used to and happy with. These were signs of her extraordinarily spontaneous relationship with the composers whose songs she sang, and with her audience.

That evening I became one of Christa Ludwig's most fervent admirers. Wherever, whenever possible, I went to her recitals or fought to hear her breathtaking appearances in opera. For me, the name "Christa Ludwig" had become synonymous with "Music." With her technique so confidently under control, Christa was free to give rein to her outstanding interpretive powers, so vital to allowing each member of her audience to develop his or her own awareness of the meanings in the music.

It was Christa who first made me aware of the great Viennese style of singing. Her voice was immediately recognizable, but had a sweet Viennese suavity to it. It was a voice which could be both lively and contemplative, a voice for all seasons, for all moods. No Teutonic rigidity. It expressed a concern for others, that generosity which Beethoven so admired and which, he said, is the essential source of all communion. It is no wonder that Christa has become a Viennese institution. What would Vienna and Viennese music-making have been without her?

A few years after that first revelation at the Musikverein recital, I finally met Christa Ludwig.

In the meantime I had continued with my piano studies and played at singing lessons to earn a schilling or two. I even founded a group, called Mosaic, consisting of flute, cello, piano, and mezzo-soprano. I myself sang with the Austrian Radio Choir as often as I could, but it was through Mosaic that I first met Christa.

Our Mosaic mezzo-soprano was quite new in Vienna and wanted desperately to meet the woman who had taught Christa Ludwig. Eugenie Besalla Ludwig was not only Christa's teacher, but also her mother. I finally agreed to phone her and arrange to play a program for her, which would include Ravel's enchanting *Chansons Madécasses*. This would enable our mezzo to perform for the famous teacher and, perhaps, milk a hint or two from her.

Madame Besalla received us graciously, listened to us patiently, and congratulated us, which was kind. To me, she suggested that perhaps I should meet her daughter, even play for her (!). She was very proud of Christa, but spoke less enthusiastically about her international career. "You know, Mr. Spencer," she told me, "my daughter sleeps in a different bed almost every night." She paused, recognized the "double entendre" of her words, then winked and said "Now, now, Mr. Spencer, no naughty thoughts."

A few weeks later Madame Besalla phoned to ask if I could play for a student who had come all the way from Holland for advice. She planned to sing some Mahler songs and the solo from his Second Symphony, "O Röschen rot." I knew the pieces, and was happy to play them. What I didn't know was that Madame Besalla had arranged for Christa to eavesdrop on the lesson from the next room. Christa liked what she heard and invited me to play for her some day.

"Some day" did not dawn too easily. First I was asked to accompany Christa for a lieder recital in Germany, but the impresario wanted someone else. Typically, Christa herself broke the bad news to me. Then Christa asked me to play for her in Turin in 1982. We were to perform Schubert's *Die Winterreise* at a festival where the complete song cycles of Schubert were programmed. I learned the whole story later. Originally another accompanist was asked, but he declared himself too busy judging a competition somewhere or other. So Christa spoke to me, which was all the original pianist needed to suddenly become available. Christa Ludwig couldn't possibly replace him with an "apprentice." Oh, couldn't she? She did. We had never performed together, and she had hardly any time for rehearsal—that spectacular spontaneity of hers—but she made an exception, for my sake, and not her own. Typical Ludwig generosity. How often have I heard her say, "If we don't let young people get wet, no one will ever know if they are swimmers—or sinkers."

After that Turin recital we performed together with increasing frequency. Musically, symbiosis took over. I discovered that the Christa who had enthralled me from the platform at that first Musikverein recital was simply the real Christa. We grew close enough for Christa to become more than a friend, more than a confidante, perhaps even more than a mother to me. I had the privilege of having in Christa a mentor such as she had found for herself in Karl Böhm.

Making Music Together

That Christa and I were on the same musical wavelength was clear from the start. For the first Turin *Winterreise* I was prepared to rehearse for hours. We had to get all of the intricacies of Schubert right. When Schubert puts eighth-note triplets in the right hand, contrasted by dotted eighths, followed by six-teenths in the left hand, should the last one-sixteenth be played with the last right hand triplet note or after it? How much rubato is acceptable? How do we handle ritardi? How much pedal? How important is it that singer and pianist come to the same conclusions on the metaphysics of the Wanderer?

We had exactly one hour.

"So," said Christa. "First we can quickly run through the 'tempi' of the opening bars of each song, though, come to think of it, the tempi might change quite a bit for the performance, so much depends on how I feel, how the acoustics of the hall respond. You know, Charles, all of those things." I didn't know "all of those things," and, worse, I had even heard that Christa Ludwig sometimes asked for complete key transpositions "on the night." I could do nothing but trust my instincts and hope for the best. What Christa needed most was to create the mood of each piece, develop an emotional con-text for it, and sense that her accompanist could be trusted to provide exactly the sound she needed to cradle her voice. This was something which Karajan had taught her. The pianist must not provide too much downbeat, or she started to push. He must not be too "passive" either, or she would feel she had no support. Her highly individual sound, its "velvet" texture, was set off to its best advantage with a particular sound from the piano.

As for the mood and meaning, that is, the metaphysics of the Wanderer, she said they were in the text, and Schubert had already captured them in his music. For example, the piano part that leads into the first song of the cycle spells out how tired the Wanderer is from trudging through the deep snow. The sound should be almost muffled, an indication of how the new snowfall hampers the Wanderer's progress. The following chords, under the melody itself, which later become the main theme of the accompaniment, shouldn't be too distinct, but shouldn't be too mushy either. Such was her, later "our," interpretation of the opening of *Winterreise*. Next she talked about the wind, and the feelings it seems to evoke in the protagonist. On through the harrow-ing "Der Lindenbaum" (no comfortable conventions here), on to the "Frühlingstraum," which I believed was best played in a "swinging" 6/8 tempo to give it charm. "No," Christa said, "what you must do is imagine that you are half asleep and dreaming already of something beautiful—'Ich träumte von bunten Blumen, so wie sie wohl blühen im Mai.' Don't let the dream slip away. Hold still. It's all happening inside you. Shall we try it so?" I understood her, and found the music coming differently to and from me. It had taken on a new perspective and sounded "right," both in these reflective passages and in the stark reality of the line "als die Hähne krähten."

So it was that we rehearsed the whole cycle in just over an hour. Quite a feat, and absolute proof of how intensively we crafted the piece together. I was in seventh heaven. My destiny had been revealed, and music, singing, interpretation and, most importantly of all, my style of playing the piano took on new value. From that day on, we never rehearsed *Die Winterreise* again, but through our many performances, the work never ceased to take on new, more intense and terrible meanings for both of us. This is what music-making should be.

On occasion I would receive a little note from Christa before, or sometimes after, a recital, suggesting how she would like me to change tempi, dynamics or agogics. What she liked she would comment on directly (sometimes even sharing her satisfaction with the audience). So we grew closer and closer, developing the unity that people have remarked on. It always surprised people to learn that, unless we were performing a work for the first time, we spent little time rehearsing. We knew the music and had our techniques so much in hand that, just by listening to each other, we could create what seemed almost like an improvisation each time. Our last *Winterreise* was different from all the others, because we still continued to create new colorings, new inflections, new panoramas of expression. In London in 1993 as Christa sang "Der Leiermann" and came to the words "Wunderlicher Alter, soll ich mit dir gehn?" I suddenly saw before me a poor weary man who seemed to be insane. The singer's voice seemed to drop away and sounded hollow, echoing suffering and disillusionment. I looked up and saw the tears which coursed down Christa's cheeks. Here was a piece which she had sung countless times, and yet it moved her, and therefore the audience, to tears.

Gottfried von Einem's cycle "Bald sing ich das Schweigen" is about a young woman who knows that she is condemned to die of cancer. At the words "Jetzt weiß ich, daß ich glücklich war" (Now I realize how happy I was), Christa wept again. "Oh," she sighed, "how terrible it must be to recognize happiness only because one is about to lose it forever."

I shared the sentiment, thinking that it is often only radical change which allows us to take stock of our joys and our sorrows.

There were pitfalls when we performed a work which hadn't been programmed for quite some time. Fortunately, I had my own system of "filing" all possible key variations or "mood markings," but sometimes Christa would come up with a request to change the key we had always used. "I know my voice will sound better that way this evening," she would say. To tell the truth, it was usually our tried-and-true previously decided key which turned out to be best. "It lets my voice soar," she would admit. Or, "it gives just the right vocal position for me to get into the piece."

Her occasional demands for changes, in what we had agreed were "our" dynamic and agogic markings, were much the same. Once in Mahler's "Rheinlegendchen" she said, "Charles, we need a forte here." Our score was marked "piano," even though the solo piano was substituting for the full orchestra in the symphonic version. "Yes, 'forte'," she repeated. "After all, you alone have to be the orchestra, and you're describing the depths and surging of the sea. 'Forte' will give the keyboard sound the intensity we need."

Every now and then she would ask for a crescendo to replace the diminuendo which I had noted down as "ours" to date, or she would ask for a pianissimo to disappear in favor of a fuller, larger sound. "We've always done it that way, haven't we?" she would say guilelessly. This could be a little frustrating, but in the end it served as a reminder of just how flexible an accompanist must be—different tempi, different sounds—these are right for the singer if the mood of the moment makes them right. Christa was always alive, awake, and ready to look at her interpretations in a new light.

A Friendship

Now Christa sings no more in public. One of this century's most important singers has retired. Her marvelous husband, Paul-Emile, has at home the wife he adores, a wife who can chatter away as she wishes, can catch cold if she's not careful, and doesn't need to treat her voice like a precious instrument. I am happy for them both.

As for myself, I miss our times together. Throughout her "farewell tour," I realized, at each and every recital, just how irreplaceable she was. We still meet regularly, and I remain immensely in her debt for all she taught me, for all she shared with me.

Christa Ludwig is unique. Perhaps, as a tribute to her and to Paul-Emile on the path which they now share outside the public eye, Mackay's text for Strauss's lovely song "Morgen" best echoes my wishes for them:

And, yet again tomorrow, the sun will rise
And shine upon the pathway
Where we shall meet
In the sun-blessed air...
Reunited
In harmony & happiness.
And,
We shall walk down
To the edge of an azure sea
Your hand in mine,
And
Silently,
We shall gaze into
each other's eyes
And let a soundless harmony
invade our souls...

[Translation provided by Charles Spencer.]

Singing Is Hard Work

(in alphabetical order)

Claques

Years ago, we had claques in the major opera houses. These were groups of opera buffs who knew exactly when to begin applauding or shouting bravo, and the less knowledgeable members of the audience would naturally follow their lead. These people were seated throughout the auditorium, and earned money for what they did. Payment bought enthusiasm. Lack of payment quashed it.

When I was first starting out in Vienna, I'd just gotten into a cab to go home from rehearsal one day, when a young man suddenly opened the door on the other side, climbed in, and sat next to me. He asked for money because, he said, he and his friends could "help" my debut in Vienna. Because I was simply too naïve to understand what he was talking about and had scarcely any money with me besides, I refused, and he climbed out of the cab. I was never approached again, and not paying the claque neither helped nor hurt me.

When I began singing in America, I learned that it was completely normal to pay the claque. It was actually institutionalized. The management simply took $20 out of my fee for the claque after every performance. I thought this was a pretty dumb thing to do because I usually sang in German operas where there were no arias that were deliberately "framed" to offer a break for applause. I could understand why singers in Italian opera would pay because the arias are separated from the rest of the music, and applause is expected. But not in German opera.

Nowadays, it seems that claques have gone out of business, at least as far as I know. Singers encourage their fans in more tasteful ways. They take them to dinner, or invite them to special events where they are appearing. For example, the great baritone George London once bought Würstel (Viennese sausages) for the people who stood in line all night waiting to buy tickets for one of his performances. This kind gesture assured their appreciation, even though they were already devoted fans.

Clothes

Choosing what to wear for a recital can be very tricky. You don't want the audience distracted by the gown, but you also don't want them to be bored after looking at it for two hours either. I've always tried to choose something timeless, simple, elegant, but a little interesting. Since I love beautiful clothes, it was often very difficult for me to control myself. I tried to remember that these were really work clothes, and the most important thing was that the dress must not distract from the music.

I already mentioned that I sewed my first evening gown from a Nazi flag. I was very slim, so I could stand before a mirror, hold the material in front of me, and cut it to size. It always fit. And if it didn't fit, I just gathered a bit of material here and there.

When I was first engaged at the opera, I made my own evening gowns from beautiful fabrics that I bought, because at that time I couldn't afford a dressmaker. When I came to Vienna, I admired the wonderful shops. Already in the 1950s, there were very beautiful ones, especially on the Kärntnerstrasse, and, above all, the wonderful Adlmüller shop. But the price of a dress from these shops was far beyond my monthly salary, so I bought clothes on the Mariahilferstrasse and other, cheaper areas. When I got my little fee for singing a concert, I spent half of it (or sometimes even all of it) on an evening gown, because at lieder recitals and concerts in Vienna, I had to put on a different dress every time. Once I wore a white lace dress, and at the next concert a white silk dress. My accompanist Erik Werba said to me, "But you're wearing that white dress again!" He didn't notice that it was a totally different fabric, and, of course, the audience didn't notice either. Werba always had very specific opinions about everything, including the color of the evening gown a woman should wear for each composer. For example, red for Hugo Wolf, and blue or white for Schubert.

Occasionally, a conductor will make the rules. At a Verdi *Requiem* with Herbert von Karajan, I wore a black evening gown without sleeves, but he insisted on a dress with sleeves. He told me I absolutely had to wear a different dress at the second concert. I told him that I only had a white one, but that didn't bother him. It just had to have sleeves.

Later, when I earned a little bit more money, I went to Adlmüller. I got over my fear of entering the shop, and said very pertly: "I'd like you to make me a dress!" I didn't ask about the price. He had his models show me wonderful evening gowns, and it was a delight. A singer, however, has to wear a dress that is suitable for her work. She must be able to breathe in it, and it must fit the piece she is singing. For *Winterreise*, I dressed quite sadly most of the time, in black or dark purple or a similar sombre color. A white dress is also possible, because it can look as serious as a completely black one.

The top half of one of my first really good concert dresses was stitched with sparkling stones. After the concert, a woman said to me admiringly: "You know, one can see so clearly how you breathe." Of course, the dress was always reflecting the light. When I breathed in, it would sparkle, and when I breathed out, it would grow dimmer. A dress that's too tight can have the same effect. I remember how embarrassed I was once when some young men came to see me after a recital and said how interesting it was because they could see where I breathed during a song because of my dress. After these two incidents, I always checked for this "bellows effect" in the mirror. Also, a dress can't be too close-fitting, or it will be too hot, especially in summer.

And the audience notices other things, too. I once wore a dress with a very low neckline, and after a concert, I received a postcard from a Catholic priest. He wrote, "Honor your body, because it is a holy shrine." He said that he'd been sitting in the dress circle on the right above me, and had been able to look quite deeply into my neckline from his seat. Since then, I was always careful about necklines too. Dresses shouldn't be too short either, because the singers always stand high on the stage, and the audience can see their feet.

As I've said, what a singer wears must not distract the audience, and Adlmüller had a very good eye for catching such distractions. He also had a sure eye for knowing what would work well from a distance. But I have to admit that his dresses were very expensive. Sometimes they were as expensive as the entire fee for my concert. Nevertheless, they were worth it. Because they didn't change with the fashion very much, I could wear them in many different cities and for many years. A singer's clothes don't have to reflect what's in vogue. Instead, she should wear a classic stage dress, and not the kind of elaborate evening dress that she would wear to a ball.

I loved beautiful clothes. Dressing in them could be a hobby that takes up almost all a woman's time. But by now I've given away almost all my beautiful dresses to younger artists, either pianists or singers. I must admit that I felt sorry to see all the beautiful fabrics and embroideries leave my closet. Every dress was connected with memories of certain performances. I can understand why older divas dress up in their vintage gowns, like old movie stars trying to relive their youthful successes. I did it myself once. I modeled my old evening gowns for my husband Paul-Emile, and I was appalled that many of them didn't fit, because I had grown fatter. So I stopped modeling!

Colleagues

I always had good relations with all of my colleagues for the simple reason that I had no close contact with them. And I was not a prima donna (unfortunately). Colleagues, especially the female ones, treat prima donnas with hostility, simply because they are prima donnas. Mezzo-sopranos are always spared these problems because they are, quite simply, more "normal" than sopranos or tenors. Baritones and basses too. Maybe it has something to do with having a high voice. Higher voices are more prone to stress, and perhaps that's why their owners are more difficult to deal with. The rivalry between sopranos and tenors is always the greatest because they have the leading parts, and, of course, each wants to be the best Tosca or the best Manrico in the world. I remember a *Traviata* in Frankfurt where the woman singing Violetta said to a colleague, who had also had great success in the part: "I'm the better Traviata. I know how to die."

There is a similar story about Renata Tebaldi and Zinka Milanov. Rumors were circulating that Tebaldi had broken her leg in the last act of a performance of Puccini's *Tosca*, when she had to jump off the roof of Hadrian's fortress tomb in Rome—onto a mattress behind the stage. On hearing about Tebaldi's supposed misfortune, her great old colleague Milanov remarked: "I've always said that Tebaldi can't sing Tosca!"

Sometimes singers are asked for advice by their colleagues. For example, someone once asked Birgit Nilsson for the secret of singing a great Isolde, because Nilsson was the best Isolde in the world. Nilsson answered, "The most important thing you need for Isolde is comfortable shoes."

Sometimes singers can be openly malicious. I've heard one colleague say to another with great pity: "Oh, you're singing that role now! They asked me first, but I didn't want it."

After our *Frau ohne Schatten* premiere in Paris, Leonie Rysanek and I attended a performance of *Norma* with Montserrat Caballé and Fiorenza Cossotto. Caballé wasn't having a very good night, and fluffed a few high notes, which made the audience restless. Cossotto saw her chance, and sang her high notes perfectly. Great success for Cossotto! After the second act, Caballé said she was ill, and the third act was canceled. We really felt sorry for Caballé, and also for her husband, the tenor Bernabé Marti, who was also singing. He only had to show his nose on the stage, and he was booed loudly. It was awful! The next day Leonie and I ate together and talked once more about this sad experience. And Leonie said: "Poor Caballé, I felt so sorry for her, I sent her some flowers—because I had so many."

On the day after the premiere of *Rosenkavalier* in which I sang the Marschallin at the Salzburg Festival in 1969 with Karl Böhm, there was a reception for Lotte Lehmann, and I was introduced to her. I knew that she had been at the premiere and when she started to congratulate me, saying so nicely, "I liked you so very much," I was really very proud that the most famous Marschallin was praising me. But I wasn't prepared for what was to come as she continued, "I congratulate you sincerely on your performance—in the *Missa Solemnis*." But my disappointment lessened a little when she gave me a small figure of Fidelio with a pistol in its hand, which she had made herself of thin wire.

Management can also be cruel. Kurt Böhme, a famous Baron Ochs in *Rosenkavalier*, was disappointed when he learned that he hadn't been invited to sing this role in a new production, and he called the director to complain. The director pacified him with the words: "But, Herr Böhme, I know, of course, that you are the greatest Ochs!" Ochs is a common term of derision in German-speaking countries: to be the greatest ochs is to be the greatest fool.

And conductors have ego too. During the party celebrating the premiere of *Così fan tutte* at the Eulenspiegel restaurant in Salzburg, Karl Böhm talked incessantly about himself and his successes to Kammersänger Waldemar Kmentt. Then suddenly he said: "I always talk about myself! Let's talk about something else, Herr Kmentt. How did you like my *Tristan* in Bayreuth?"

I've often seen a colleague happily showing off the bad reviews of another who sang the same role, along with their own good ones in the same part. After a performance, colleagues will come backstage and say, "With such a loud orchestra, it's impossible to hear you at all!" Or with pretended pity, as if you were ill, "How did you feel this evening?" Or you hear from dear colleagues how good a costume looked on you, but not one word about how well you sang.

Colleagues are simply not friends. Acquaintances are made at premiere celebrations and in Vienna at Heurigen, but you seldom find a real friend. Especially at the big opera houses, where there is no permanent ensemble, singers come together for their performances, and afterwards go their separate ways.

At a gala performance of *Rosenkavalier* in Hamburg with Anneliese Rothenberger as Sophie, Walter Berry as Ochs, Elisabeth Schwarzkopf as the Marschallin, and me as Octavian, there were lots and lots of flowers, especially for Schwarzkopf. When Walter and I left afterwards to go to our hotel, the Vier Jahreszeiten (by the way, one of the most beautiful and best managed hotels in the world), Schwarzkopf was standing completely alone on the street, waiting for a taxi. She was surrounded by all the baskets of flowers and bouquets, which had been brought out onto the street in front of the artists' entrance for her. There she stood, the great Schwarzkopf, alone, without help. No colleague, no fan, no enthusiast from the audience, none of those who asked for autographs or signed photographs—no one took care of her!

We singers are all thin-skinned, and we're all afraid of failing and showing our weaknesses. We disguise ourselves with arrogance or indifference, according to our dispositions. Colleagues who incessantly make jokes are the most afraid. Others talk about sex and money all the time. They are also afraid. And we all have the same fears: losing our voices and not having enough money to live.

In provincial houses, singers are more likely to find friendly colleagues. Competition isn't so obvious, and you are together in most of the opera productions during the season. Since my Frankfurt days, I have been friendly with a colleague, the former soubrette Trude Kortegast, who is now more than 80 years old. We are like school friends. Memories of the old days connect us.

But life in smaller houses can be cruel too. Singers are often fired in their early forties, before they get the tenure that exists in many opera houses. Every small house would prefer to engage young singers, and that's why older ones are shunned. I have had colleagues who later became car salesmen, and I knew a dramatic soprano who had to go from door to door selling ladies' underwear. A wonderful soprano from Frankfurt, whom I admired greatly in *Tosca* and other roles, was given a job in the music score archives. Others became prompters or dressers until they qualified for a pension. At the big opera houses, where one earns enough money to be able to put something aside "for later," and where most of the time there is a retirement fund, as in Vienna, a singer has more security. But all singers share a fear of not being able to make a living, which sometimes makes us seem unapproachable. But deep inside we are all humble about our vocal gifts.

Education

"O, die Natur schuf mich im Grimme,
sie gab mir nichts als eine schöne Stimme."

[Oh, nature created me in anger,
she gave me nothing but a beautiful voice.]
(M. Claudius)

Opera singers, like several other kinds of professionals, focus single-mindedly on their work. Perhaps this concentration on the voice is why opera singers have developed a reputation for being dumb. "Dumb, dumber, tenor" is a common phrase in musical circles, and the same with baritones, only an octave lower. "Soubrettes—cute but dumb" and "the higher the soprano, the dumber" and so on. Of course, it doesn't matter if a singer passes a qualifying exam to attend a university or even studies there because singing has nothing to do with academic achievement.

Vocal studies are very long, seven to eight years, and, I must add, very interesting. Singers don't only learn technique, that is, how to breathe right, but also how to use their muscles to support the breath on which the tone rests. Of course, singers have to learn many roles by heart, and how long it takes depends on each singer's musicality. Then singers must connect the words and music with technical things, like where to take a breath, where to sing gradually louder (crescendo) or softer (diminuendo) so a phrase is sung as effectively as possible, and how to color vowels and adjust the unique coloring of their voices without distracting the audience. One example is the "ä" in the German word "Mädchen." If a singer sings a clear open German "ä" (as in the American pronunciation of "medicine"), it sounds almost ridiculous. So the singer colors the vowel in a bit and sings a German "e" (as in the American pronunciation of "made") instead of an "ä," that is, "Medchen" (Made-chen). There are so-called I- or A-voices, which, especially in higher registers, sing mainly these substitute vowel sounds and not what's written, without the listeners particularly noticing.

Singers also change the position of the tone in certain registers, just as instrumentalists move their hands on string instruments, and this change is hidden by a tiny coloring of the vowel. A singer must "cover" certain transitions, which means not singing a flat, clear "a," but more a vowel in-between "o" and "a." This doesn't mean, however, that Baron Ochs in *Rosenkavalier* should sing "Papo, Papo" instead of "Papa, Papa" since too much "o" would suggest a common word for derrière to a German-speaking audience.

It takes a few years before a singer has thoroughly mastered a role, and then things continue to change because the body keeps changing. In addition, singing other roles can also change things and make new difficulties, so singers must rework all their roles constantly, even the ones they have mastered thoroughly. I myself had a particular difficulty in the alto aria of Bach's *St. Matthew Passion:*

Erbarme mich,
Mein Gott, um meiner Zähren willen!

The word "zähren" extends over many bars a few times like a solfeggio on the first syllable "zäh." As I sang the *St. Matthew Passion* for almost forty years, my notes at this spot in my score look quite funny. I never sang "zäh." For a few years I sang it more as "ze," a few more years as "zö," then as "zo," while thinking of "zä," so that it wouldn't sound like an "o." I always sang the vowel that suited me at the moment and wrote it in the score. Making the audience think you are singing "zähren" while singing a totally different vowel is not only a lot of work, but also a great art. It demands continuous attention. Singing really is hard work. The audience only hears a two-hour performance, and there everything must sound effortless, and, as a result, some people say, "Singing is easy for her. There's nothing to this. It's not difficult at all. She just stands there and sings!"

My mother's teacher told her: "If the audience can see that it's difficult, then you haven't worked hard enough. The greatest skill is to hide the skill!" Singers should really be married only to their profession, because you can never switch off. You are always thinking about this vocal position or that. How can I interpret it better? How can I sing it better? It's difficult, almost impossible, to concentrate on anything else. Perhaps you can distract yourself for a short time with a crime novel or a TV show. I like to work crossword puzzles and play different versions of the card game Solitaire. You can be silent while doing these things, and, in spite of the distraction, still be thinking about the details of your singing. To read a serious book, you need a clear head without constant worries about the state of your voice. So singers are condemned to remain specialist idiots—unless they come to their senses one day and escape. And I believe that it isn't very different for conductors, especially because the arms of these poor people are more robust than our vocal cords. They can conduct daily, practice or make recordings in the morning and afternoon, and then conduct a concert or an opera in the evening!

The singing profession, if one is "in the swim," may require up to six hours a day of rehearsal for new productions for four to six weeks, depending on the opera. Then, in addition to this, what is easy to overlook: each singer's own preparations, which means warming up at home. In order to sing properly without hurting ourselves, we singers must be awake for about four hours before singing, so the blood has enough time to circulate fully through our vocal cords. We must always remember that we are using a muscle, and straining it in a totally unnatural way. We are like athletes, for example, tennis players. Before starting a match, tennis players have already completed a few hours of training exercises. And when we don't have rehearsals, but only a performance in the evening, we are tense all day, only living for the evening, and unable to think about doing anything else. We also can't exhaust ourselves physically because we have to be in top form in the evening, when "normal" people are taking it easy after a day's work. For all these reasons, it's really difficult for singers to educate themselves or develop other interests. When a singer has a wonderful talent, but no sophistication from schooling or their parents, it's easy to see how the impression that singers are dumb can be created.

Even conductors are not always intellectually educated people, as one might assume. My father told me about a bass who was singing King Philip in Verdi's *Don Carlos* when he himself was a young singer. At a rehearsal this bass asked the conductor quite innocently what an Escorial (the huge residence that Philip built near Madrid) was since it's a word that appears repeatedly in the text of Philip's aria. A bit embarrassed, the conductor answered: "Well, it means something like dear God."

Karl Böhm told me a story about a tenor who was singing Tristan. In the last act, after the fevered fantasies in which he incessantly talks about Isolde, she finally enters, falls into his arms, and sings "Tristan!" The tenor must then quickly sing "Isolde" before he dies. To Böhm's surprise, the final "Isolde" wasn't sung. When the conductor asked his Tristan later why he hadn't sung the final word, the tenor said "At that moment, I couldn't remember the name of that damned woman!" Dumb, dumber, tenor.

Sometimes an early success runs ahead of a singer, and he or she has to limp after this sudden fame, which has fallen like gold coins from heaven.

Such a singer often doesn't know how to handle this good fortune, and behaves in a conceited and arrogant way from ignorance and secret doubts. Visible signs of these delusions of grandeur are driving the most expensive car, arriving late for rehearsals, reprimanding the dresser for trivial things, and just generally acting like the Great Star.

On the other hand, there are well-educated singers who manage to complete university studies and even earn doctoral degrees before, or at the same time as, their vocal studies. But if singers have too much intellect, they often want to use it while singing. They start to construct every tone like a doctoral dissertation, their singing becomes artificial, and they feel far superior to their colleagues because of intellectual arrogance. I would say this: ideally, singers should have a good balance between intellect and intuition. And singers must never forget that vocal intelligence is the most important thing, along with constant attention to the themes of the different operas and to the times in which they take place. These things can make the operas come alive for singers. Also, from wearing the costumes and wigs of a different age, we get a sense of history, in case we didn't get it at school. We can also discuss our roles with the stage director, and learn how to examine a character psychologically, which helps a singer slip into the character of a person from a bygone age. And if singers can grasp the music they are singing intuitively and make it meaningful, they will excite the curiosity of the people in the audience, who will want to learn more. Sensitivity and intuition are very important qualities in a singer.

During the last few years, the level of education for singers has grown much higher. If aspiring singers attend a specialized music school or a university with a vocal department, they receive a good general education as a base. They also learn all kinds of useful things like how to read a score, harmonic theory, and even the languages needed to sing various operas. And at the end of their schooling, they have a master's degree, although sometimes not the right vocal technique.

Learning languages is very useful, since nowadays we sing in the original language. Although I didn't speak Italian, French, Hungarian, or Russian, I sang in those languages, and I even sang in Japanese once. I remember how difficult it was for me because I had to learn how to pronounce the text phonetically, and I didn't know exactly what the words meant. Then there was the problem of combining the sometimes strange vowel and consonant sounds with my vocal technique. Italian is made for singing. Words like "amore, sole mio, o dio" have wonderful sounds (and wonderful vowels!). French, on the other hand, is a nightmare, with nasal vowels such as "on" and "en," which sit between the nose and the soft palate, while singers are used to placing their tones on the hard palate. There are also amusing vowel nuances such as "mon coeur," which could be sung with an open French "u" (which has no exact equivalent in English), as "mon cur," but that sounds much too close to "mon cul" (my backside!). Germans are also used to singing a rolling "r," which the French don't use when they speak, but, occasionally, do use when they sing. The question is, when, exactly?

When we were singing Mozart's *Le Nozze di Figaro* in the original Italian at the Vienna State Opera, the great Italian bass baritone Tito Gobbi was in the audience. He came backstage at the end of the performance and said that he was very sad because he had always believed that he knew German well, yet he hadn't understood a word of the opera. Our Italian sounded like incomprehensible German to him!

When Karajan came to Vienna in 1958, he decreed that all operas had to be sung in the original language. This led to some odd performances of *Carmen* and *Aida*. The chorus only knew *Carmen* in German and couldn't relearn it very quickly, but the soloists were told that they had to sing in French. So we sang "l'amour" while the chorus sang "Die Lieb." In *Aida* both the soloists and chorus were scheduled to sing in Italian, until suddenly the Aida canceled and her replacement only knew the role in German. So in the trio with Radamès and Aida, I sang to Radamès in Italian and to Aida in German. It was a lot of fun.

Another time I learned the role of Marfa in Mussorgsky's *Khovanshchina* for the Hamburg Opera in Russian, and for months I suffered with the two different Russian "l's." One "l" sounds a bit thicker down in the throat and the other is like a German "l." In addition, there was something guttural that sounded like "wui" in German. After the final performance, my dear language teacher came to me and said: "Your Rrruuussian was torture for the ears!"

One problem for singers at specialized music schools and university departments is that pure voice lessons often are taught only once or twice a week, while other kinds of lessons, which I personally consider unnecessary, are taught instead. To me the most important thing for a singer is to learn how to sing because proper technique and correct breathing are "the legs on which the table has to stand." It's true that today it's unthinkable for a coach at an opera house to play every note on the piano because the singer doesn't know how to read music. In the past, the opposite was often the case. Leo Slezak learned only how to be a very good locksmith as a young man, but he nevertheless made a great career as a singer because of his beautiful voice.

Surely being naïve can help a singer. To put on a costume and make-up, stand on a stage and sing, and make operatic characters believable for an audience—that's quite a special, strange profession. Sacha Guitry said that all actors are liars. True, we lie to the audience about everything—love and hate, the risqué and the chaste, even about life and death in three-quarter time, but the audience delights in our lies. As Richard Strauss says in *Capriccio*, his "conversation piece for music in one act":

> Eine Opera ist ein absurdes Ding.
> Befehle werden singend erteilt,
> über Politik wird im Duett verhandelt.
> Man tanzt um ein Grab,
> und Dolchstiche werden melodisch verabreicht.

> [An opera is an absurd thing.
> Orders are sung,
> politics is discussed in duets.
> Graves are danced on,
> and stabs are delivered melodically.]

How could an intellectual choose such a profession?!

One needs talent to be a singer, but by talent I don't only mean a good voice and musicality and the ability to learn easily. I also mean a gift for discipline and hard work, and a lot of other things too; for example, good feet and a healthy back, so you can stand a long time—really, overall good health. But, of course, all of us have a weakness somewhere. Who has everything—a beautiful voice, good looks, great musicality—and the luck necessary to make a career? If you asked me who is the artist who has 100 percent of the talent needed for singing, I would say Placido Domingo. He is a tall, good-looking man with a beautiful voice, which is sexy for a tenor. He is very musical, and has wonderful phrasing. Admittedly, he was never a tenor with a brilliant high C, but he doesn't need it because he has so many other advantages. (But, of course, this means he doesn't have 100 percent of the talent needed either!) Callas was a singer whom I admired and loved. Every note she sang was a jewel to me, yet her voice wasn't exactly beautiful. Zinka Milanov had a wonderful voice, but she was not an interesting person to watch on the stage. As I said, there is always a weakness somewhere. But we are talking about one percent or two percent missing from 100 percent of the required talent, and I think it's exactly that—the weakness, the missing one percent or two percent—that is possibly the most important gift. Why? Because overcoming that weakness is what can make a talented singer into a true artist.

The tenor Karl Terkal sang at the Vienna State Opera. He had a secure, brilliant high C, he was never hoarse because he was always in good shape vocally, and he mastered all his roles easily. The problem was that he lacked charisma and personality. Julius Patzak, on the other hand, didn't have as beautiful a voice as Terkal, and he had a crippled hand, which he always hid very skillfully on stage. Still, Patzak made a great career and Terkal didn't. Patzak was an incomparable evangelist in Bach's passions and a great Palestrina in Hans Pfitzner's opera, and he himself said: "If I had a voice like Terkal, I would never have made a career." There may be some truth in this. Singers who have 100 percent of everything in the beginning are always sure of themselves. They think they are omnipotent and always the best. If singers have to work to overcome obstacles, they can learn from them and grow.

Fans

Frau Pollak was a typical Viennese, the kind I love very much. She was small and round and a bit motherly, and contrary to what the unforgettable satirist and music expert Hans Weigel said in his funny-nasty way about the golden Viennese heart, hers was not made of stone. She and her family had suffered a lot during the Nazi era, and now she, the only survivor, got by on a small pension. Still, she always had enough money to go to an opera or a concert. Although she could only afford the cheapest seats or even standing room, she came tirelessly every evening. She was *the* fan of Walter Berry and myself when we were married, and after we were divorced, she divided her affection between us.

Frau Pollak came to every one of my performances, and at premieres she even came in a long dress, under which I could glimpse her comfortable shoes. Since she had to walk or take public transportation to get to the theater and was already "of a certain age," these shoes were indispensable. When there was a knock on my dressing room door before a performance, I always knew who it was, and without looking or asking, I'd say, "Please come in, Frau

Pollak!" With highly colored red cheeks, partly from the fresh air and partly from being "made beautiful," she entered and always brought a small flower, a few pieces of candy, or a small painting of the role I was singing, done by her friend Fritzi Schlesinger. Now and then, I must admit, these visits made me more nervous, when I was already nervous enough, and I often thought that too much love can be a nuisance. But Frau Pollak was so ingenuous and so kind that I simply couldn't say anything. She even traveled by train to London and Paris, not in the sleeping carriage, but as cheaply as possible, so she could attend important performances of mine there. She was well known at the ticket windows because she always asked for "the best, but cheapest" seat. She would never ask me for my courtesy tickets, as so many other people do who only call when they want free tickets. She came in snowy, icy, or rainy weather. Nothing could stop her.

Then one evening Frau Pollak didn't come. I asked the dressers if they'd seen her, and they said that only a small flower had been delivered in the afternoon accompanied by a short letter. In it she said that she didn't feel well, but she hoped to be better by the next performance. Suddenly something was missing. The habit of seeing Frau Pollak's round face, at first always a bit inquisitive, her asking if my voice was in good shape, and then wishing "toi-toi-toi," had become dear to me. I missed her, and I looked forward to seeing her again soon.

At my next performance, she told me that she had gone to the doctor, and it was nothing, and she should eat vegetarian. But she felt very tired, and her red cheeks were now pale and her eyes not so shiny. Her visits became fewer because too often she felt weak. Finally, she telephoned one day to say that she was at home in bed, coughing, probably with some kind of flu. I cheered her up as well as I could and told her that she would have to be healthy again before the revival of *Falstaff*, which was scheduled soon.

Then came the call from the hospital. "I'm so weak that I can barely hold the telephone receiver," she said. I talked about my many stage and orchestral rehearsals for *Falstaff*, and promised to visit her immediately after the first performance. But when I came to the hospital the next day, she had already died. A doctor said to me, "Odd that no one visited her. It's not until now that everyone is coming." It was lung cancer. Frau Pollak never knew what her illness was, and it had progressed very quickly. She had never smoked.

Still today I blame myself for having come too late. Prevented by my voice, as always, and devoured by my profession—living only for "The Theater"—I didn't return Frau Pollak's love when she needed it, out of ignorance. How many people say, "I'll do it tomorrow, after…." Tomorrow has to be today, that's what I learned. But Frau Pollak continues to live on in my heart as my dearest fan, and I can still see her in front of me, when she visited us in Paris and spent a few days with us. How happy she was! She said, "This is the high point of my life!"

The typical Frau Pollak-like fan is difficult to find in small theaters. I didn't know about the large groups of fans and the innumerable autograph seekers until I started to sing in Vienna. And, of course, all this made me very happy. I've seen a new group of fans emerge about every ten years. It starts with boys and girls about fifteen or sixteen years old. In Europe this is a year or two before the Abitur (examinations at the end of grammar school, which are used to qualify students for higher education). I once received a letter from a worried mother, asking me to tell her daughter to pay more attention to her exams!

Some fans just want an autograph. Others worship you from afar, and a few of these I have had for more than twenty years. They usually communicate by letter, as, for example, my Angelika. She is a mother herself and has a profession, but, in spite of these commitments, she traveled to my recitals whenever she could, and afterwards wrote me letters and described her exact impressions of the performance. She discussed the nuances of almost every song, sometimes only one phrase or word in it, and talked about how I emphasized or pronounced it in a special way. Sometimes it was frightening to find out that my singing had such an effect, and I learned a lot from the reactions of fans who were "schooled" in my singing for so many years.

Another female admirer of mine is Sonja. She is a young voice teacher whose hobbies are taking photographs and writing poetry. She writes wonderful poems and has for many years made calendars for me with her photographs and poems. It's a wonderful present every year!

For many, many years I have also been in contact with two children, who now are no longer children, in England. The boy was dyslexic, and the girl had several operations for cancer on her face. The mother owned phonograph records of mine and played them for the children, and the odd thing was that after listening they felt more free, and reacted better psychologically, and the boy's dyslexia improved somewhat when he heard music and the sound of my voice. Although we corresponded for many years, the mother had never heard me in person. Not until about three years ago did I met her personally, and her children are now grown, and both have professions. These are the kinds of contacts that really make me feel that my singing has a purpose.

I also once received a letter from a lady who lost her singing voice because of a serious illness and, from that time, never wanted to hear any music or go to an opera or concert again. One day an acquaintance said to her, "You have to listen to this recording by Christa Ludwig. It's beautiful." So she did, and then she wrote me a letter saying that, because of my recording, she was inspired to listen to music again, and she was very happy about it. Me too.

There are also people who write to me, "We're happy that you don't sing any more, so that you can finally lead a normal life." These are fans who don't regret the end of my career, because they see me as a woman, and not only as singer. There is a lady in New York who became my fan at a performance of *Parsifal* at the Met. She wrote me a letter, we started to correspond, and then one day she offered, like many fans, her help. And she could really help because I'd just bought an apartment near Carnegie Hall in New York, and I needed pots and pans and towels and everything else. Since that time, Regina has kindly taken care of my apartment (and now she is editing this book).

Although large groups of fans are rare at mid-size and small theaters, there are opera enthusiasts there. Decades ago I met a young woman in Hanover, who from her earliest years had a great love of opera and hardly ever missed a performance. Our acquaintance resulted in a working relationship. After taking a position in a bank for a short time, the young Hannagret Büker first joined the renowned management of Hans-Ulrich Schmid, and then, a few years later, established her own artist management, which still exists today. Over the years, the young opera fan became the owner of an important agency for singers and other musicians.

Then I have fans, now in their thirties, who know me from my recordings. One of these is the pianist Tzimon Barto. When we first met, he said, "Christa, I grew up with all your records, from when I was seven or eight years old. I love your recording of the *St. Matthew Passion*, and it would be my greatest wish to accompany you once in a lieder recital." Since I knew what a tiger he was at the piano, I thought to myself, "Oh God, this won't work." An accompanist, although he has to be on the same musical level as the singer, must always play in the background, not at all as he does at a solo recital. So I said to him, "It's not possible. You'll steal the show!" But he replied, "No, I will behave myself."

I told Hannagret Büker about the possibility of my playing with Tzimon Barto, and she was very enthusiastic, especially about the suggestion that he should accompany me in *Die Winterreise*. We only had one rehearsal, but it was obvious from the beginning that Barto is a wonderful accompanist. Unfortunately neither of us ever had time to prepare another program besides

Winterreise. Because he had a wonderful empathy for the sound of my voice and for the piece itself, Barto's playing in the Schubert piece was something special. Sadly, we gave our last recital together at the State Opera Unter den Linden in Berlin in May of 1994.

In 1971 I sang Octavian in Moscow with Karl Böhm and the Vienna State Opera. It was the first time *Rosenkavalier* was given in Moscow, and it wasn't in the Bolshoi but in the Kremlin. Unfortunately, I felt that the audience didn't really understand the opera. I also sang in Beethoven's Ninth Symphony, again with Karl Böhm. After those performances, I had a new fan, a critic who wrote me long letters in Russian, which I always had to have translated. He stayed loyal to me for more than ten years. When I celebrated my fiftieth birthday, he sent me a large plaque from an evening at the Conservatorium in Russia, which he dedicated to me in honor of my birthday. Later I also got to meet him in person.

I love my faithful fans, and I wish I could have mentioned all of them here.

Hobbies

The Vienna opera and concert manager Roman Vladarski once said to me, "You should take up a hobby, so you have some other interest besides your voice and your profession!" I readily took his advice, because I had seen how miserable my father was after his retirement from theater management. He didn't know what to do with himself. He didn't have what is commonly called a hobby or any other interests outside the theater. When he was a manager, he was always the first one in the office in the morning, returned home only briefly for lunch, after which he returned immediately to the office, and came home the last of everyone in the evening after the performance. Everything was the theater, the theater! Even at home he lived more or less in the theater. Dusty laurel wreaths with long bows covered with gold writing hung on the walls in the living room. Photographs in costume stood on the grand piano, along with theater programs printed on white silk. When I was a child, I wasn't allowed to snigger at this, but only admire, and, good God, how I hated all that junk. My mother always said that singing doesn't last forever, so even as a child I knew about the sword of Damocles that dangles over every singer's head.

Before I started to read "wise" books in my fifties, trying to find the connection between the spiritual world and the physical one, I gave hobbies a try. Generally, I gave in to my domestic tendencies, and tried knitting, sewing, cooking, etc. I find walking and hiking terribly boring, and, although I like to look at nature and I admire a beautiful garden, I'm completely an "eye person" and prefer to let other people do the work. But what I really love is everything there is to do inside a house, even mindless work. For example, I love ironing. Not for too long, but isn't it wonderful to see how a wrinkled piece of fabric straightens out? I also like to knit—I mean I also *liked* to knit—because I found it wasn't good for the vertebrae in my neck. I even bought a knitting machine, but that is work and not a hobby. Instead of enjoying myself, I sat in front of this beastly mechanism, counting how many stitches I needed, and please be exact, because once the wool is inside, there is no room for mistakes. Be careful you don't drop a stitch! What satisfaction did I get from knowing that it only takes one second of foot pressure to do a row, and that afterwards, a child's sweater comes out?

"But Christele, you miss the point by using a machine," Leonard Bernstein said to me once. His wife Felicia knitted incessantly at one of our rehearsals at Tanglewood. Knitting is good for the nerves because one releases tension through the hands, and I discovered how satisfying it is to sit in a chair, watch TV or have a conversation, and get on other people's nerves by clicking away with my needles. For a few years, I was in a real knitting frenzy, and I outfitted my whole family with knitwear. Whenever my husband thought that one sleeve was longer than the other one, I'd say, "It doesn't matter. Just fold it over." Or he'd say, "This shoulder is wider than the other one," and I'd say, "It doesn't matter. Just stand a little crooked."

After I tortured my family and friends with my knitted gifts, I gave up, and found another hobby—rug knotting. To my great relief I now had no sleeves or collars to worry about. Just one square—no difficulties at all! I knotted everywhere, even on the long car trips to concerts in different cities. I didn't give the rugs away, but instead laid them out everywhere at home, where they were stepped on, which, of course, is a rug's fate. They looked nice, until my mother's cat came along and chose one of the largest ones to make herself immortal on. The cat was old and grumpy, and didn't care to go out or use her litter box anymore. No, she preferred my rug. It stank terribly, and one day rage overcame me and I washed it, and all the colors ran together. So all my hours of work ended in cat-astrophe!

Then for several years I had a rage for embroidery. When I start making something, I always stick to it. In spite of that, many a tablecloth sat a long time in the cupboard before I continued embroidering it, especially because I found cross-stitching extremely boring. Large and small cloths flowed from my hands, Easter cloths with Easter eggs and Christmas cloths with Christmas bells, it was always the same. Then one day a visitor said, "What, have you *such* cloths?" The tone was so pitying and disparaging. "Not something as old-fashioned and bourgeois as that!" I was very hurt, and have never embroidered since. What a waste of time!

Only one hobby have I kept—cooking. Please note: not for more than six people. More than that, and cooking degenerates into work. But cooking is fun. One needs love and imagination for it, and it's an art. With me it's more like a "happening" than a meal, and sometimes I even succeed, and then I'm prouder and more satisfied than when I sang beautifully. I have all kinds of machinery. One machine makes pasta (although it is better for my figure if I don't eat the results). I pour in all the ingredients, choose the pasta shape, and the noodles come out ready-made. Terrific! And equally terrific is my bread-making machine. Again I put in all the ingredients, and the machine stirs, kneads, lets the dough rise, and bakes it. Then, after four hours, it goes beep, and the bread is ready. Sometimes it's even edible. I have many wonderful machines, but don't worry, I'm not going to mention all of them. I also have yards and yards of cookbooks full of recipes for tasty dishes from all over the world. Then I have others with titles like *Iß dich schlank* (Eat Yourself Thin) and *Gesunde Vollwertkost* (Healthy Foods), but a bit further away hidden in a corner!

Here's my recipe for roasted calves' liver, a delicious dish. I got it from a book that said it was by Alexandre Dumas, the author of *The Three Musketeers* (published 1844!):

Take 1 kilo of very good quality calves' liver in one piece. It should look like a roast. Dumas suggests (but I don't do it) that you use smoked fatty bacon instead of lard. Cover the bottom of your roasting pan with strips of bacon (I use oil and butter), and then, on top, put the liver, diced carrots, clove-spiced onions, a bit of diced garlic, and a spice packet. Season with coarsely ground black pepper, salt, and a little nutmeg. Cover the liver with bacon (always smoked fatty bacon!), and add two glasses of mild red wine mixed with two glasses of grapefruit juice or freshly pressed grape juice. Bake all this in a preheated oven at about 200 degrees for 40 to 60 minutes until the liver is "English" (pink on the inside). If you need liquid, add more of the red wine-juice mixture. With this roast, serve chestnut puree, seasoned to taste with a little nutmeg, salt and pepper, and peeled steamed grapes without seeds. Add a touch of love and imagination, and don't think about cholesterol. Enjoy your meal!

Cooking is fun, but one needs time, and, above all, dear friends who know how to appreciate a good meal with good conversation and, last but not least, a good wine.

Still, after all these hobbies, I must admit I've learned only one thing irrefutably. I only know (or imagine I know) how to do one thing really well—and that's sing.

One day my colleague Hilde Güden, full of pride, told me about her hobby—her garden—and about everything she planted. In particular, she described her vegetable garden, and insisted that I see it. I was struck dumb with admiration! Hilde Güden was a high-class, well-groomed woman, who was busy with a lot to sing and had an active social life, and still she found time to take care of a vegetable garden? How admirable! When I arrived at her home to see her garden, dear Hilde was standing very elegantly in white trousers and white jumper (very chic!), giving her gardener instructions: "The carrots a bit to the left, and the tomatoes over here..."

We also had quite a large vegetable garden once, which neither my husband Paul-Emile nor I had time to take care of, but in which the gardener planted many tasty things. When we looked at the little piece of earth, we were filled with pride. We were surprised that we had so many strawberries and raspberries and yard-high, fully grown salad vegetables, although we ate these things daily! The solution to the mystery was that our maid preferred to buy all our fruits and vegetables at the market, because it was so much work to pick them. So, from then on, we gave up on vegetable gardens!

So, when I think about it, I don't really have a hobby, not even listening to music at home. I am like Dr. Murke in Heinrich Böll's novel: I prefer the "gesammelte Schweigen" (gathered silence). Dr. Murke worked at a radio station, and, when at home, preferred to listen to his own private tape, which contained a collection of the silent gaps between the musical selections on the tapes he played all day at the station. I love to live very naturally with everything that makes life lovable and livable. As long as I practiced my profession, I recharged my batteries on my days off by doing nothing. Today people have forgotten how to do nothing. Does one incessantly have to watch TV, or listen to the radio, or play sports or games? Isn't it wonderful to put your hands in your lap for once and watch nature in peace? I love my summer friends with their blue, glasslike wings—two dragonflies flying over the water. Or, toward evening, a family of swallows, flying and bathing over my swimming pool. Our dog tries in vain to catch rabbits, and I admire the supple lizards on the wall of the house. I say "Good Morning" to my hibiscus blossoms every day, because in the evening they are already withered. Life is so rich in its diversity—one only needs eyes to see it. How beautiful is a raindrop hanging on a leaf, and watching the changing cloud formations is very restful. My days off flew by. I was never bored. I simply *lived*. I'll have to wait and see if I still like such a contemplative existence when I don't sing anymore for a few years. But I've had enough restlessness in my professional life, and I don't want to make any more plans for the future. By doing that, one lives even more quickly, because everything only really exists in the future tense. My motto is quite simply—live now!

Management

When young singers look for engagements, they usually only get them through agents. And I must say that it's often very hard for agents to "find a taker" for an unknown singer. My father used to tell me about the famous Viennese agent Hugo Gruder-Guntram, whose recommendation alone could get a singer an engagement—without an audition.

Nowadays agents are necessary, and they take a relatively high commission. In America you have to pay your agent 20 percent for arranging a recital, and sometimes even more. In Europe, the commission used to be 10 percent , but now local agents take 15 percent to 25 percent. For young singers, this is a lot. They receive very little in fees at first, and a quarter of it goes to the agent, and then 25 percent or 30 percent for taxes. Nothing much is left!

I myself never had bad experiences with agents. Ballhausen was *the* agent in Germany when I was starting out, and he brought me to Vienna. The only problem was that the fee he negotiated for me was much too low. When I realized this and saw that I couldn't possibly manage to live on what I was earning, I went to the State Opera management myself, and they doubled my fee without hesitation. I then wrote to Ballhausen and told him that I could do better myself. But, despite this, I continued to pay him for three years as we had agreed because he had opened the doors for me in Vienna.

Agents know theater managers. The manager of an opera house or a concert hall will say to an agent, "We want to put on some lieder recitals. Who can you offer us?" This works very well, and agents have a lot to do with arranging recitals and concerts, especially in America. My American agent was the highly respected Ann Colbert, a German journalist who immigrated with her husband to New York. They opened an agency called Colbert Artists Management, at first only for chamber music players, but later also for singers and other musicians. When I signed with them, Colbert had the biggest names in classical music under contract: Elisabeth Schwarzkopf, Hermann Prey, Dietrich Fischer-Dieskau, the flautist Jean-Pierre Rampal, and Sir Georg Solti. The agency never grew as big as others, who represent as many as 200 or 300 people, but instead Colbert chose to concentrate on a small group of high quality artists.

Mrs. Colbert could always be reached day or night, even on Saturday and Sunday, which is very important for artists. Once I got stuck in a snowstorm in America, and my plane arrived very late. The concert organizers, who were supposed to meet me, had left. I had no idea what to do, so I called Mrs. Colbert. As always, she had a solution, whatever time of day or night it was. Her agency took care of everything, decided what flights I should take, arranged my tickets, reserved my hotel rooms, and paid for everything in advance. I never had to worry about anything. I should add that Mrs. Colbert has retired, and the management of her agency has now been taken over by her longtime associate, Aggie Eisenberger.

I never experienced the Colbert-style of management in Europe, where management offices are closed on Saturday and Sunday. If a singer becomes ill in Europe on a Saturday night and is scheduled to sing on Sunday, no one is ready to help. In America, there was always someone available, and that's why I believed that agents there really deserved their 20 percent.

The amount of money that star singers are paid is a subject that can often fray nerves. I read in the Metropolitan Opera Annals that Caruso received $2500 for each of his appearances at the Met during the 1909/10 season, and he paid no taxes (there were no income taxes back then), and a new car only cost between $175 and $200! When you compare Caruso's situation to Pavarotti's today, Pavarotti's million dollar fees don't seem quite so huge. And the legendary Jenny Lind received $100,000 for a concert appearance, just as Pavarotti did for singing in places like Madison Square Garden in front of 25,000 people and more. People were saying, "My God, he's getting $100,000!" and admittedly, that sounds like a fortune for one concert. But when I compare his situation to hers, it seems that Jenny Lind earned a lot more!

Contracts have a special place in the professional life of an artist. They represent an obligation, also a joy, and sometimes a disappointment.

Erika Köth told me that she was invited by letter to sing Sophie in *Der Rosenkavalier* during the opening week of the rebuilt Vienna State Opera in 1955. She gladly accepted, made a note of the date on her calendar, and then learned from the newspaper that Hilde Güden would be singing Sophie instead. When she complained to the management, they simply said that a letter is not a contract!

Something similar happened to me more recently. I got an offer from the Vienna State Opera to sing Ulrica in a new production of *Un Ballo in Maschera*. I had already sung the role in Vienna because, in my later years as a singer, I could do justice to the dark timbre that this part demands. Because I had a guest contract for a certain number of performances during the season, I was given all the performance dates, and I kept these dates available. How astonished I was when I received my ratified contract in which no dates for *Ballo* were included. When I asked what happened, I was told tersely that Claudio Abbado had decided to hire another singer. Of course, this is his right, but shouldn't somebody have told me?

When conductors say to singers after a successful evening, "Now you must sing this and that with me," singers should never believe them! In the happy glow after a successful evening, conductors often promise a lot of things—and then the next day they promise the same things to other singers. But such things also happen to conductors. Karl Böhm told me that he usually found out if and when he would be conducting in Vienna by reading the newspapers! And this way of doing things is not at all limited to Vienna.

Lisa Della Casa had an unpleasant surprise in Salzburg once. She sang her wonderful Marschallin under Karajan at the opening of the new large Festival Hall in July of 1960. I heard that a film would be made of this performance, but with Elisabeth Schwarzkopf as the Marschallin. When I ran into Lisa on the street in Salzburg during the festival, she started to talk about the film, and she told me how much she was looking forward to being in it. I quite naïvely said to her, "But don't you know that Schwarzkopf is supposed to be singing the Marschallin in this film?" She had no idea that someone had simply booted her out. But, as one opera director used to say to me, "Contracts are made to be broken" (just as Wotan always did in the Ring).

Sometimes these things border on the absurd. Once I was scheduled to sing Cherubino in Switzerland, but something else came up at the last minute. My agent said to me, "Things aren't so bad. We'll get Hanna Ludwig instead. Ludwig is Ludwig. And we'll say that you're having a baby." Later the reviews were sent to me, and they said that Christa Ludwig had sung, when, of course, it was Hanna! Ludwig is Ludwig.

Sometimes it happens that even with a contract you end up with nothing. This has happened to me, too. Near Nîmes in southwestern France, there is a castle called Pondre. I was contracted to sing at this castle by Michel Glotz, my manager in Paris. I flew there, accompanied by my husband Paul-Emile, and when we landed, we were supposed to be picked up by the concert organizer. As we walked out of the airport, we couldn't believe our eyes. Waiting for us was a car that looked as if it had come out of the previous century. We were invited to get in, but first I had to clear a place for us among the empty beer and soda cans and cigarette boxes on the back seat. The car was filthy and stank terribly of cigarette smoke, and I felt as if my feet were in a garbage can. Very astonished (really almost in shock), we drove to a hotel, which was also dreadful and very garish.

The next day, which was the day of the concert, Paul-Emile decided to rent a car and go to see where this Castle Pondre was and report to me what it would be like to give a concert there, because I never practiced beforehand in the places where I sang. My accompanist Charles Spencer went with him, and when they returned, I asked how it was. The only reply I received was, "Well, you'll see."

In the evening we drove to the castle in our rental car. There weren't any signs, but Paul-Emile knew the way, and suddenly we saw a handwritten note on a wooden board which said "Castle Pondre Festival." When we finally arrived, we had to walk a long way through the grounds from our car to the castle, which once must surely have been beautiful, but were now mostly a ruin, completely dilapidated. We also thought it was odd that the concert was scheduled to start in ten minutes (I always liked to arrive at concerts at the very last minute), and there was no one around.

A wooden table had been set up where people could buy tickets, and one or two concertgoers were standing there. Maybe everyone was seated already? We were told that I would be singing an open-air concert in the castle courtyard, and there were chairs and platforms set up so that the audience could sit in rows that climbed higher and higher, as in an amphitheater. Paul-Emile thought that about thirty or thirty-five people had come for the concert.

"Is that all?" I asked.

"Yes, that's it," he said, "And there aren't any posters anywhere or anything else that says that there's a concert. Nothing."

We asked the person in charge, and he said, "Well, we never really do anything like that."

In the room I was given as a dressing room, I sat down on a chair, which collapsed immediately, and the other chair in the room had only three legs. The toilet was so old-fashioned that I didn't even know what it was. Charles and I were desperate. "My God, what do we do now?" I thought. "Do we go home? But now that we're here, Charles and I should get our money. I'll sing."

So we went out onto the platform. The few people in the audience were very nice, and the concert went very well.

Afterwards, we were told that we were invited to a meal, and we were led into a big "hall," which used to be a stable in the castle. There stood two barrels with a board across them, and on this board were a few paper cups of wine. There was also a salami, which we had to cut ourselves, and a bit of cheese, but no plates, knives, forks, or napkins. The castle owner told us to help ourselves, but we told him that we had to leave because Charles had to go on to Barcelona immediately. Of course, we thought that we would now be paid, but the person made no sign that he intended to give us any money.

I said, "Will we see you again? Perhaps at the hotel tomorrow?"

He said, "I don't know if I can make it tomorrow."

So we left without receiving a penny, and today Charles and I are still waiting for our money from the "Castle Pondre Festival." Musicaglotz has written more than twenty letters, without receiving a single reply, so naturally the question of whether or not we should sue came up. I spoke to one of my agents in Germany, and she said, "Yes, I know about these things. The same thing happened to us once at a concert in Germany. We sued, and it cost us so much money and so much stress that it wasn't worth it."

Something similar happened to me when I was scheduled to sing in *Elektra* in Lisbon. The opera was canceled two months in advance, but still the whole cast had reserved the dates for four or five performances plus rehearsal days for Lisbon, and it was too late to schedule anything else. Since the opera was bankrupt, any money that was left went to the bankruptcy court, and we got nothing. But thanks to the persistence of the Musicaglotz management, I got a wonderful surprise two years later. I finally received my fee for all the canceled performances!

Marriage

My God, I feel sorry for all the unfortunate people married to singers!

The Long-Suffering Wife

Although I pity anyone married to a singer, I'll talk about the wife of a singer first, since traditionally wives are supposed to be devoted to their husbands and their husbands' careers, and leading a life in the shadow of a "star" should be more "normal" for them.

Perhaps as a young girl, the future wife of a famous singer imagined how wonderful her life would be—invitations to parties and receptions every evening, lots of foreign travel, beautiful clothes and jewelry, and many other marvelous things. She could share in his fame, and become something of a celebrity herself. But how different the reality is. Her idol may admire her when she experiences his sunny side in the Green Room after a successful performance, but, woe, when they start living together! Living with a singer quickly frays the nerves, and is really hard work! Soon the beloved singer-husband shows himself as he really is, and she gets to know the side of his life that is carefully hidden from outsiders. Perhaps she thought her singer-idol's voice is naturally in good shape all the time, and he's always cheerful and certain of victory and success. But at home she soon finds out that he's a demanding partner.

Years ago I spoke with wife of Ludwig Suthaus. Hans Beirer and Suthhaus were considered true heldentenors at that time, and Suthaus's daughter had a very beautiful voice. When I asked Mrs. Suthaus if her daughter would also become a singer, she said, "No, for God's sake! I can't go through all this again!" Suthaus, by the way, may have been the cleanest man who ever lived, because whenever you called his house, Mrs. Suthaus would answer and say, "My husband can't come to the phone. He's taking a bath." I myself broke the habit of giving such excuses long before I retired. Even if I happened to pick up the phone, I just said, "I'm sorry. I can't speak because I have to sing." Very daring, but talking on the telephone is dangerous for singers, because one speaks differently into the receiver than one normally does. If people didn't understand that I couldn't speak on the phone, then they weren't true friends, and I didn't attach any great importance to their ever calling back.

I knew the wife of a famous colleague whose duty it was to always inspect their hotel room in advance. Could it be darkened for sleeping during the day? Was it quiet enough? Could the air conditioning be switched off? If not, the windows had to be taped over with black paper and the opening from the air conditioner blocked off. I certainly sympathize with the desire to control the air conditioning. When I sang at the Schubertiade in Hohenems, I stayed at a hotel in Feldkirch. The air conditioning couldn't be turned off, and it blew icy cold directly across my bed. I pulled the comforter over my head, so that I wouldn't have to breath in this cold, dry air all night, but it didn't work. In the morning I woke up as hoarse as a raven, and had the greatest difficulty getting my voice back in shape before the evening's concert through hours of inhalation therapy, oil compresses around the neck, and special humming exercises.

If a woman is considering marrying a singer, she should try to find out as much about the realities of his professional life first, so she can know what to expect and not be disappointed by her idol's life. I know of a case where a young bourgeois married woman was enthralled by a male singer and felt compassion for him because she thought he was so misunderstood by his wife. She left her husband and married this charming, successful singer after his own divorce. He showered her with furs and jewelry and bought her a fancy car, and they always flew first class to his guest appearances all over the world. But it soon became obvious that he was often nervous and on edge. If he had a head cold, she had to take care of him, mother him day and night, pity him all the time, and endure all his moods. She trembled with him before the evening's performance, hoping that everything would go well. She also had to be housewife, mother, and secretary, and answer all his phone calls and letters. Her dream life soon came to an end. She found out that her singer-idol was very human after all, and, disappointed, she left him, after living through several of her husband's extramarital adventures, which he needed to bolster his self-esteem. The beautiful clothes and other material things, which other women long for, quickly became unimportant because the essential things were missing—unconditional love and understanding between partners.

I believe that all singers, male or female, love themselves first, as actors do too. People say that it's more in a woman's nature to give love, and that women are very vain. But have you ever watched men in the bathroom? They need much more time in front of a mirror than women!

The Derided Husband

I sing the praises of singer-wives—and also singer-husbands, who are sometimes smiled at so condescendingly. It's not traditional for a man to lovingly make his wife's life his own, give up his own profession, and live off the money his wife earns. "You let your wife work and don't do anything yourself? Ugh! How disgusting!" is what many people might say. But it only looks that way from the outside, and I feel even more sorry for these poor men than I do for the women who are married to singers. Almost always the husbands of singers had satisfying professions that they gave up for their partner's sake. Sometimes they were also singers, perhaps not too talented, and together the couple decided that her bigger career was more important, and he gave his up. So now this poor man is tormented by this from all sides. His own family and friends say, "How could you do it! You could have made a great career as well!" Non-friends, often the singer-wife's colleagues, look down cynically on this pitiable person and say things like "Have you gone walkies with the doggie yet today?" or "Quickly, quickly, get a coat for your wife so her income doesn't catch cold!"

The husband of a singer is totally dependent, and must ask his wife for every penny, because she is the one who works, earns the money, is successful. She is the splendid one who has to be kept happy.

Many female singers (as well as male singers and actors) take their roles home and continue to play them. So the poor husband lives less with his wife than with a demonic Carmen, a sickly Mimi, or a crazy Lucia di Lammermoor. Female singers often have very sensitive nerves, and are what men call hysterics. Such women are often unbearable marriage partners at home, and only care about their voices. The poor man, apart from being a husband, is also a nurse, courier, secretary, bodyguard, dog-walker, and chauffeur. He has a lot to do, but can't risk speaking his mind freely, because she is the important person, even in financial matters. My sympathy goes out to all these poor creatures!

Separate But Unequal Careers

When the husband of a singer continues to practice his profession, it's a completely different situation. A very successful businessman would never quit, and his adored singer-wife becomes like a red rose in his buttonhole, someone he can display proudly to his friends. If the singer-wife is lucky, this kind of husband is so fascinated with her profession that he respects her wishes in everything, gives her complete freedom, and now and then flies to one of her performances, full of admiration. She lives in a golden setting. Her husband provides a house and all the help she needs, so she only has to worry about singing. She can keep the money she earns, and doesn't need to worry about household expenses. If she has children, they have a nanny, and, of course, she has a chauffeur. She lives with her husband now and then, but, otherwise, they love each other by telephone from a distance. Everything is wonderful, everything is glittery and shining. I must add that only a few happy female singers have such marriages. But are they really happy? They are almost always alone.

There are also businessman-husbands who love to outshine their wives, and don't understand at all the stresses of singing. I had a colleague who once told me sorrowfully how serious her disagreements with her husband were. He didn't understand why she couldn't attend an important party or host his business friends in the afternoon before a performance. He'd say, "What do you mean you can't come? You are only singing!" Either a singer gets rid of such a husband, or she gives up her profession. And if she does decide to quit, thorns of self-reproach are always in her heart, and she thinks, "Because of him I gave up singing!"

Singers Inc.

Then there are couples that I call "Singers Inc." Two singers get married, and the situation looks ideal to outsiders. Joint engagements, double fees—fantastic! No nerves and worries about money, because one of them can always sing when the other has a head cold. Now and then such marriages succeed, especially if he's the more successful one and she travels with him unnoticed and sings smaller roles. Because of her smaller career, she can take care of "the great one" and admire him, and he can generously praise her smaller roles, engagements, and fees while secretly considering them second class. He is always the greatest.

But if both are on about the same level, life is quite different. They are not only a married couple, but rival colleagues, even if they're both very different vocally, for example, a bass and a soprano. It's always "Anything you can do, I can do better." Who had the greater success? Did they shout bravo louder for you or for me? Who got the best reviews? The one who gets panned complains, "This idiot critic doesn't understand at all!" while the other, who was praised, has to be happy in secret, but is nevertheless downhearted because the review comes from "that idiot critic" who doesn't understand anything. Then there are logistical problems. Who warms up first at home? Who takes a bath first before joint performances?

A "Singers Inc." couple has the good (or bad) luck to be together all the time—at rehearsals, at performances, on trips. And they are not immune to the manipulation of fans, who sometimes play one off against the other by saying, "Oh, you are much better than your wife (husband)." Even with all the togetherness, love letters flutter into the house, and each one finds time for extramarital escapades, which, of course, the other finds out about from colleagues who "mean well." In addition, the only topic discussed at home is the profession, and everything is doubled—the joy, the anger, the nervous tension, and the conflicts. If one partner is angry with a colleague, conductor, stage director, or manager, then the other must be as well. And one can't embellish a profession-related story without the other interrupting immediately and saying that he or she was right there and "That's not at all the way it happened." So the story is ruined.

A "Singers Inc." relationship is very difficult, and I admire those who are tolerant enough to stay together. I personally believe that it's best for a female singer to live alone, if she doesn't find a partner who accepts her and her profession, and also understands and loves her privately as a woman, just the way she is. I can speak from experience because my first marriage was to a singer, the bass-baritone Walter Berry. We weren't at all unhappy, but he didn't have a wife in me, nor I a husband in him. We were both "devoured" by our profession, a profession which reaches into the most intimate parts of a singer's life.

As Lilli Palmer says in her book, one asks in Hollywood, "Are you happily married, or do you paint?"

A Final Word

I always remember what the wife of Mario del Monaco said when she noticed that her husband, the famous Italian tenor, had started flirting with a young lady. As the flirting grew more and more obvious, she went up to the girl and said: "On the day before a performance, he shouldn't. On the day of a performance, he may not (it makes his throat slimy). And on the day after a performance, he can't. He sings twice a week, and the one day in between belongs to me!"

Prima Donnas

My God, I so wanted to be a prima donna! But I was always only a seconda donna.

To be called a prima donna in the opera world, you have to have seven successes and seven scandals every year. Scandals are much more difficult to come by than successes, because a good scandal requires that you do something out of the ordinary. What that something is really doesn't matter. The important thing is that the press and the public want to talk about it. If Callas treated her mother badly, or she flew first class while her husband was in coach, people said, "Oh, how terrible!" If Jessye Norman told the management that she wasn't satisfied with a normal dressing room, and they had to make special arrangements for her, everyone chattered about her "unreasonable demands." It's always the same. Truly, it's a lot of work to be a prima donna. You have to travel with an entourage, and live in a large hotel suite. Destroying furniture like rock groups is also useful, since the tabloids must always have something new to write about. Wherever they go, prima donnas live for the press. And they always smile, smile, smile! An enormous ego is required to declare that "I am the greatest," and you need to keep a publicity machine running that would make Coca-Cola proud.

A prima donna always gets the most beautiful dressing room. Often only she has a sofa or a comfortable chair, and a piano. And, of course, she gets the most money, the kind of fees that other singers can only dream about. With all these temptations, is it surprising that I tried to become a prima donna too by singing soprano roles, like Leonore in *Fidelio*, the Marschallin in *Rosenkavalier*, Kundry in *Parsifal*, and Ariadne? And I almost succeeded. For a while, I had the best dressing room and sang the leading parts, but in my heart of hearts, I just wasn't made for it. For me the circus that goes with the role of prima donna was just too much. Besides, I'm very lazy. So I just remained a seconda donna.

Until recently, prima donnas often traveled with their own special costumes, and they wore them even if they didn't match the style of the production they were singing in. When my husband, Paul-Emile Deiber, was directing Bellini's *Norma* at the Met, the stage set and costumes were done in an antique style, and Joan Sutherland, who sang the opening night, wore the costume that had been designed for the production. But when Montserrat Caballé took over the title role, she made it clear at rehearsals that she didn't intend to follow the original blocking and would stand anywhere on the stage that she pleased. She also made it known that she wouldn't wear the costume from the original production, either. She would use the costume that she had brought with her, which was more suitable for the third act of Verdi's *Un Ballo in Maschera*, where the heroine wears a beautiful nineteeth-century ball gown. Paul-Emile tried to reason with her, but she just kept repeating, "I always stand here, and I always wear this costume." All pleading and persuasion were useless. In desperation, my husband went to Gören Gentele, who was then the Met General Manager. His response was, "Caballé sells out the house. It doesn't matter where she stands, or what she has on."

Male singers can be prima donnas too. I remember very well a rehearsal for *Werther* by Jules Massenet at the Met, where Franco Corelli was to sing the title role, and I was to be his Charlotte. Again my husband Paul-Emile was the stage director, although we weren't married then. The set was in place, and the entire cast was in costume and make up, and everything went well until the third-act entrance of Corelli, our primo tenore. Paul Emile's idea was that Corelli should enter slowly, and the spotlight on him should gradually grow brighter, which would fit the mood of the scene and the music. But when Corelli realized that he would not be in full spotlight immediately upon his entrance, he flew into a rage, threw down the book he was carrying, ripped the wig from his head, called for Lauretta, his wife, and left the stage with Lauretta and their poodle in tow. What a great *éclat!* Sir Rudolf Bing, the omnipotent general manager, had to come down from his office, and only after he calmed the tenor down with his fabled diplomatic skill did Corelli return to the stage.

Along with everything else, Corelli was especially nervous about singing the role of Werther. Although he'd been very successful in the French repertoire earlier in his career with the role of Romeo in Gounod's *Roméo et Juliette,* he was really a dramatic Italian tenor, and a great one. I think he was uncertain about returning to the French repertoire, even though he sang his glorious aria "Pourquoi me réveiller" so ardently that he made me cry. His fear of the part steadily increased and reached a climax on opening night when, a quarter of an hour before the performance and already in costume and make-up, he declared that he couldn't sing.

Paul-Emile came to my dressing room very agitated. What to do? Who is the cover? Opera houses like the Met always have a "cover" or substitute singer available who can step in at the last minute if someone cancels or becomes "indisposed" during the opera and cannot continue. On this occasion the "cover" was Enrico Di Giuseppe, who had participated in a few rehearsals, but who was not ideal for the role. For one thing, he had a light voice, which was very well suited for Rossini, but not for Massenet. And, worst of all for me, he was almost a head shorter than I was!

In such a crisis, the most important thing is to stay calm. Since Corelli was several inches taller than I and we looked great together, I had been planning on wearing very pretty high-heeled shoes. But now I searched frantically for my flat ballet slippers, which I would wear in the desperate hope that I wouldn't appear farcically taller than my substitute Werther. A pity!

The opening was delayed for half an hour so the new Werther could put on his costume and make up. The audience grew restless, and then was bitterly disappointed by the announcement that Corelli was suddenly indisposed and wouldn't sing. All of us in the production were sad, too. For weeks, everything had been beautifully rehearsed. All the staging and gestures worked very well for me and for Corelli, my tall Werther. Now, suddenly, I had to make myself as small as possible. Whenever I could, I sat down or leaned back with knees bent in the arms of my diminutive Werther. Di Giuseppe sang very beautifully and effortlessly in the Italian style, but without any real excitement. The audience felt this lack of excitement too, since they were used to sitting on the edge of their seats, waiting to hear if their beloved Corelli would hit his high notes or not.

Luckily, the performance went well in spite of everything, and Corelli sang all the rest of the performances with erotic passion and great success. Only on opening night did his nerves fail him. From experiences like these, I've come to believe that opening night performances, opening night audiences, and opening night critics should be done away with altogether. The best performances are always the later ones, when only "normal" people are in the audience. Such audiences are generally much more knowledgeable and appreciative of the music than the elegantly dressed opening night crowds.

Today, star tenors sometimes let their colleagues rehearse for weeks, and arrive only for the final rehearsal. But there are signs that the era of prima donnas and primi uomini is coming to an end. Certainly it is easy for people to cheer a familiar name, because knowing the difference between what is good, and what is very good, is difficult. I won't deny that every singer has the right to make a great name, but it's also absolutely wrong to pass over those who are equally good, but who are not well-known, or those who are just starting out and haven't had the time to make a great name yet. Once, at the Salzburg Festival, a man from Hanover came to my dressing room and spoke very enthusiastically about my performance. I asked him if he had heard me sing in Hanover that same year, and he answered no, he never went to the opera in Hanover because the company there was just average. I was really angry with his stupid snobbery and unfair opinion, and I told him so bluntly and to the point!

Public Relations

Often when I sang in North or South America or Japan, I would return home to Vienna and always hear, "Where were you? What were you doing? One doesn't hear anything about you at all. Were you sick, or were you on vacation?" I had sung somewhere else, and had a huge success, but at home no one even knew I was still alive. So I decided to hire a public relations manager. When I was singing in *Die Frau ohne Schatten* in 1966, I met Maurice Feldman, who handled public relations for Karl Böhm. He asked if he could work for Walter Berry and me also. Because it always annoyed me that no one knew what we did abroad, we agreed, and Maurice started to take care of our public relations.

Now a delightful time began. Every morning we received a registered letter with some kind of article or other with references to us marked with a thick, red underline, and reviews, which Maurice had partly written himself, because he had great influence with many newspapers. One day, however, I was very embarrassed. I was sitting on an airplane when I opened up a newspaper and read that Golda Meir had kissed me when I sang in Israel. I hadn't even seen Mrs. Meir when I was there! Many newspapers also reported that I didn't wear any make-up at all, and they carried stories about my evening gowns—how many jewels and semi-precious stones they had, how they were sewn, and how heavy they were. All of this was supposed to be of great interest to Americans, but to us Europeans it was a bit too much.

Maurice also had pictures of us taken with famous people whom we never saw again after the five minutes it took to do the photos. The great painter Salvador Dali was one example. Maurice invited us to the Regent Hotel in New York. We arrived, Dali arrived, we all said hello, sat down, the photos were taken, and then we all left. The pictures from this little session were sent everywhere, and were snatched up by newspapers like warm rolls at breakfast. They wrote how unique it was that we knew Dali. Then Maurice circulated the story that Dali insisted on painting me, but only in Spain under a warm, southern sun, and I didn't have time.

The most implausible stories were spread around about us, which goes to show that publicity should never be taken seriously. Maurice was a very, very nice man, and when he worked for us, my fees went up by leaps and bounds. My recitals were sold out because people read this and that about me in the papers. Before we came to a new city in America, stories about us that were never true, but which created interest, always appeared in the newspapers. It was as if Maurice did commercials for us, just like for Coca-Cola.

After Maurice died, I stopped employing a public relations manager, because I found the situation too ridiculous. It's strange how newspapers and magazines devour these small stories, and their readers believe them. You have to be talked about, or you're considered uninteresting.

Recordings

I loved making recordings because I could repeat a passage or an entire piece as often as I wanted when something went wrong. The tape recorder is patient. Unfortunately, this also meant that I needed a lot of patience too!

Totally different rules apply in the recording studio than in the opera house or concert hall. For one thing, the audience only hears. A singer's physical presence, charisma, gestures, facial expressions, external appearance—everything is lost. The listener is really "all ears," and because of this, a singer must interpret the personality of an operatic character or the meaning of a song much more emphatically than would be necessary (or advisable) on the operatic stage or concert platform. If it's raining in a song, a singer must make the song sound like it's raining, a sunny day must sound like a sunny day, and the listener must actually hear the smell of a flower, so to speak.

The rules for making a recording are much more subtle and technical than giving a sad passage a slightly darker tone than a happy one. The articulation of all the syllables in the words, and especially the consonants, has to be adjusted exactly for a highly sensitive microphone. A big concert hall swallows consonants, and they have to be pronounced more obviously there, something that would sound absolutely ridiculous in a studio recording. A good example is the last word in the famous final phrase of the song "Die Nacht" by Richard Strauss. It goes like this:

> O die Nacht, mir bangt, sie stehle
> Dich mir auch.

The last word "auch" must really be sung A-U-CH, and the CH must be articulated very emphatically and gutturally on the concert platform, much more than in normal conversation, or else the audience only hears "ow." If one articulates like this in front of a microphone, the recording would sound terrible, especially to listeners who understand German. However, there are now very famous singers who have made it a habit always to articulate with too much clarity, so that their style is very artificial and all naturalness is gone. Unfortunately, it's very difficult to point this out to these singers because, first, no one else has the courage, and, second, the singers won't listen because it's exactly this over-articulation which captivated audiences at the beginning of their careers. Singers need good friends with honest hearts to save them from becoming too artificial.

One good thing about recordings is that a singer never has to sing too loud. Even if the orchestra is extremely loud during the recording, the technicians and the producer can always manipulate the tapes later, so the human voice dominates. Because of this, singers can make the most beautiful sound their voices are capable of, without worrying about volume, and the best qualities in their voices are heard. The danger, of course, is that singers start to compete with their own (earlier) recordings. How often are listeners in the opera house or concert hall disappointed when they hear live for the first time a favorite singer, whom they know only from recordings. It's just like with photographs—professional lighting and only showing the best side of the face is not reality! Many excellent singers have small voices, like Rita Streich, for example. The quality of her timbre was wonderful, and it was coupled with a very high degree of musical intelligence. But her voice wasn't big, and in very large houses, her voice didn't carry beyond the first few rows. She was perfect for recordings, however. Unfortunately, because of her success, she was invited to sing in opera houses and concert halls all over the world, and the listeners at her live performances were very disappointed, because her voice was so small.

The opposite kind of singer is Birgit Nilsson. Her voice was so enormous and so strong—like metal—that she could effortlessly drown out any large orchestra and fill huge opera houses with her sound. But recordings couldn't do justice to her timbre, because her voice was so big that recording tape was incapable of capturing it accurately.

Many singers with small voices use recordings to make very successful careers. The tenor Josef Schmidt, for example, made the song "Heut ist der schönste Tag in meinem Leben" (Today Is the Most Beautiful Day of My Life) world-famous. He had a small voice, as did Mario Lanza, and both men made "microphone" careers. I was very surprised at what happened when I took part in a Peter Alexander TV show in Europe in which Peter and I sang some German folk-song duets. We recorded the duets in advance, and they were played back during the broadcast while we lip-synched the words, which, by the way, was difficult for me because I wasn't used to this technique. When we recorded the duets, I noticed that Peter kept his microphone extremely close to his mouth, so much so that I could hardly hear him singing, although I was standing right next to him. Later, when we listened to the recording, I couldn't believe my ears! His voice sounded so beguiling, his interpretation was so intimate, and every breath had such expressive power that I, who had sung "normally," sounded absolutely colorless and insignificant and without any finesse, compared to him. Many of his colleagues, all famous singers of popular music, also know how to use the small but beautiful sound of their voices to perfection.

It's interesting to understand the art of making recordings. You sing into the microphone, as if into a human ear, but that ear is incorruptible. You can't cheat! It often happened that I was disappointed when I listened to myself, even when I thought I'd sung and interpreted well. I could already see it in the faces of the recording technicians and the producer, or I heard, "Well, how did you feel?" Uh oh. I knew immediately that something wasn't right. Often it was because of the tempo. When you sing slow songs for a recording, the tempo has to be a bit faster than in the concert hall. On the other hand, the tempo has to be a bit slower with fast songs.

A talented record producer can conjure up just the right effect. He can make a loud voice softer, or a soft one louder, which is easier, by the way. Sometimes vowels I thought I had colored correctly would sound different during playback, as if the pitch was too high or too low. A tiny lightening up of a vowel could make the tone sound higher, and a small darkening, lower. Unfortunately, I felt that I could hear all my mistakes too clearly at a recording session to be really happy about the result, and many of my colleagues feel the same way. With our own ears we hear ourselves very differently than the "ear" of the microphone "hears" us. For this reason, we are very dependent on the judgment of the record producer. Walter Legge, one of the greatest record producers of all time, had such a fine ear and wonderful feeling and love for singers that we could have complete confidence in his opinions. Under his care, we achieved the best results.

Towards the end of my career, I had a terrible experience while making a recording of *Les Contes d'Hoffmann*. I was asked to take over the role of Antonia's mother, though the part had already been recorded by another singer. Actually, the whole opera had already been recorded with other singers, because originally a movie was planned, but the project fell through. Now the recording company wanted different singers in several roles. I was in Vienna, so I agreed to go to sessions there. When I arrived, I was astonished not to see any other singers, or an orchestra or conductor either. I was given headphones, and told to stand in front of a microphone and sing. Now, the mother in this opera almost never sings a line by herself, but only appears in a trio with a soprano and a baritone. All alone, I had to try to sing my part in a tempo that had already been decided and recorded, and I had to follow the previous singer's tempo variations, as she sang the mother's music. This gave me, and I am quite a musical person, great difficulties, to say the least. I had to more or less put on musical shoes that didn't fit me. Also, I couldn't hear the orchestra very well through the headphones, or my own voice either, as I was singing.

When listening to the playback, I almost had a stroke! Aside from the places where the orchestra and I weren't together, which is normal at recording sessions, my voice sounded totally alien to me—like the voice of Mickey Mouse! My timbre was missing. There were no overtones. What I heard didn't have the remotest similarity to my own voice. I was horrified. The technicians calmed me down by saying that I wasn't making the recording in the same hall as the original recording, and all halls have a different acoustic, which, of course, is well known. (By the way, the soprano recorded her part in London, and the baritone, his in New York.) So they were only recording a "trace" of the sound of my voice, which is why I sounded like Mickey Mouse. "Everything will be taken care of by the technicians," they said. "Don't you worry."

When I returned home, completely unnerved, I phoned the recording company and told them that I didn't agree with their way of doing things, and I wasn't confident that they would be able to do anything at all with what I had recorded. It would be best if they found another singer. After further animated discussion, we agreed that I would do the recording again with better sound. But when I went back for another session, the circumstances were exactly the same. The only difference was that I was more experienced in using the headphones and in knowing how to adjust myself to what my predecessor had recorded. When I listened to the playback at the second session, the sound was a bit better. It still wasn't my voice, but everyone assured me solemnly that, without any doubt, everything would be resolved in a first-class way. If only I hadn't believed them! When I later heard the finished recording, I was horrified again at what had been done to my voice, and I condemned that recording to the deepest, darkest corner of my closet. I am terribly ashamed that this discordant recording of me exists!

The biggest difficulty today, apart from finding a first-class producer, is getting all the singers together at a recording session. One can only come on this day, another on that one. Because of scheduling problems, playback procedures similar to the one I was forced to use in the *Contes d'Hoffmann* recording are more and more the norm. A quintet is recorded by three or four people the first time, or a duet with one singer alone. Singers are added on different "tracks" later. The most important things are the famous names on the cover and that the actual recording should take as little time as possible, so it doesn't get too expensive. How can a recording possibly have a homogeneous style, a feeling of collaboration, of "making music together" under these conditions?

I remember how Solti made recordings, and how he worked with every singer. To be honest, I'm happy that I don't make opera recordings anymore, because when I made recordings enough time was allowed. For example, when I sang Leonore and Jon Vickers sang Florestan on the recording of Beethoven's *Fidelio* that we made with Otto Klemperer, the sessions took place over the course of a good two weeks. Many critics consider this recording a "classic," and I sometimes think that the pace at which we made the recording is what made it so good. All the singers' voices were in good shape, and they stayed that way, because we weren't asked to do too much on any one day. It was a joy to make recordings like this—to make beautiful music and to take one's time doing it.

Listening to recordings at home was considered something special in the days when the *Fidelio* with Klemperer was made. The idea was that the record companies should strive to produce the best recording of a particular piece with the best interpreters available and with optimum sound quality. Nowadays, the over supply of recordings hasn't really brought any enrichment. As the recordings become more and more sophisticated sound wise, listeners find themselves gladly reaching back to old records in which the sound may not be first-class, but the interpretation is.

How wonderful it is to hear an old recording of a pianist like Gieseking performing Mozart, or Furtwängler conducting a Beethoven Symphony, or voices like Kipnis or Björling, or *Bohème* or *Otello* with Toscanini conducting. How happily does one give up modern technology! Many music lovers today prefer to buy "live" recordings of opera and concert performances because they can experience some of the original spontaneity, even though the performances may not be 100 percent accurate. These recordings are more authentic than the sterile canned ones produced by the sophisticated computerized technology in today's recording studios, which home stereo equipment can't hope to reproduce anyway. The pianissimo sounds are so quiet you can't hear them, while the fortissimo sounds crack the plaster in the ceiling.

But miracles still do happen today, such as James Levine's recording of Wagner's Ring Cycle with the Metropolitan Opera Orchestra!

Regimen

Preparation

I'm often asked what singers do all day when they have to sing in the evening, and first I have to say that each individual is totally different. I can only speak for myself. My own preparation for singing really never ended, because I almost always sang every two or three days. This meant an eternal "save oneself for the next performance" existence.

The first commandment for me was "Thou shalt not speak too much." When I spoke, I got hoarse. So most of the time I had to do without friendly get-togethers. Laughing, talking, smoke—all these things irritated my mucous membranes, and I felt this in my voice. Perhaps I was especially sensitive, but female singers in general aren't as hardy as their male colleagues.

For me, direct preparation for an opera performance began the previous day. After midday at the latest, no one was allowed to speak to me any more, and I withdrew. This was really very pleasant, because I could do some uninterrupted reading. Almost everyone today complains about lack of time. I had time, time to read, time to contemplate. In the evening I ate very lightly, only a cup of yogurt or an apple. I often watched TV, a good way to fall asleep quickly because the eyes get tired.

On the day of the performance I stayed "alone with myself," and had a little breakfast. The first thing I did after waking up, while still in bed, was sing "mi-mi-mi"—is the voice there? If the weather was nice, I'd go for a short walk, possibly half an hour. Then I got myself in voice. Carefully, not up too quickly! Very easy scales, very slowly, five minutes, then pause, again a few minutes, then again a pause. This could take from twenty minutes to three-quarters of an hour, depending on the state of my voice that day.

After "warming up," I had an easy-to-digest lunch of fish or veal. Because I was used to it, I always drank a glass of wine, but only one. Then I went to bed again, and tried to relax completely and sleep, but not for too long, so that my voice didn't "fall asleep" too deeply. About three or four hours before the performance, I'd get up again, take a long, lukewarm bath, which calmed me, and switch on the radio and search for jazz, rock, or pop—anything that didn't remind me of serious music. Next I'd get myself in voice a bit more, rehearse a few pieces from my part, but not too much—I got smart about this from hurting myself when I was young. Finally, I'd leave for the opera house, so I'd arrive about one to one-and-a-half hours before the performance to put on my make-up. Most of the time I brought something to eat—oranges and jars of honey or glucose. For a long time, I drank molasses with lemon in hot water, but later I preferred fizzy tablets of vitamin C and calcium dissolved in water.

Preparation for a lieder recital was a little different because I had to study the song texts. I did that in the mornings and afternoons, because I forgot the texts very easily.

I must confess that I was less careful when I was young, and the difficulty of the part made a difference too. When I sang Marie in *Wozzeck*, for example, I could even lie in the sun and swim until midday, because that role requires no bel canto singing. There are no long phrases, but usually just *Sprechgesang* (spoken-sung phrases). Nothing that required difficult breath control.

How often did I sit in my hotel room and look through the window and watch life on the street! If I was lucky, I saw a river or a park sometimes. From my apartment in New York on the fortieth floor, I had a view of Central Park, and, beyond it, a mass of pointed skyscraper roofs. The dusk of early evening was the most beautiful time. The apartment houses on Fifth Avenue slowly lit up, and seemed almost transparent. These silhouettes looked like Brussels lace, and reached into the sky like the Dolomites. In Hong Kong, I've watched the bustling activity on the ships between the city and Kowloon.

When I sang in the evening, I couldn't, as I've already said, do a lot in the daytime. When I went out, I quickly returned to my hotel room, because the noise and the smell of the cars was too awful, and there were so many tourists on the street at summer festivals like Salzburg. So all I had was the view from the window, and the solitude of my hotel room. Of course, I lived in anticipation of the performance, but, nevertheless, time moved slowly. I couldn't always read or write letters, so I looked through another window or at TV, and experienced real life vicariously, separated from the world. Many female singers live this kind of lonely life, as if in a convent. If singers want to be in first-class voice, they can't exhaust their bodies, even though the vocal cords are only tiny muscles, eight to twelve millimeters long. We singers say "my voice and I," because we have a split personality: "I'm doing fine, but how is my voice?" Nothing is as bad for singers as having an off-day with their voices. No toothache or headache is taken as seriously as a tickle in the nose or a scratchy throat. When I woke up from the anesthetic after an operation, the first thing I did was "mi-mi-mi" to see how my voice was doing. I lived in constant fear of a cold or some other infection, and no one was allowed to come close to me if they might be a carrier. What else could I do but withdraw, instead of nurturing human contacts and experiencing life up close. I only had the view through the window.

Dr. Reckford, my unforgettable throat doctor in New York, always warned me to sleep and be silent a lot, and, above all, not "run around." By that he meant that I should avoid the everyday tasks and duties of life, because singers who run around town all day have no voice when they stand on the stage in the evening. My mother believed the same thing, and she would put me to bed on the days when I had to sing in the evening. She said it was to keep my body at an even temperature. The theater itself is very dangerous. The mucous membranes get a terrible shock when you sing on a hot stage, and then go into an ice-cold dressing room. Equally dangerous is smoke. Everything has an effect on the vocal cords, the most sensitive spot for a singer. That's why we have to hold cloths in front of our mouths, which explains the often comical-looking scarves singers wear.

Eating and Drinking

Singers have to stay as fit as athletes. Like them, we can't eat everything we'd like to. We have to have only enough in our stomachs when performing so that we don't feel hungry. Every singer has his or her own little rules. For example, they say that chocolate causes too much phlegm, which is bad for the voice. I often think about the great tenor Leo Slezak's advice. He warned his colleagues: "Don't eat or drink anything cold, hot, or crumbly!" And, by the way, nothing bubbly like champagne or soda. If you breathe deeply with champagne in your stomach, you'll burp. Everything singers eat and drink should be the same temperature as their throats, never hotter or colder.

A singer should never eat cabbage for lunch. It causes flatulence. Also drinking coffee causes a swollen stomach. Tea makes the throat dry, and honey brings mucus. There are heaps of such prohibitions. Red wine doesn't agree with me. It gives me a dry throat. But white wine makes me very lively. Of course, singers shouldn't drink cognac or other strong liquor before a performance, because it destroys their concentration.

They say Caruso always ate a sizable portion of spaghetti with olive oil before he sang. I did the same sometimes. Although the oil reaches the stomach through the esophagus, it still has a positive effect on the larynx and vocal cords. When I felt that my throat was dry, I'd reach for a small bottle of the finest olive oil and take a sip, regardless of the taste.

A singer has to eat and drink well to calm the stomach and also the nerves. Eating well also keeps the mucous membranes moist and oily, and forms a protective layer on top of them. But, of course, one then risks gaining weight, and this worries many singers. Maria Callas wanted to lose a lot of weight and took medication to do it, which made her extremely nervous. I envied Grace Bumbry, who managed to keep her slim figure for so many years.

The subject of medication, tranquilizers, and stimulants could fill a long chapter. When a singer is fine vocally, he or she doesn't need to take anything. But the time always comes when "the voice" causes singers to become more nervous, and then they get a lot of different advice. I concluded after many years that nothing really helps when one is very nervous.

Sometimes singers are jittery because of the weather conditions in some cities. I would wake up in Munich, and there would be Föhn, a warm southern wind from the Alps. One look at the sky and I already had butterflies in my stomach. And because of this, my voice started to tremble. True, there are pills that are effective against weather sensitivity, but you have to take these the day before. How can a singer, who is traveling all the time, know what the weather will be like in the next city? And the pills that cure the nervousness also dry out the throat. I suffered a lot from migraines, and I knew there were few medications that helped without making my throat dry.

A lot depends on the right nourishment. In my earlier years in America, I made do with canned vegetables. Then someone convinced me that this was wrong, and I started eating raw vegetables, drinking fruit juice and taking vitamins. And I've continued to do these things for more than 20 years now. I still take high doses of vitamins. Even if it doesn't do any real good, at least I believe in it! In America I even learned to give myself vitamin injections (of course, only intramuscular). I practiced with an orange because I didn't want to go to a doctor's office and wait just for a vitamin injection.

There are many other things that my colleagues believe in, from strychnine in homeopathic doses to the very dangerous cortisone. If a singer is insecure, he or she is liable to try anything. The best thing for these feelings, however, is (and always will be) good preparation before a performance. Fischer-Dieskau said, "There are two positions for a singer: either vertical when he is singing, or horizontal when he lies in bed." I can only confirm this. When I traveled for an extended period, I spent all my time, except for the performances, in silence. If I didn't have any distractions, I didn't have any vocal problems either!

All this sounds like a terrible subordination of everything to the voice. Like slavery. But it's true. This is exactly how the singing profession is.

The Morning After

On the morning after a performance, I usually woke up quite early because "it" wouldn't let me sleep. At night, while half asleep, I always continued singing. Passages I didn't sing very well, I repeated ten times the right way, and, of course, I then remembered how to do everything correctly. The applause, the high I felt after a successful evening, was already long gone.

The day began without make-up and spotlights in front of me. Masses of flowers lay in water in the bathtub, waiting to be taken care of, and they were the last memory of the previous evening. I always felt it was a shame about all these flowers, which were given to me so lovingly. If I stayed in a hotel for a day or two, I tried to divide them up in several vases, which shocked the maids who were at a loss to know how to clean up. If I had to leave immediately, I gave them away, and that really was best. Porters, secretaries, taxi drivers, maids—everyone could enjoy them, except me! Sometimes I took a few bouquets with me if I was traveling by car. Wrapped in wet newspaper, they sometimes kept until I got home, or until I got to the hotel in the next city.

When I carried a bouquet, every passenger on the plane smiled at me, customs officials were pleased, stewardesses gave the bouquet an empty seat— everyone enjoyed seeing the flowers. But all too often I had to leave them behind, like everything else in my life. Like the evenings when I sang— already in the past! "Alles zergeht wie Dunst und Traum" (Everything dissolves like mist and dreams) as the Marschallin says in the first act of *Rosenkavalier*. Always again a new day, another performance, and always so quickly again in the past.

To wake up in the familiar and loved world called "home"—how wonderful that is. Not to see the flowers cut and arranged in beautiful bouquets, but in a garden. Not to leave them behind, but to know that, as every flower withers, a new bloom will come in its place. Not to have the gardener plant flowers and trees, which you never see blooming because you are in Rome or Helsinki, "die Aprikosenblüte ist lieder vorbei, die Kamelien schon verblüht" (sadly the apricot bloom is over, the camellias already withered). It's wonderful to enjoy the change of seasons in one and the same place, not to fear the cold and rain, and not always to connect them with a head cold. It's wonderful to look forward to a new day with anticipation, without pressure, without always packing and unpacking suitcases! Waking up from the fleeting dream of the world of the voice and success, waking up to a consciously lived and experienced reality—or is this also only a dream?

Superstition

We singers are all superstitious, some more than others. Let me tell you about some of these superstitions.

Never go back if you forget something. That nothing happened to me when I forgot my passport at home and had to turn around on the way to the airport was pure chance. Never go back to your dressing room during a performance to quickly blow your nose just once more. I'd never do that! I'd ask the people at the security desk to call the dresser and ask her to bring me a handkerchief.

Never let anyone sew anything on your costume once you are wearing it. Use only safety pins. And make sure everyone knows that they should have their tongue between their teeth when they are pinning. And always return the pins later, if you want to avoid future problems.

Never use new make-up unless absolutely necessary. Of course, sometimes you have to buy new make-up or brushes or mirrors or make-up remover, but definitely never throw away the little talismans that your fans give you. And for God's sake, never spill any powder! If you do, you'll never get new engagements. And I don't want to hear anything about a broken mirror. Singers get seven years bad luck just like everyone else.

Never walk underneath a ladder backstage, or leave a nail lying on the floor. And never whistle in a German theater. There they whistle instead of boo, and you risk being whistled at if you whistle yourself. I wouldn't risk whistling in any theater in any other country either.

I hope I haven't forgotten anything. We theater people are constantly surrounded by evil spirits, and danger lurks everywhere.

My father was terribly superstitious. When I was a child, he taught me never to put my left shoe on first, or put my left arm into the sleeve of any garment first. If I stumbled on a stone on the street, I was taught to quickly go back and walk over the stone again without stumbling.

My father was superstitious about nuns. In the very Catholic city of Aachen where we lived when I was a child, there were many of them, and it was difficult to avoid them. Nevertheless, if my father saw a nun on his way to the theater in the morning, he returned home immediately. And if he came to my first day at school and saw that I would be taught by a nun, I had to quickly change schools.

In Giessen we had the bad luck of moving into our new house on Monday, and everybody knows that Mondays are unlucky. To make matters worse, a cricket took up residence in my parent's bedroom and chirped incessantly, bringing us to the point of despair. Everyone knows that it's bad luck to chase away or, worse, kill a cricket, but my mother found the cricket's hole in the wall and plugged it. The cricket didn't chirp anymore, and surely that's why we were bombed out of this house in Giessen during the war.

I was also taught to be very superstitious about numbers. If I had to sing or take an airplane on Friday the 13th, I was extremely nervous until the performance was over, or the plane landed. Numbers are quite a strange thing. My parents seemed to be associated with the numbers 11 and 13. My father was born on July 11th, and my mother on May 13th. There were 11 years between their birth dates, and they lived together for 26 years, and were married for 22 of them. We were bombed in 1944, and my mother came back to Vienna in 1955, after a 33-year absence.

For many years, I felt these numbers were propitious. Remember that my debut at the Vienna State Opera took place on December 26th. When I traveled, my sleeping compartment always had to have the number 11 or 13, and I always sat in seats with one of these numbers at the theater or the movies. Important agreements had to be signed, if possible, and flights booked that would arrive or depart on days with these magical numbers. Even my hospital room had to have one of these numbers!

Over the years, a belief in the power of numbers gradually left me. It's true that I'm still careful, although 11 and 13 don't seem to matter as much anymore, and no other numbers have made a special impression on me. I can't help myself, but I still think that we humans are subjugated to a magical numbering system, even though I'm no longer dependent on it.

Many singers have dependencies on people. In Vienna there was a very well-respected voice teacher, who, in my opinion, didn't teach a really first-class technique. But apparently this women had incredible charisma, because one famous singer had her as a teacher, and always insisted that she sit in the front row at important performances. Otherwise, she wouldn't be able to sing. My good spirit was my dear Viennese throat specialist, Dr. Kürsten. If I sang in Vienna, the security of having him close by made me very calm. And I always felt uneasy in other cities until I could at least tell him on the phone how my throat and voice were behaving, and hear him say that everything would be fine.

Dependency on a person is understandable, but a dependency on things is superstition. I don't believe that dear God will help singers give a good performance if they make the sign of the cross before every entrance but aren't prepared. It happened to me. In my grammar school in Germany, children who played instruments had to perform in little concerts from time to time, and I played piano. One time, I hadn't prepared anything, and I couldn't play a single piece without mistakes. Since I'd been raised to be very religious, I prayed to God fervently for his help the evening before, and again on the morning of the concert. Very calmly, and with great faith that I would have help from heaven, I sat down at the piano. But, behold, no help came. I stumbled over the keys, and was very embarrassed. The teacher said, "Christa, next time you must practice more!" I desperately wanted to hide, and I was mad at God for letting me down. But from then on, I knew I could only succeed by practicing, and I vowed to do it.

And I don't really believe that a cup of coffee before each performance of the Marschallin would have helped me, or a glass of Hi-C fruit drink would have made me sing Lady Macbeth any better. But I wasn't able to sing a lieder recital for years without drinking a glass of water with a fizzy tablet of vitamin C and calcium dissolved in it first. But I know these things are imagination. Because I felt good when I drank it the first time, I thought I needed it every time I sang.

Because I was always very nervous before *Fidelio*, I started taking a valium in the afternoon before a performance, but sometimes I'd forget. Later I would suddenly remember that I'd forgotten my tranquilizer, and then I just *had* to get nervous, because, of course, I knew I had to be nervous if I hadn't taken it. The old saying is true—it's all in the head! My nerves came from fear, which, in turn, came from insecurity. We singers never know how a performance will go. We can wake up in very good voice, but that's in the morning. Things could get worse before evening! It's also possible that we could be bothered by dust, dryness, or drafts on the stage. In any case, we only know for sure how we'll sing after we've sung!

Once I had a dependency that caused me great difficulty. One day in

Berlin in 1962, I received a letter from a stranger, who said that I would lose my voice very soon because my technique was totally wrong. The writer claimed that he was an astrologer, and he would be able to help me with advice and predictions. At first I didn't know what to do with this letter. I was annoyed, but I was also afraid, and, after some hesitation, I wrote back, and we met. He was a tall, gaunt man, with a sensitive face and very long, thin fingers, which made his hands look like rakes. He impressed me with his strange but strong personality, and he persuaded me that I absolutely had to study with him immediately if I didn't want to lose my voice. He also asked for the exact minute of my birth.

Suddenly I became dependent on this "spider" who said he knew about the voice and the stars. He had me vocalize on "nü-nü" with my tongue hanging out, and nothing else. Since I often sang at the Deutsche Oper Berlin in those days, he always got free tickets. He also charged high fees, and, worst of all, he prepared a daily horoscope for me. I'm sure you can imagine how I reacted when I had to sing my problem-child role of Fidelio and he gave me a bad horoscope for that day. Of course, I canceled the performance!

After I finished singing all my performances in Berlin, the "spider" insisted on coming home with us to Vienna, so my hanging-out nü-nü tongue wouldn't lose the good habits he had taught it. So I paid for his trip, he slept at our house, ate and drank with us, and continued to get paid a lot. He also went to the Vienna State Opera with my free tickets, and was of the opinion that my voice had already gotten a lot better, and that through him I would have a chance to sing longer than "the day after tomorrow." My then-husband Walter Berry was not taken in by all this, and the "spider" noticed, but didn't tell him anything about the early end that was coming for his voice. Now and then he gave Walter lessons, but Walter didn't need them because his voice is magnificently "placed" by nature, which is even obvious when he speaks.

When we returned to Berlin for more performances, we were astonished to find a one-page advertisement for the "spider" in the opera program, in which he praised himself as the voice teacher to whom even Christa Ludwig and Walter Berry came for help. Really, this was too much—using us for advertising without asking! Suddenly my eyes opened, and I saw the kind of power he had over me, and how he had played on my most vulnerable spot, namely, my fear of losing my voice. Thank God I was cured. I didn't sing "nü-nü" with my tongue hanging out anymore, but I did get hooked on astrology. True, I never again had a daily horoscope prepared, but only an annual one, and I was always astonished how accurate it was.

I believed in horoscopes for almost ten years, and tried to console myself with them and adjust myself to them. I know that I got caught up in these things because of the insecurity in my life. During the crisis years of my first marriage and then of my voice, I was addicted to questioning the stars and blaming them, of course. For me it was easier to know that it wasn't my fault when something was troubling in my life, but only the fault of the stars. Certainly it wouldn't hurt to be careful when the stars were in a bad aspect. Perhaps I could avoid a lot of difficulty. So I thought it might be of some use to ask the stars. Over the years I lost this belief, as I became more secure. But it's very difficult to be cool, calm, and collected, and to criticize yourself and change faults into virtues, without help. To make your way, you have to leap over many obstacles on the "road of life," until you reach your goal, or until you realize that the road itself is the goal.

Travel

How wonderful it is to travel! But only for a few years. People say that one good thing about the singing profession is that you can see and experience the whole world. But can you? What have I seen? Airports, the roads into town, hotels, concert halls, and opera houses. What else? I was in Japan several times—how fabulous it sounds! But I saw nothing in Tokyo except the Hotel Imperial and the Nissei Theater. I had a ticket to fly to Kyoto, the imperial city, but I caught a head cold and ended up staying in the hotel in Tokyo. Only towards the very end of my career, when I was in Japan for a concert, was I able to see more of the country and its culture, which I love very much.

Once with Walter Berry and our son, I made a real trip at the end of a guest appearance in Buenos Aires. We wanted to see South America, so we visited Machu Picchu and Lake Titicaca. My young son Wolfi, unseen by us, ate an unpeeled apple, got a stomach virus, and then couldn't cope with the altitude at La Paz. The poor little guy had to endure the trip with an oxygen mask and antibiotics. But it was still a great experience! I would like to see the Grand Canyon once, but, otherwise, I don't care to travel anymore, because

I've been traveling ever since I started singing. At first I only made short trips within Germany, but gradually my trips grew longer and longer, climaxing in a 29-hour flight to Buenos Aires, when we still used propeller planes. Japan is also a very long flight. Sometimes I traveled by boat for the rest and to adjust more easily to the time differences. A few times I sailed to North America, and also once to South America and back, and that was an unforgettable experience. I remember the warm mist as we crossed the equator. But the games we played on board were stupid, as was the crossing-the-equator cere- mony. I traveled very elegantly in luxury class because the trip was paid for by the Teatro Colón in Buenos Aires. Though there were almost no passengers, there were ten waiters around the table at mealtimes. Caviar, pâté de foie gras—all these wonderful foods for only seven passengers! I was spoiled, and I came home ten pounds heavier.

In 1966 the whole household—which meant my mother, Wolfi, a secre- tary, and a cook—traveled with Walter Berry and me to New York. We had 23 big suitcases, not counting "carry-on" bags. After all, we would be staying in New York for six months. This was something like the Israelites moving out of Egypt. In Vienna we rented a small truck to go to the train station, and in the train we had four sleeping compartments, and one was only for suitcases. In this manner, we traveled to Paris and from there on to Cherbourg, where we were to embark by ship for New York. But in Paris we had to change stations. The Parisian porter didn't believe his eyes, but he helped us to find another truck which transported the suitcases, while we traveled by taxi. When we arrived at the other Paris station, there was no truck to be seen, and our train to Cherbourg was scheduled to leave shortly. We grew more and more worried as we looked at the clock. And none of us could speak French! Where were our suitcases? Just before the train departed, they finally came. Quickly we got on the train—with all 23 suitcases—and hoped nothing was missing.

The boat to New York was delayed for several hours in Cherbourg. Since our son was only seven years old, he had to be entertained. We searched for a toy. Eating and drinking would have shortened the wait, but there was only one shabby cafeteria. Finally we were allowed to board. Now where could we put all our luggage? The cabins were much too small for us *and* 23 suitcases, so we had to send most of them off to the baggage room. But in which suitcases were the clothes we had bought to wear aboard ship? Of course, we had to dress differently for lunch and dinner, sometimes even in formal evening clothes. On the ship one could only appear in traveling clothes the first night.

Finally we got everything sorted, had dinner, and fell into bed dead tired. Well, not quite. The beds turned out to be our biggest problem. They were very narrow, and I actually fell out of bed during the first night. So I put a mattress on the floor, and there I slept better. Overall, the crossing itself was wonderful, but the arrival in New York! Every—yes, every—suitcase belonging to the passengers was opened and searched by customs officials. We waited for hours and hours to get through customs. And then we had to find another truck for the suitcases. On the trip back, we went through the same thing in reverse. These are trips one doesn't forget easily!

Shorter trips from one concert to another by car or plane also brought surprises: an unexpected snowstorm, lightning outside the plane, canceled flights, hour-long waits in the airport, sitting inside of snowed-in trains. These are the joys of concert travel! Then, when you arrive very late and dog-tired at a hotel, often they've given away your room because the management didn't think you were coming. By the time you get a room, the restaurant has closed. Is there 24-hour room service? No, the kitchen is closed. Or, if the plane is on time, your suitcases have probably landed in another city. That happened to me once in Amsterdam: no evening gown, no nightgown, no toothbrush. And no music for the concert, either. From such experiences I learned to carry the most important things, if they weren't too heavy, in carry-on bags.

At the beginning, I enjoyed these trips, and gladly put up with all the difficulties. But then one day, I had enough, and dreamed only of staying in one place for at least three months.

For a while we had an apartment in Gran Canaria, because there the weather is very nice, and the climate is the same all year. A doctor advised me to live in such a place, where the weather is less changeable, because of my migraines. For this, Gran Canaria was ideal, but then I always had to make long flights to get to my concerts. And Iberia employees, just like those of Air France and Alitalia, go on strike a lot. It was always a nightmare for me when I had to stay overnight in Madrid, instead of continuing my journey, because the connecting flight had been canceled. Or the airline would overbook the flight, and I would simply be told: "Your seat has been sold!" Unfortunately, I didn't know enough Spanish to complain.

Once I had to fly to Frankfurt for a live interview on television. I had my credit card in my hand baggage, and no cash except for a few marks, because I expected to fly back immediately. There was a good connection from Las Palmas to Valencia, and then I would continue my journey on the same plane to Frankfurt. I arrived in Valencia on the 14th of July, and this time Iberia wasn't on strike, but Air France. The air space above Marseilles was closed, and we were locked in a waiting room for several hours. No one knew what was going to happen, and I was sitting on the floor because there weren't enough chairs. Finally we were told that we would have to stay overnight in Valencia, but my live interview in Frankfurt was scheduled for that same evening, and I had no way of getting there in time. It was Saturday, everything was closed, and I had no Spanish money. I used my credit card to make a phone call and cancel, and to buy a ticket back to Gran Canaria. Finally, I arrived home twenty hours later without having accomplished anything. I really got fed up with such adventures!

The Men in
My Life

Better Every Day

In 1971, I met "Er–den Herrlichsten von allen" (He—the most magnificent of all), as it is so nicely put in Schumann's *Frauenliebe und leben*. That January, I was still very depressed after my divorce from Walter Berry in June of 1970. Reluctant and unprepared, and with a severe head cold, I flew to New York for the rehearsals of the French opera *Werther* by Jules Massenet at the Met. I had to sing Charlotte without knowing French, and I hadn't even studied the part yet! An unfamiliar opera, conductor (Alain Lombard), stage director, and even an unfamiliar ensemble, since my Werther was to be Franco Corelli, a singer I knew only from attending his performances as a member of the public and from the recording of *Norma* I made with him and Maria Callas.

But then I went to the first stage rehearsal "und sah ihm in die Augen" (and looked him in the eyes, as Isolde says), namely my stage director Paul-Emile Deiber. I thought, "This can't be happening. I'm a mature woman. How can I fall head over heels in love with a man I've never met before?" And how could I fall in love with my stage director—I, the one who always attached great importance to avoiding "hanky-panky" with the conductors and stage directors I worked with? Franco Corelli was not at all thrilled when Paul-Emile showed him over and over again how to hug me passionately. Paul-Emile was also very patient with my lack of knowledge of the French language, offered to work with me in private—and then we got married! At the age of 43, I got to know not only French culture, something previously unknown to me, but also the huge differences between being an actor and being a singer. By the way, I didn't know when we met that my stage director, and soon-to-be husband, was also an actor at the Comédie-Française.

For actors, the stress is definitely on "play," while for us poor singers it's more on "work." I envied Paul-Emile so, because he could play tennis in the morning before an evening performance, have supper with friends after the performance, and then act again the next day. I loved to see him play Cyrano de

Bergerac or King Lear on stage, and I was amazed to hear him use rhythm in his speeches to color the words, just as a singer would do, which, of course, is easier in French than in German. My favorite role of his was the Beggar (who might also be a god) in *Elektra* by Jean Giraudoux. The text he spoke connected so harmoniously with his character that I was very impressed. It was a joy for me to be kidnapped away from music to the theater by him for awhile. In addition, I was incredibly lucky that Paul-Emile is a music lover and music expert, who played the violin when he was a boy and always went to hear performances at the Paris Opera, in the standing room, of course. He owned all my records because he was a fan before we met. He knows a lot more about music than I do because for the most part, I mostly know only the music I sang.

Paul-Emile's knowledge of music and understanding of singers made him decide to become an opera director. He knew that actors could express themselves with both speech and body language without restriction, while singers are always subservient to what the music requires. The art of singing takes precedence. Body movement and positioning on stage must be in harmony with the music, but they are secondary. This is what Paul-Emile kept in mind when he directed opera. He aimed to serve the work, and direct the singers in the spirit of the music. He wasn't one of those directors who stage themselves instead of the piece, and who sometimes don't even know the piece they are staging. He always stood as a mediator between the score and the singers, and also between the conductor and the singers, in order to achieve the best possible result both dramatically and musically.

Now we have been married for more than 25 years, and every day our life together gets better. He, the poor man, had no idea what it was like to live with a singer. With tolerance and kindness, he always gave me the peace I needed and encouraged me, but also stopped me from taking on engagements I hadn't thought through completely. Whenever time allowed, he listened to me with "long ears" and was a good critic. Certainly I had to travel alone a lot, especially in the years when he managed a theater in Paris. But when I needed him, as friend and advisor, he was there to ease the burden of traveling and being alone, especially in the last years when I sang.

Paul-Emile and I met at an age when people are more tolerant of their life partners and don't want to change them. We didn't want to repeat the mistakes we had made in our previous marriages (instead we made other mistakes). But I believe that no singer, and especially not me, really wants to live alone, even though privacy is as important to us as bread. We singers need to relax and renew our strength. We need to feel safe and to feel the warmth of human contact and have an understanding partner, but we also want to be alone when we have that certain thick feeling in our throats, and we don't want to speak or interact. However, it isn't possible for singers to call on their partners only now and then when it suits them. For this reason, singers have to have partners with an instinct for knowing when they are welcome and when it's better for them to withdraw. And this instinct has its roots in love.

My Silent Wife
by Paul-Emile Deiber

The human voice—it's the most beautiful instrument in the world, that's certain! But it's an instrument whose use demands great human effort. This effort is ignored by members of the public who come to an opera or a recital with terribly strict standards created by listening to recordings.

A recording and its perfection are the fruits of long hours of work and patience before a microphone, as well as a recording console. The mood, the communication among the participants, the recording technology and its influence, all play a part. For one reason or another, this passage will be redone tomorrow, that note will be improved, if someone or other has the impression that it can be done better. The director, sound engineer, and technicians get together to create a montage since they have the leisure to choose among several versions, taking one measure here, one measure there, changing—if necessary—the color of a passage or a single note. The result, obviously, is often close to perfection, technically, at least; but the rest is a matter of taste and leaves the door wide open for controversy.

And it's an ear used to this kind of perfection that's taken to a concert or an opera!

Permit me to draw attention to the conditions that surround the human instrument that we are talking about. And, to understand the problem, a comparison might be helpful. Yehudi Menuhin cherishes his violin like a child; he takes very good care of it. I've seen the great virtuoso get into a car and refuse to let the chauffeur take his precious instrument. Yes! Menuhin, kept his violin on his knees for a trip of a good half-hour. And yet the case was firmly closed, padded also, and the instrument protected from shocks and changes in temperature. What's more, for a long trip, a special box will cover the case, and the strings are loosened.

The singer is, at the same time, both the instrument and the virtuoso. To take care of his voice is to take care of himself. He has to protect himself (retire into his case), avoid all unnecessary fatigue, shun all dangerous contacts, and refrain from any unnecessary use of his precious cords. By the way, do you know that these two little cords, capable of drowning out the orchestra of a Wagner or Verdi, are no longer than twelve millimeters and are only as thick as a woolen thread?

These few facts should be enough to destroy the detestable legend of the capricious diva, but let's go on a little further and look at the motivations of our idols.

If Placido Domingo doesn't sing Otello tomorrow, it's because he knows he can't do it. And if Jessye Norman cancels a series of appearances at the Met, it's because she feels that her performances risk not being on the same high level as her reputation. The decision of these two is not taken by chance or by caprice, but by listening to their consciences (listening to their voices, should I say?) and out of respect for the public. And when a singer is indisposed, he suffers through a terrible war of nerves, where doubt and uncertainty alternate with waiting in hope of total recovery. An ordinary flu—cured by staying in bed for three or four days, and leaving a normal person tired for only a week—means no work at all for a singer for an entire month. Winter means permanent danger, and forces the singer to avoid public places: restaurants, theaters, cinemas, not to mention smoky nightclubs.

All these precautions have a sound basis: the singer wants his voice (his instrument, his daily bread) to last. And he knows—and this deserves to be considered also—that it will not last as long as he. How many famous voices have we known that disappeared after a very short career! Many actors still walk the boards after they are 80, even until they are 90 years old. But singers? Short careers are very frequent, so it's important to reach an international level as quickly as possible. And for that five years of study are indispensable, followed by five years of singing all around the world. If luck decides to be his ally, our singer will reach his goal, and then he must maintain his reputation. At each engagement, he must not only give his best, but more. His performance must equal his previous triumphs or the perfection of his recordings, which may have won prizes the previous year and been unanimously praised by the critics.

"Love your profession, it's the most beautiful in the world." With these words, Debureau addressed his son in a famous piece by Sacha Guitry. Do those who possess the most beautiful instrument in the world also consider their profession the most beautiful? Only a yes-and-no answer seems valid. Yes, when they think of the joy of singing for an audience which shouts its satisfaction and cheers endlessly. No, when they think of the sacrifices that giving such a performance requires.

And here the memories flood into my mind. It's impossible to forget the premiere of *Frau ohne Schatten*, a certain *Rosenkavalier*, *Les Troyens*, triumphant lieder recitals at Avery Fisher or Carnegie Hall. But I also see myself arriving at the Met for the premiere of *Werther*. Horrors! It's twenty minutes to eight, and I'm dragged into Franco Corelli's dressing room. I find him in costume and completely made up, but he doesn't want to sing! He doesn't want to, or he can't! Stage fright? Warmed up his voice too much in the last hour? Quickly we send a message into the auditorium for the charming Enrico di Giuseppe, and we throw him onto the stage. And he sings, and very well. A miracle! But what a life!

Should I tell you about the daily visits to the throat specialist? About microwave treatments of the larynx, after which a singer is forbidden to speak for several hours? And the sun? Forbidden: might swell the vocal cords. Swimming? Not recommended: chlorine might dry out the mucous membranes. Sport? Dangerous: one might breathe in cold air, which could lead to an infected windpipe.

So what's left? What does a singer have to do to sing well, to be in voice and give the dear audience what it expects? Well, here it is: Three days before the concert, he must retreat and live the life of a Carmelite or a Trappist. In his hotel room he will read, watch television, listen to the radio (knit or embroider if our singer is a diva). He won't smoke (that goes without saying), and he won't receive anyone, conversation being the worst danger. These precautions taken, he has a chance to reach his ultimate goal (for a tenor that's called the high C). And, after all his efforts, no thoughts of a late dinner in town or attending a few society parties (see above).

This is the life of the "Schweigsame Frau" (nothing to do with the "silent wife" in the opera by Richard Strauss!). I have forgotten to say that I write these lines because Christa Ludwig did me the honor of giving me her hand 25 years ago. Yes, I married a "silent woman," but I'm not complaining about it—oh, no! I was her admirer before I met her, and I still am. I also know that she imposed this silence on herself, and has suffered because of it. So I want her to speak finally, because she adores talking, and loves her family and friends. We need her to speak to us now, after she has sung for us.

Yes, dear Molière, I'm a fool, as you have Sganarelle suggest in *Le Médecin malgré lui*. I no longer want my wife to be silent!

From Wolfi to Wolfgang

When I was 14, my school class helped out at a day care center and kindergarten for a month, so we could learn how to take care of babies and handle small children. I was very enthusiastic about this because I didn't have any brothers or sisters at home, and I thought that this experience would help me be a good mother. My dearest wish was to have a child of my own someday, and I particularly wanted a son. I preferred the naïve little Adams to the "eternal Eves."

When I began singing, my goal was to have a child by the time I was thirty. Many years later, I met Walter Berry in Vienna when we were both singing in *Carmen* and *Le Nozze di Figaro*, and we fell in love. Since both of us were single, I thought, "OK, now I can get married and have a child," and I achieved my goal at the very last minute. My son was born on the 4th of March 1959, and I turned 31 twelve days later.

We decided to call our son Wolfgang, but I don't remember whether it was after Goethe or Mozart. Of course I wanted to nurse my baby according to the latest thinking, and that was whenever he was hungry. But little Wolfi was almost always hungry. I had hardly closed my eyes to rest when he woke up and was very lively. As long as I didn't have to work, I could live with this "schedule," but when I started to sing again, we had to hire a nanny.

Wolfi's nanny quickly brought order to our laid-back lifestyle. Everything was done according to a strict schedule, and she chased us away from the baby's bed because we were full of germs from the street! After a year she left us, since she only took care of very small babies, and after her, Wolfi had a string of nannies. One of these plunged him in cold bath water, and for months after she left, he would scream bloody murder whenever he saw a bathtub. While another was on the phone with a friend, Wolfi hung upside down in his baby swing. A third fed him chocolate constantly, so that he was a connoisseur who preferred Lindt chocolate exclusively by the time he was two years old. Shocked by these experiences, my mother decided to give up her position as Professor of Voice at the Vienna Musikakademie and take care of Wolfi herself. My own wish to be a good mother was sidetracked by the demands of my profession.

Walter and I had to travel constantly. When we would come home and ask Wolfi, "Where's daddy?" and "Where's mommy?", he would point at the pictures on the wall and say, "That's daddy" and "That's mommy." He didn't recognize us at all. When he wanted to play with me, I often couldn't speak because I soon had to sing at a rehearsal or a performance. When he had a cold, I couldn't be with him. Because of all these things, I missed out on a lot. Suddenly he could sit, then stand, then walk. My mother faithfully wrote down what he said for us, and all the new words he learned, but I only knew these things secondhand.

Certainly it must have been difficult for Wolfi to understand his singer-mother when he was a small child. Why doesn't she speak? Why does she make signs with her hands? Why does she write notes on pads all the time? Why is she always whistling? One whistle for yes, two whistles for no, and even a whole whistle-sentence! What does she mean, "Mommy has to sing tonight, and that's why she can't speak to you"?

When Wolfi was at school, he often complained that neither his father nor his mother came to school gatherings. I only saw him once in a fairy tale play. We weren't there when he graduated from the American School in Vienna, and we weren't there when he received his Austrian Matura. Only his grandmother went. My mother even played soccer with him. It's true that Walter took him skiing a few times, but usually we just weren't home, and this was very sad for both Wolfi and us.

It's very difficult to know if it's better to practice a profession or bring up a child. My mother always chose to take care of Wolfi, and, in the end, I chose to practice my profession. But that didn't mean that Wolfi and I had no relationship. True, that relationship always seemed a bit distant, but I never felt that we were disconnected. And when we're together now, it's wonderful, and I'm happy that I have a child.

I probably blame myself unjustly if I say that I wasn't a good mother, especially because of the way other singers bring up their children. I once read an interview with a famous Italian singer who said that she herself is a wonderful mother, and that her husband and child come first, and singing last. When I met her and asked where her child was, she said "in boarding school"!

I was very fortunate that my mother was always what we call in German a "Tiger-Mother"—very protective and caring—and she was the same for my son. For me, the most important thing is to teach a child not to be afraid of other people. And one must be honest with children, and tell them the truth. All other ideas about child rearing are a matter of fashion. Often more value is placed on teaching children how to hold a cup of tea or greet someone than on teaching them how to be decent people with honest hearts.

But my son Wolfgang grew up like a prince. He had everything he wanted because his parents always felt guilty that they weren't with him. Because he lived with my mother in a big house in Klosterneuburg, just outside of Vienna, he always had a lot of servants. Everything was brought to him, and his room kept tidy. All he needed to do was throw his things down somewhere, and someone would pick them up for him. That probably explains a lot of his personal habits today. He was always driven to school by a chauffeur, because the American School was in Saalmannsdorf and there was no school bus and my mother couldn't drive. He was a bit embarrassed by this because the other boys and girls were brought to school by one of their parents, and only he had a chauffeur. He didn't like it when people said, "Your driver is coming!"

Walter and I divorced when Wolfgang was still quite young, and he coped with it well. Later he figured out how to play us off against each other. If one parent said no when he wanted a moped or a car, then the other one would surely say yes. I always kept the house in Klosterneuburg for my mother and my son, so Wolfgang could grow up in the surroundings he was used to.

My mother thought that every child should start to play the piano at the age of six. But Wolfgang didn't like this idea at all, and it was impossible to get him to sit at a piano. He preferred the guitar, so we bought him one along with lessons at a conservatory. Every morning he practiced the guitar from seven to half past seven, before leaving for school. Then one day when I was in America, he called me and said, "Could you please bring me an electric guitar, a Gibson?" So I bought a Gibson, even though I didn't know exactly what it was. With this Gibson, I went through customs, and, of course, the customs officer asked, "Did you buy that in America?" I said, "No, no, this is my Gibson, I'm a guitarist, a jazz guitarist." So I was allowed to take it with me without tax, and Wolfgang got his first Gibson.

Later my son started a band with friends. This group of young people assembled their huge pieces of equipment in our house and made a terrible noise, until the neighbors complained. And no one spoke when they sat at the lunch table. Instead they wore their headphones and swayed in time to the music, while devouring twenty Wiener schnitzel. But because they were all teenagers, I thought to myself, better noise and schnitzel than drugs, until we got over this difficult (and very noisy) period.

Also, as many parents know, teenagers like to look "different," with strange hairdos and odd clothes. Once I took Wolfgang (he had outgrown Wolfi) to a premiere at the Salzburg Festival, and he wanted to wear "his" clothes because his "good suit" itched. "So just go like that, then," I said to him, and we were quite a strange-looking couple. I was in a big evening gown, and he was dressed as a hippie. The next day, after seeing everyone dressed up at the festival, he told me he thought that maybe it would have been better to wear a suit after all. I believe that children should make their own decisions in small things, like what to wear. To me the inner natures of children are what's important, and helping them develop characters that make them honest, strong, and courageous. The exterior things are unimportant. I was happy to see how Wolfgang developed as a person with his own views, and our contact is, and always has been, open and honest.

Very early, Wolfgang had his own taste in everything. What we, his parents, suggested to him, he tried out politely, and rejected whatever didn't suit him. Opera was an example. When he was twelve, he came to a dress rehearsal of *Lohengrin* in which Mommy and Daddy were singing, but he wasn't very interested, and only asked afterwards, "Why didn't daddy kill the golden knight immediately? Then we could have all gone home early!" Later when he was about twenty, I asked him if he wanted to come to my last performance of Lady Macbeth. His pithy reply was "But, you know, I heard you in that already."

After he graduated from the American School, he passed his Austrian Matura easily, and studied psychology for a while at the university. But he soon decided that what he wanted was to make music.

At twenty, he began to live on his own, even though he never managed to live on the money that we gave him every month. I think it took him about eight days to run out, and after that he would only eat noodles. Certainly it was a good thing that he left home and lived independently, so he could learn to take care of himself, until he started to earn his own money. But this period of readjustment was difficult for him. Although he knew that his parents made a good living in their profession, he didn't understand how much hard work was involved because we didn't tell him this when he was a child. We worked at home, and he always heard us singing, but for him singing wasn't work. It was fun, a joy.

Wolfgang has a totally different kind of talent than his parents. He has a beautiful bass-baritone voice, like his father, and he studied singing first with my mother, then in the conservatory. But he had a problem. He always wanted to be like his parents, but he learned too much about technique from us, and always wanted to sing everything correctly from a technical point of view. This focus on the technical robbed him of a certain spontaneity in his singing. But he has other talents. He can compose music, and write lyrics. He also has a great sense of humor, which he probably inherited from his father. He is very quick-witted, and likes puns. These talents are very useful in his profession as a composer of musicals, and he also writes songs and slogans for commercials.

The tolerance that I showed for Wolfgang's individuality has been rewarded, especially since, with time, he has come to understand my profession and its difficulties. Today it fascinates me to see how baby Wolfi has become Wolfgang the man, with his own personality. He has found himself in his profession, which is simply different from that of his parents. He makes a totally different kind of music than the music he always heard at home when he was a child. He has even taken a different first name, Mark, which he likes better than the one we gave him.

Wolfgang and his wife Johanna, who is Dutch by birth, have a son, Kevin. Since both Wolfgang and his wife went to the American School in Vienna, they speak mostly English at home, and their whole way of life is a bit American. Their son is also going to the American School, which is a wonderful place for children to grow up and to learn, and Kevin is being raised "internationally." But instead of living in New York, Los Angeles, or San Francisco, they have chosen Vienna. Anyone who understands Viennese charm, as they do, knows that Vienna is a wonderful city to live in.

Whistler Mother
by *Wolfgang Berry*

My mother has a rare gift for making herself understood. While people in her situation might use too many words, she reduced her communication to a few whistles, or, if paper was handy, to fragments of whistle-thoughts written in big, not-to-be-misunderstood letters. As a child I had difficulty reading these whistle-thoughts at first, despite the large print, so I grew up hearing a lot of clever whistling from my mother.

My whistler mother cleverly combined tragic melodies with cheerful, playful tunes, in order to let me know her opinion in as legato a way as possible. Because I wasn't adept at the great art of serious whistling myself, I was limited to the direct, rather banal way of communicating known as speaking.

Since my mother sang more than she whistled, and sang more than she talked, I was always hoping to be sung to once in a while. I was very disappointed when my grandmother Jenny explained to me that "singing is worst thing for the voice"!

That knowledge didn't give me any peace. Perhaps if my mother changed her profession from singer to whistler, she might be able to sing something for me at home sometime, because I liked to hear her sing.

I learned to read her.

Crisis and
Change

Stages: A Hesse Poem

Probably everyone has a big crisis in their lives, often when they are about 40 years old. Professionally, you have crawled up the mountain, and, as Wozzeck says, "Es schwindelt einen, wenn man hinunterschaut" (One gets dizzy, when one looks down). You see how easily you can fall. Suddenly you live more consciously and start to question yourself, your profession, and your success, and you start to doubt yourself.

> Die Zeit, die ist ein sondebar Ding.
> Wenn man so hinlebt, ist sie rein gar nichts.
> Aber dann auf einmal, da spürt man nichts als sie.

> [Time is a strange thing.
> As one lives from day to day, time means nothing at all.
> But then suddenly, one is aware of nothing else.]

So says the Marschallin in *Rosenkavalier*, and it probably happens to everyone something like that. Suddenly you pay more attention to time and its passing, and negative thoughts day after day build to a crisis. Clever sayings like "If life hands you a lemon, make lemonade" don't help at all. Hermann Hesse talks about these times of crisis and change in his poem "Stufen,"[3] and I'd like to quote it here because it means a lot to me:

> Wie jede Blüte welkt und jede Jugend
> Dem Alter weicht, blüht jede Lebensstufe,

---

[3] "Stufen" [Stages] appears in *Das Glasperlenspiel*, 1943. The English translation provided here is literal. For another translation, see *The Glass Bead Game*, tr. Richard and Clara Winston, New York, 1969.

Blüht jede Weisheit und auch jede Tugend
Zu ihrer Zeit und darf nicht ewig dauern.

[As every flower withers and every youth grows old, so every stage of life, every wisdom, and also every virtue flourishes for a time and may not last forever.]

Es muß das Herz bei jedem Lebensrufe
Bereit zum Abschied sein und Neubeginne,
Um sich in Tapferkeit und ohne Trauern
In andre, neue Bindungen zu geben,
Und jedem Anfang wohnt ein Zauber inne,
Der uns beschützt und der unds hilft, zu leben.

[The heart must at every call from life be ready to depart and begin anew, with courage and without remorse go into other, fresh relationships, and every beginning contains a magic, which protects us and helps us to live.]

Wir sollen heiter Raum um Raum durchschreiten,
An keinem wie an einer Heimat hängen,
Der Weltgeist will nicht fesseln uns und engen,
Er will uns Stuf' um Stufe heben, weiten.

[We should cheerfully walk from room to room, cling to nothing like a home; the World Spirit does not want to fetter and limit us, it will lift and broaden us stage by stage.]

Kaum sind wir heimisch einem Lebenskreise
Und traulich eingewohnt, so droht Erschlaffen;
Nur wer bereit zu Aufbruch ist und Reise,
Mag lähmender Gewöhnung sich entraffen.

[Scarcely are we settled into a routine and comfortably accustomed to our surroundings, but that weakness threatens; only one who is ready to break away and travel, may strike out against paralyzing habit.]

Es wird vielleicht auch noch die Todessstunde
Uns neuen Räumen jung entgegensenden,
Des Lebens Ruf an uns wird niemals enden...
Wohlan denn, Herz, nimm Abschied und gesunde!

[Perhaps even the hour of death may send us to new, fresh rooms. Life's call to us will never end.... Come then, heart, say farewell and be strong!]

But if you are in the very bottom of a deep trough between two waves, no piece of literature helps, no matter how wise it is, nor does the well-meaning advice of friends (if you still have any). You have to pull yourself out of the bog by your own pigtail like Münchhausen did once upon a time.

Anatomy of a Vocal Crisis

My crisis hit me very suddenly. Well, perhaps not all that suddenly, when I think back. It was more like a glass of water that "suddenly" overflowed.

In December 1971, I suffered a burst capillary, which means that a small blood vessel broke on one of my vocal cords. It was caused by my repeating Kundry's screams too many times for a recording of *Parsifal*. This was apparently the start of all my misery, but it was quickly forgotten at the time after a short rest period.

About eight months later, after singing *Das Lied von der Erde* with Karajan in Salzburg, I went to Munich to take part in an opera gala at the Summer Olympics. I rehearsed the aria and duet from *Samson et Dalila* with James King and orchestra, and the next day I was scheduled to rehearse again for a television broadcast. But what a shock I had the next morning. I woke up completely voiceless, even though my voice had been in great shape the previous day. I immediately went to Dr. Bötte, a throat doctor at the clinic of the famous laryngologist Dr. Zimmermann at the Starnberger See. He told me that there was bleeding on one of my vocal cords, and I needed to rest for at least a week, and I shouldn't speak either. I had to cancel the beautiful opera gala, and I bought an erasable writing tablet like children use, so that I wouldn't have to speak at all. Try it! Try not to speak a word when you're not alone at home. It's terrible! No one could read my handwriting, or understand my sign language. It was very upsetting. One evening I sadly watched my colleagues on TV at the opera gala. This was really bad luck! Also financially it was difficult, because I'd already bought a painting at a gallery for the fee I had expected to earn. I still do this today, by the way—I spend money I haven't earned yet.

After a little more than a week, my voice was fine again, and I flew to Edinburgh to sing *Das Lied von der Erde* with Karajan at the festival there. Everything went well, and the memory of the bleeding faded from my mind. Soon after, in the fall, I started rehearsals in Paris for a new production of *Frau ohne Schatten*. My first big mistake was not being careful enough with my still very sensitive vocal cords and putting them through the strain of singing the Dyer's Wife, a role that was really too high for me. But it's easy to say this afterwards. At first, everything went wonderfully. No problems. The cast was the same as at the Met, and the production was again a great success for all of us, partly because this was the first time the opera was done in Paris. But during the last performance, something terrible happened. While I was singing in the last act, a note broke quite dreadfully, and afterwards I could only "sing" one octave lower very quietly, really not audibly, until the end. I didn't think it was a burst capillary, only that my voice wasn't in very good shape that day.

Next came my second big mistake. I didn't go to a throat doctor because the one I trusted and who knew me, Dr. Kürsten, was in Vienna, and I was simply too lazy to fly there. I preferred to fly to my husband Paul-Emile in Geneva, where he was staging an opera. We had a few beautiful days together, and I thought my hoarseness would soon end. It was Christmas time, and I was happy with the presents which I had bought for my family in Vienna, where I always spent Christmas day with my mother and my son.

Finally I traveled to Vienna, and went to see Dr. Kürsten, who said that the changed color of one of my vocal cords could be related to bleeding. Because he didn't know what had happened in Munich six months before, he told me just not to sing or speak, and everything would soon be fine again. I should explain who Dr. Kürsten is. He's not merely my throat doctor, but my psychologist-throat doctor, a specialist to whom singers come from all over the world. We often meet in his office, where the waiting room walls are covered with beautiful photographs of smiling singers from all the world in their most famous roles, all of them "poor devils," I often think, because we wouldn't be at the doctor's office if we didn't have problems. And because Dr. Kürsten has treated the same singers for many years, he knows exactly how this one or that one reacts, which parts they can still sing with minor problems, and which they can't. He also comes to singers' dressing rooms during a performance, "holds their hands," and possibly gives them a small "oil change," which means he puts a drop of oil on their vocal cords to make them more supple. He always takes the time to explain to each individual exactly what, where, and why, and—this is very important—he has no inhibitions at all about telling the opera management that his patient can't sing that day. It doesn't matter how much the management insists that a singer must sing to save the performance. He remains adamant. It's thanks to him that I sang as long as I did, and that I succeeded in some very risky vocal "adventures" without too much damage.

Also in New York there was another such "singer's doctor" Dr. Reckford. Actually his name in Vienna, where he first practiced, was Rechnitzer. Most of his family died in concentration camps, but he was lucky and immigrated to New York. He told me that Americans couldn't pronounce Rechnitzer, so he thought that Rech sounds like Reck in English and the nitzer "muß fort" (had to go). Since "fort" sounds like "ford," he called himself Reckford.

Dr. Reckford told me a wonderful story about how singers wear blinders like racehorses, figuratively, and often don't care about anything else but their voices. On the day that Hitler marched into Vienna on March 13, 1938, he was treating a cantor in his office on the Opernring just as Hitler and his troops were going by. He had to allow the space in his windows to be used for "cheering" without charge because he was Jewish, while others could sell their window space. The cantor was complaining that he could sing all the notes well except one. Dr. Reckford, who was then still Dr. Rechnitzer, said to him, "Why do you care about one note? How do you know that you'll be allowed to sing at all in the synagogue now? Don't you know what is happening on the street? Aren't you worried about what Hitler and the Nazis are going to do to us?" The cantor looked very worried and replied, "Yes, Doctor, that is really terrible, but why do you think I can sing all the notes, except one?"

Dr. Reckford was a singer's doctor of the old school, with very old medical equipment. When I came to his office for the first time, I was shocked at seeing these obsolete dinosaurs in his examining room; but, in spite of them, he could still tell what was wrong with us singers very well. He treated not only singers from the Met, but also stars from Broadway musicals. He had a loud, beautiful bass voice, and his laugh was really a roar. He had studied singing himself, and played the piano brilliantly. He also knew which parts singers could still sing with small physical problems, and which they couldn't sing at all, and he would come to the opera in the evening to hear with "long ears" how his patients were doing, and possibly "drop some oil." After a misunderstanding, I stayed away from his office for a while, which, by the way, was my third big mistake during my vocal crisis. Later, when he was very old, he only saw a few of his longtime patients, and he treated me just three days before his death. I was terribly shocked when I telephoned his office, and the operator said, "The doctor has passed away." But he had a merciful death. He died in his sleep.

After Christmas 1972 in Vienna, I flew to New York at the beginning of January, where I was scheduled to sing Lady Macbeth. When I was warming up in my apartment before a rehearsal, again a note broke off terribly, giving me a feeling similar to the one I had during the performance in Paris. After a short time, perhaps an hour, I was completely voiceless. Now I started to get very nervous. What was this? Why was this happening to me? What was wrong?

Since I had had a misunderstanding with Dr. Reckford, the Met management sent me to a famous specialist, Dr. Gould. In his waiting room, he had many photographs of celebrities hanging on the walls, not only singers, but also politicians, even John F. Kennedy. He had many small cell-like rooms, which looked like telephone booths, and in each one was a chair. He went from cell to cell, and when he came to mine, he didn't even say hello. He just looked in my throat and filmed my vocal cords. He didn't even ask me to moo, or meow. Not a peep! I waited for a while, and then an assistant came and told me that I wasn't allowed to sing, and I should come back in two weeks. I'm sure it's easy to understand that this doctor's visit was the one of biggest disappointments of my life. I received no guidelines about what I should do, no medication, nothing at all. Of course I didn't wait two weeks without knowing what was wrong with me. Instead I flew as quickly as possible to Vienna to "my" Dr. Kürsten. Naturally, I had to cancel Lady Macbeth, but the worst thing was the result of my examination, which showed that again a capillary had burst, and again my vocal cord was bleeding. That was in January 1973, and now many difficult months followed.

Without speaking, in my sleep, at breakfast, no matter when, my capillaries burst. On my vocal cords, I had a "tree" with delicate capillary "branches," and they all burst. I think that everyone can understand what something like this means when it happens to a singer. It's hell! With Dr. Kürsten, I went to the famous voice specialist Dr. Zimmermann at the Starnberger See, so that he could also look at my vocal cords with a microscope. Both doctors came to the same conclusion. Don't do anything. Wait. (Laser treatment didn't exist yet.) For God's sake, do nothing. Don't try to remove injured cells with injections, a treatment similar to the one used to cure varicose veins at that time.

"Do nothing? Will I ever be able to sing again? How long will it take?" Questions and more questions!

"Of course you'll be able to sing again, but we can't tell you when."
How could I live like this? My professional life was at its peak! First I had
to cancel all my engagements, which meant no income at all. And what
would I tell people? As Hilde Güden said to me once, singers can have all
kinds of illnesses, but they can never tell anyone that anything is wrong with
their voices, or it will be the end of everything. The uncertainty was terrible.
When would I be able to sing again, if at all?

I tried to sing now and then despite my illness. I made two recordings of
Schubert songs in 1973 and 1974 (accompanied by Irwin Gage) in between
episodes of burst capillaries, and my vocal cords began to bleed again after the
last session for a *Samson et Dalila* recording. It was a horrible time. My savings
started to melt away because my income stopped but my expenses didn't. If it
wasn't for the positive attitude of my mother and husband, I probably would
have stopped singing and changed professions, I was so desperate. The only
consolation was that, when I sang, the timbre of my voice sounded
unchanged and had not suffered from the scarring. To add to my misery, my
menopause came prematurely with all its unpleasantness, which every woman
understands. With a singer, menopause also influences the vocal cords. They
swell from the lack of estrogen, and one can't sing.

My troubles continued to multiply. In the aftermath of my divorce from
Walter Berry, I quickly lost more than 30 pounds, which certainly looked very
nice but wasn't very good for my health, and I developed a skin condition.
When I ran my fingers over any part of my body, immediately huge thick lines
appeared, which itched terribly. I now believe that my nerves, really my soul,
didn't only cry, but it screamed, and my sorrow manifested itself physically.

As consolation I always heard, "Be happy that you didn't get a stomach
ulcer, and that no capillaries burst in your brain." I read all kinds of wise books
and tried to find out why all this was happening to me. And all I read was that
everything was for the best. Now, when I look back, I believe that if I had
continued singing—fresh, happy, free, without problems—this and that part
at this or that opera house, I would never have had the time to find myself.
Only because of the enforced rest periods did I come to think clearly, and
finally master my nerves by learning autogenic relaxation techniques. I threw
away all my sleeping pills and tranquilizers, didn't take medication for everything so quickly anymore, and changed my diet. As my years of change started, I transformed the way I lived my life.

At the Salzburg Festival in the summer of 1974, I even dared to sing the
Dyer's Wife again. I was still a bit hesitant, but I sang much more carefully
than before, and scheduled more free days between performances. As with all

my engagements, I insisted that another singer share the performances with me, so that I wouldn't be the only Dyer's Wife available. But my problems with menopause increased. Back then the doctors didn't know much about how to treat these problems, and I was like a guinea pig. I received estrogen, but because I didn't want to have a hysterectomy, I bled for many, many weeks, which made me very weak.

The mistake that women and singers make is not talking about these problems. The subject is taboo, because a woman would be admitting that she is getting old. My mother had stopped singing long before menopause, so she couldn't give me any advice. My vocal cords were often swollen, and felt as if they were made of glass. They seemed extremely fragile whenever I wanted to sing.

All my problems reached a crisis at the Salzburg Festival in the summer of 1975, when I caused a scandal by canceling and leaving Salzburg abruptly. At the premiere of *Don Carlos* under Karajan, I sang Eboli, in spite of the fact that my voice was in bad shape, and I had great difficulties in the big aria "O don fatale." I was very shocked at my performance, and felt so bad physically and psychologically that I didn't think I could continue singing. I'm not the kind of person who wants to fight against an obstacle. I prefer to go around it. Besides, I was worn down by many months of continual problems. So I resigned myself to the idea of canceling, and traveled home in a state of panic.

Probably I hurt myself most by canceling. Whatever the newspapers wrote, and most of them weren't very friendly, didn't matter to me. But I returned home only half a person. I sat in a chair for hours, without thinking, without doing anything, but just staring into the air. Psychologically, I felt lower than I ever had before, even during all the past years of my crisis. But very, very slowly, I recovered. When I first started singing again, I preferred to stand far back on the stage, and I didn't sing any loud notes. I started to put all my big, strenuous roles aside, and I followed a policy of taking very small steps one at a time, and I tried, slowly but surely, to pull myself up again. If someone had told me back then that I would be singing for another twenty years, I would have laughed and shook my head in disbelief. But I changed my repertoire, didn't use my voice recklessly, considered my parts carefully, and canceled an evening whenever I didn't feel well, no matter what people said. I treated my vocal cords like a person whom I respected and took good care of. I managed to control my problems with menopause, and started to live a little more normally in private life. I found the strength for activities at home, and the harmony of my private life showed me that there are other, more important things than singing.

I didn't escape into private life, but I realized that life goes on after singing, and it would be terrible for me to find myself in an empty room after I retired, without knowing how to go on living. Looking back, I have to say that my years of crisis were a positive experience. They helped me as a person to find myself, and to recognize what is really important.

Singing Is Your Destiny

I probably would never have led the life I did without the influence of my mother. I really owe everything to her. Along with vocal technique, she taught me discipline, perseverance, diligence, and self-confidence. She also taught me to acknowledge other people's success without envy. She was an extremely strong person who always had a positive attitude towards life and a strong belief in God. She used to tell me: "You have received your talent from God; show your gratitude by doing everything to develop that talent. You have a duty to grow from a singer into an artist, and to give many people joy. This is your destiny. It doesn't matter what profession a person practices. He must always do his best."

My mother was firmly convinced that I had to hand on what I had been "given," whether it was by singing or through financial help, wherever weaker people needed it. For years my mother was the absolute center of the family; she gave singing lessons tirelessly, helped with advice and practical help in everyday things, and was the guiding spirit for my son Wolfgang. If she left the house when he was a small child, he would scream terribly. If I left the house, he hardly noticed.

For many years, she came to every one of my rehearsals and performances, criticizing with wit and intelligence, but in a strong, Prussian way, which often led to ill feeling with both of my husbands. Certainly she wanted to continue her career, which had ended prematurely, through me. But she also wanted to protect me from repeating the mistakes that she had made. She also felt this way about my private life. I should put all my energy into my profession, she would say, and put my profession before my private life. Because my father was a real macho pasha, his rule had been: "I come first, then comes Christa, then other things, and only after all this your singing." She couldn't use her talent to the fullest, and she wanted to protect me from this same fate. Certainly she did what she thought best, especially considering how poor we were after our house was bombed during the war and we lost everything. My talent was the only way we had to escape our poverty. We had to work hard, and leave nothing to chance. And according to her religious beliefs, my talent was not a matter of luck. Everything is pre-determined, and I had to fulfill my destiny. Because I'd been given this talent, I had to accept my destiny gratefully. So I took on all the hard work with great discipline, without looking left or right, and I followed the road before me.

My mother helped me develop discipline by her example, because she herself was very disciplined. She totally subordinated her life to mine in order to help me through any difficulties I had. She was also what we called "Prussian" back then. She didn't allow herself any personal comforts. In her nature, there were no "gray zones." Everything was black and white. "If something isn't absolutely true," she used to say, "then it's a lie!" Because of this attitude, she was often in a "clinch" with several people, since tolerance was quite foreign to her, and her lack of flexibility unfortunately became stronger with increasing age. She became like the lines say in "Auf dem Flusse" in Schubert's *Winterreise*: "Mit harter, starrer Rinde/Hast du dich überdeckt" (With hard, stiff crust/You have covered yourself).

I often wonder why people become so inflexible as they grow older. Everything can't be blamed on hardening of the arteries. My mother certainly was not senile. Perhaps we develop a fear at a certain age, earlier for some, later for others. We cling to opinions and convictions that we have collected throughout our lives and that we judge to be right, and we no longer have the courage to take up others. We stiffen like old trees, which break more easily than young, supple saplings. Until a few years before her death, my mother always lived with me, and we had a totally different relationship than just mother and daughter. Until the end, she was my "guru." Singers have very intimate relationships with their voice teachers because they have to be totally honest and open with them. Why is a singer tense? Why does he or she have a shaky tongue or voice? Why are they so overly nervous and frightened? A teacher must find out.

Along with teaching pure vocal technique, a voice teacher must also be a psychologist. For that the teacher has to know the student well, in order to always say the right words at the right time. Birgit Nilsson once said, "An

As Carmen in Otto Schenk's new production at the Vienna State Opera in February 1966

At concert that opened the Large Festival Hall in Salzburg with Leontyne Price and Herbert von Karajan in July 1960

During rehearsals for *Tristan und Isolde* at the Salzburg Easter Festival in March 1972 with Kurt Moll (second from left) and Karajan (far right)

Rehearsing a "tension triangle" for Ortrud and Elsa (Anja Silja) in the Wieland Wagner production of *Lohengrin* at the Deutsche Oper, Berlin in December 1961

Joke photo made at Bayreuth for the ailing Wieland Wagner in 1966 where Brangäne seemingly asks which potion shall it be—love or death

Curtain call as the Marschallin in *Der Rosenkavalier* with Leonard Bernstein and Gwyneth Jones (Octavian), Lucia Popp (Sophie), Walter Berry (Ochs), and Ernst Gutstein (Faninal) at the Vienna State Opera in March 1971

Rehearsing the "Lamentation" from Bernstein's Jeremiah Symphony in Berlin, August 1977

Performing the "Lamentation" with Bernstein and the Israel Philharmonic in Berlin, August 1977

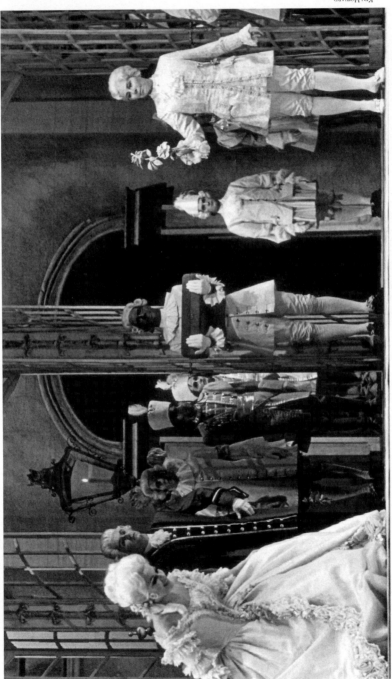

As Octavian with Helen Donath (Sophie) at the San Francisco Opera in September 1971 (the last year in which Christa Ludwig sang Octavian)

As Octavian at the Teatro Colón,
Buenos Aires, in September 1969

As the Marschallin at the
Vienna State Opera in April 1968

As the Marschallin with Tatiana Troyanos (Octavian) at the Salzburg Festival in July 1969

A dream performance of *Der Rosenkavalier*: Christa Ludwig as both the Marschallin and Octavian

Son Wolfgang (second from left) and his friends practice as his mother and dog Gypsy look distressed

Backstage after the premier of *Die Frau Ohne Schatten* at the Metropolitan Opera on October 2, 1966. Leonie Rysanek and Walter Berry are in costume, and Dr. Karl Böhm and Sir Rudolf Bing are to the left of Mr. Berry.

Rehearsing with Charles Spencer

With Charles Spencer after a performance of *Die Winterreise* in the church of Saint Leon sur Vézère in August 1990

As Lady Macbeth with Sherrill Milnes (Macbeth) at the Vienna State Opera in April 1970

As Claire Zachanassian in
Der Besuch der alten Dame
with Eberhard Wächter at
the Vienna State Opera in
May 1971

As Klytämnnestra at Deutsche Oper, Berlin Farewell on February 17, 1994 with Gwyneth Jones (left) and Gabriele Lechner

With Pierre Boulez (center) and Paul-Emile Deiber after a New York Philharmonic concert in February 1972

After a joint recital of lieder and poetry readings with Paul-Emile Deiber in Paris on May 21, 1984

Rehearsing Charlotte in *Werther* at the Met with Franco Corelli (in costume) and Paul-Emile Deiber in February 1971

Just married–March 3, 1972

At home with husband Paul-Emile Deiber in France in 1993

Finally free!

unhappy bird doesn't sing," and my mother said something similar, "Singing is an expression of joy." So voice teachers have to know how their students feel about things. Was a student brought up to be humble or arrogant? Is he or she too ambitious or too modest? What's going on in private? Is everything going well, or is a marriage on the rocks? It's hard to believe, but all this is noticeable in a voice. You can hear hardness of character in a voice, or whether a singer is more balanced, or whether or not they have great doubts about their abilities. All these things a voice teacher must sense or find out through conversation, in order to help the students overcome in small steps any problems they have.

So it was quite natural that my mother was also my confidante and friend, and we had an unbreakable bond between us. Even more important were her philosophical and spiritual ideas. Because she didn't have a lot of formal education (back then the attitude was still "girls don't need that"), she developed intense interests and further educated herself. Because she was very religious, she studied religion, but she went beyond strictly conventional religious ideas.

I was raised in her religious spirit, and I was fed with her thoughts from childhood daily, even hourly. Then, at a certain age, I naturally formed totally opposite opinions, saw everything spiritual as imagination, and wanted to convince my mother that my ideas about life were right. In this way, my mother was much more to me than a "Nur Mutter" (only a physical mother). But this is natural. For a while, I think every child sees its mother as an "Übermutter" (supermother).

In any case, my mother was for me an unusually controlling personality. I was closely connected to her, and she held on to me, so that, despite two marriages, I could never really let her go. There was also a time when I blamed my mother, and told her that she had taken my life away from me and ruined a lot of things for me. For example, during the wonderful years from 18 to 24, I didn't know what it was to be young, and I worked only to develop my voice for the future. I was refused everything that other young people had, and the situation remained the same throughout my entire professional life. During my first marriage with Walter Berry, my mother didn't dominate only me, but also Walter, and I stood in between, until Walter rid himself of the situation. When I later married Paul-Emile, my mother couldn't play the dominant role any longer, since all of us had grown older. She lost some of her natural authoritarian strength, and Paul-Emile was a mature, experienced man. I myself had slowly developed away from the "Prussian" way of living, and learned to love the in-between, the gray shades of life.

At about the age of sixty, I finally had the strength to free myself from my mother, which was really necessary, as I suddenly developed a stomach ulcer. When I asked the doctor where something like this came from, he said from stress. It could be treated, but it would always come back. Having gone through the school of my big crisis, I wasn't satisfied with this explanation. What did he mean, "it will always come back"? If my ulcer had come from stress, then it should also go away if I found out the cause of my stress. In quiet moments, I looked inside myself and searched and searched. Then it came to me that my mother, whom I loved more than anything else, was putting pressure on me psychologically.

The unusual relationship between my mother and me, which I had never questioned before, suddenly became clear to me. I realized that I had developed feelings of guilt towards my mother. Because she didn't want to live with Paul-Emile and me, she stayed alone in her small apartment in Vienna. Wolfgang, my son, who already had a family of his own, lovingly took care of "Jenny," but I was seldom with her. Although I telephoned her daily from all parts of the world, I wasn't there. Wolfgang and I were the only people she lived for. She often said to me when I visited her, "You know, Christa, you don't have to speak at all. I know you can't speak a lot when you sing. You only have to sit here." As I left her, I would see her standing in the doorway, so old, small, and fragile, and she would say, "Hopefully I will see you again." My heart always broke at those words.

During the few days I had between concerts, I never knew where to fly, to my mother or to my husband. Paul-Emile, of course, tried to understand and often said, "You must take time for your Mama." But I also needed days to rest completely by myself. Flying from one place to another made me terribly tired, and I wasn't just overtired, but almost dead of exhaustion. My fatigue pulled me towards Paul-Emile, and we felt we were too often apart. We wanted more time together to share our lives. But there was always my tie to my mother, whom I was leaving alone, of all times, in her old age, although I had her to thank for everything. It's true that she wasn't totally alone, because my half-sister Annemarie, who lived a few blocks away in Vienna, visited her almost daily. I also did everything humanly possibly to see that she was well taken care of, but she only wanted me. On the phone, she'd say, "When are you coming? How long can you stay? What? You fly so far away? To Japan? To America? Hopefully we will see each other again." It was so sad, and when I think back on those phone calls today, I'm unhappy all over again!

Surely this constant feeling of having a bad conscience towards my mother was the cause of my stomach ulcer. When I realized that, a natural egoism won out. I had to decide between my mother and my husband, and, for the first time in my life, I separated from her inwardly. It became clear to me that I shouldn't be sharing my life with my mother, but with the partner of my choice. Every person has a right to his own life and the need to find his own destiny. It took quite a while for me to totally cut the umbilical cord, but when I did, my stomach ulcer also disappeared and didn't return.

Certainly my mother must have felt that I distanced myself from her, although I still flew to Vienna to visit her, and we spoke on the phone daily. But the connection between us had been too strong for her not to sense my pulling away. She'd always been the center, the most important person for her daughter and son-in-law, and now it was difficult for her to get used to this new situation, and she suddenly felt superfluous.

Her character hardened more and more, partly because of her dependency on younger people, which is unavoidable in old age. She once said to me, "Christa, the worst thing is that one always has to say yes." She became suspicious of everyone, my mother of all people, who had always been convinced that everyone was basically good. All the wisdom that she had taught me suddenly disappeared. I was unhappy and "angry" with her because she changed so much. There were days I couldn't love her at all because she herself immediately cut off any love that I tried to show her. Her shell became harder and more rigid. She became envious, which she had never been before, envious of those who could hear and see better and who could walk better. Was this still my mother, whom I had loved so much for so many years? When we spoke about Austria, she'd say, "You have no say in the matter. You have become French." Aha, I thought. So that's how the wind blows. Memories from her youth during the First World War made France the "enemy country" in her mind And now her daughter was married to—a Frenchman!

She started to criticize me, the color of my hair, my figure, my singing. Everything came from the big wound, which I had caused her by not allowing her to "possess" me anymore. Remarks like "I'm useless. No one needs me anymore. Why am I still alive?" became more frequent. And it was because of this, and also because of her old age, that her will to live weakened more and more. In the spring of 1993, on the Wednesday after Easter, her strength left her, and she became bedridden. At this time, the Vienna State Opera was rehearsing a new production of *Götterdämmerung*, in which I was to sing Waltraute. Since I noticed that my mother spoke more and more frequently of the fact that her grandmother had died at 94 years of age, and my mother had celebrated her 94th birthday on May 13th, I simply didn't have the heart to think of my profession. I canceled everything in order to stay with her. Because she didn't have a specific disease, I saw her go through several stages—from not understanding what was happening ("Why can't I get up? I'm not sick"), to fighting against the situation to resignation. Because she didn't drink anything but water, her face grew smaller and smaller like her world, and her movements were limited to feeling for her handkerchief. When she heard music, she always wanted me to play my recording of Schubert's song "Die Allmacht" because it contains the line "Groß ist Jehova, der Herr!" (Great is Jehovah, the Lord!). It was as if she wanted to confirm this to herself, and once she uttered a muffled cry, "The only life is in God!"

In the weeks before her death, I felt that my mother's body held her spirit back more and more, and I was reminded of the old Prioress in Poulenc's opera *Les Dialogues des Carmélites*, who says on her deathbed that nothing she lived for or believed in helped her at the hour of her death. The waiting and the feeling of helplessness were awful. For the first time I became aware of how powerless we all are in the face of death. Our whole lives are organized and planned, and then suddenly there is a wall that we cannot climb over.

For hours I looked into my mother's face, which had become small and smooth, with eyes that already stared far into the unknown, and I couldn't understand what was happening at all. She was so dear, so helpless, so old. We held hands as I sat by her bedside, and we both cried and listened to music together for the last time, a violin concerto by Max Bruch. And so we said farewell to each other, closely connected as in earlier days, connected by music, which she no longer wanted to hear after that last concerto. Suddenly she asked me, "Are you my mother?" and I knew that her senses were gone. One morning she just stopped breathing.

My God, I'm crying while I write this. But for me my mother isn't dead. Daily, yes daily, I say, "Mama thought such and such." But I can't phone her anymore, and tell her how I sang, which note was good and which one went wrong. I still hear how she'd say, "Then you haven't worked enough yet." She lives on in me, and as I said farewell to my mother, I also began to say farewell to singing. That is fine, because now Paul-Emile takes care of me in the spirit of my mother, and he has kept me from practicing my profession longer than my strength allowed. And I hope that my mother is satisfied with her daughter now, because I've done everything to fulfill my talent. I couldn't have done more.

Limitations

It's difficult to recognize your limitations, because it's not easy to admit to your weaknesses. Singers aren't always in first-class voice, and we know we are subject to conditions that change daily. So when something doesn't go very well, we think, "Well, today my voice wasn't in very good shape." At the next performance, we are a bit nervous, but everything goes fine; then later, not so well again. When a singer is young and has a fresh, young voice, it's simple to "sing over" certain things with a little pressure or more breath, but these little tricks don't work anymore as we get older.

Singers have thousands of excuses. I didn't sleep well. The weather is bad. I'm getting a head cold. I've got an allergy. The conductor's tempo was wrong. There are so many physical and professional things that can bother a singer—and then add difficulties at home or all kinds of bad news. Any of these can "strike the voice dumb."

Making excuses can go on for a few years, before singers realize that things aren't as they once were. We are engaged for the same roles, we still sing them; possibly the critics have a few reservations, but, in spite of everything, we are still successful in pleasing an audience—except for a few people who truly have the ears to hear the difference. We can also replace diminished vocal capacity with more intense acting and clever interpretation. Little by little, however, we are astonished to find that singing isn't easy anymore: a particular note doesn't sound as beautiful, the placement of a high note is no longer quite right, a passage we used to sing piano must now be sung mezzo-forte, and many other little things.

At this point, there are only two possibilities. Singers can admit their difficulties to themselves and wisely, with dignity, stop singing some roles. Or, without considering their vocal cords or the possibility of negative reviews, they can simply continue to sing the same roles and say, "My contracts are my critics, and as long as I'm engaged everywhere, I'll sing this role." I don't believe that this second attitude is the right one in the long run. I can, of course, only speak for myself, and other singers may think differently; but I believe that it's better to change roles. "Leicht mußt man sein!" (Light one should be!) as the Marschallin says. There are enough roles, and, in the end, it's impossible to compete with the singing of one's early years.

It's natural for a muscle to weaken, and for us to need glasses. Athletes stop playing professionally, and there is no need to be ashamed of getting older. Also, our audience stays loyal to us as we age. To admit to them and to ourselves that we are normal people is better in the end than pity or backbiting. But probably the most difficult thing is finding a person who can be trusted, who is honest, and who doesn't give undeserved praise. Singers can't judge for themselves how they really sound. A tape of a performance doesn't always reflect the reality. And singers don't look right in some parts after a certain age. To me, a 45-year-old Carmen or Octavian simply looks ridiculous. Even if outwardly some singers look younger, the timbre of their voices gives them away.

Mezzos like me have it easy, because we can play ageless women and old witches after our young mezzo roles. We have parts where we use a cane, or are blind, or where we die of old age. But the poor sopranos, especially the soubrettes! They always have to be (or have to seem to be) young, because most of the time they are the love interest for the tenors. With the exception of a few roles, mezzos are usually condemned to play the mother of one or the other of these two. But I must admit that I always found it much more interesting to try new roles than to travel from opera house to opera house singing the same role over and over again.

Walter Legge once said to me that a singer should concentrate on five roles, and make a world career with them. I think that might be possible for about ten years at most, but, after that, singing the same five roles gets very boring both for the singer and the audience. I think it's better to sing roles that suit a singer's age, rather than always singing the same ones.

Farewell
Thoughts

The Need to Say Farewell

As I'm writing this, I'm on tour with the Schleswig-Holstein Youth Orchestra. It's the 25th of August, 1993, and today Leonard Bernstein would have been 75 years old. In his memory we are giving concerts of his music in several places. I'm singing the "Lamentation" from the "Jeremiah," his first symphony, and I love this piece very much. I gladly do everything to honor Bernstein, except the traveling, which is a terrible experience as usual.

Today we're in Rimini. This evening we were supposed to play a concert in the open air, but it's raining, so we'll be giving the concert in a movie house instead. It's unbelievably sultry, and I'm sitting in my hotel room and looking out over miles of long sandy beach full of rows and rows of empty deck chairs, closed umbrellas, and wet changing cabins. Over a quiet gray sea hangs a gray sky that looks like a dirty linen cloth.

It's a miracle that I can still sing and cope with all this traveling at the age of 65. But the years are passing quickly, and I don't have a lot of time left to live "normally." When we decide to plant a tree in our garden at home, I always say to the gardener, "Please, buy a big tree. I can't wait twenty years for it to grow." Two years ago, my husband gave me a little dog, and the first thing I did was calculate whether or not he could outlive me.

When I began to wonder if my profession was worth my not having a life, I knew it was time to stop. Why continue to wake up every morning and sing "mi-mi-mi" to see if the voice is still there? Why keep suffering the constant fear of catching a cold, of having to cancel, of failing? The older I get, the more I feel I have a duty not to disappoint my audience. My standards are getting higher and higher, yet I know that the "bloom" of my voice can't possibly be what it was thirty years ago. Despite that, I still try to find the most beautiful sound. I become very self-critical, and am often frustrated because I can no longer sing as I did when I was younger. It's true that I can now replace pure beauty of sound with a more insightful interpretation, and give my singing a simplicity that only comes with maturity. But then there's my vanity as a woman. For many years now when I have sung in concerts where I used a score, I have needed glasses, and I tried all kinds of stratagems to avoid wearing them. First, I tried to learn everything by heart. Then I wrote everything out in large letters. But finally I couldn't do it anymore. I gave up and wore glasses. Terrible!

I always loved to wear high heels with my evening gowns, until it happened that I couldn't walk after standing for an hour and a half without moving from one spot. I think the first time this happened was when I was singing *Winterreise* in the Arena Herodes Attikus in Athens. Because my feet hurt so much, my accompanist Charles Spencer had to support me, and we left the stage very slowly. Since then, I was only able to wear flat evening shoes.

Because of my life as a singer, I naturally gained weight. I sat in the taxi. I sat at the airport. I sat in the plane. I sat in my hotel room. And because I was bored, I ate. I would have needed an awful lot of discipline to stay slim, unless I had the right metabolism, and I definitely don't! Because of my weight gain, I had to start wearing a different style of evening gown, what I call my "walalaweia" gowns, which are very flowing and not form-fitting. ("Walalaweia" is, of course, one of the phrases the Rhinemaiden Woglinde sings at the very beginning of *Das Rheingold.*) The gowns are still beautiful, but....

I'm 65 years old in every respect, and I can't change that. So in February 1993, I began to give farewell performances. Whenever I agreed to an engagement in a particular city, I said, "This is the last time." And at the end of 1994, my life as a singer will come to an end. I say goodbye to the stage, and hello to my private life. As my son said in his telegram to me when I gave my farewell recital at Carnegie Hall, "Say Farewell to Broadway, but Welcome to the World." So far I've been relaxed as never before at every one of my farewell performances. I gave my best, and then looked out into the hall and said "Adieu" without sorrow, more or less relieved. To practice this profession for 49 years is enough, and I say to the audience as Venus says to Tannhäuser: "Zum Überdruß is dir mein Reiz gedieh'n?" (Are you surfeited with my charms?).

Was It Worth It?

"Would you live your life the same way again?" I'm often asked. I would certainly do several things differently, but it's futile to think about it. Has it been worth it? This is a more serious question. Is "das Lied, das aus der Kehle dringt" (the song, which out of the throat comes) really a "Lohn, der reichlich lohnet" (reward that rewards richly), as Goethe says in his poem "Der Barde"?

I must say first that I'm extremely grateful to destiny, which has gifted me with talent—and not too much of it. Geniuses must always struggle with their talent, and are more or less consumed by it. I had just enough to be successful, so for me it was measured out just right. I am equally satisfied with external circumstances, because I had the good fortune to meet the right people, and to be in the right place at the right time. Through my profession I met interesting people, and I traveled. I was overwhelmed with flowers, rode in elegant chauffeured limousines, lived in the most beautiful hotels, and bought clothes from expensive fashion houses. I gave interviews, got photographed, and was given numerous medals and honors. I now have crates full of photos, reviews, and other memorabilia.

But, looking back, I ask myself if all of this isn't just superficial, a material reward. The only important thing is what my profession and my life have made of me as a person. Above all things, I think I've learned tolerance towards everything and everyone. Through my travels, I've learned that people from other countries and from other races are exactly the same as I am. Prejudice is taught to us by the media, and we learn it from being brought up wrongly. Scandinavians aren't necessarily more diligent than Italians, and Austrians don't need to look down on Turks. As Karl Böhm's son Karl-Heinz once said, "If I walk towards the blacks in Ethiopia with open arms, they will also open their arms." I always think that this kind of tolerance towards the people of other nations starts with a knowledge of their culture, and that it's more important to teach this in school, rather than to stuff children with facts about war and such things.

It's certainly very pleasant to live in a certain luxury, although for singers this is a chimera, since most of our time is spent in rehearsal rooms without windows. And as we singers know, earning good money for a period of time is not the same as being rich! Flowers and exaggerated praise and invitations to embassy receptions are over quickly when fame fades. How lonely was Callas when she died in her apartment in Paris. How alone she must have felt when she heard her voice on records and tried to recapture her youth. Of what use are all the pictures and reviews? What do I do with my oh-so-expensive evening gowns and other showy clothes? No, that's not what's important, but one only knows that after one has had it all. How great was my longing for all these material things when I was a young girl!

The "reward that richly rewards" is, of course, the incomparable feeling of producing musical sound, hearing it, and experiencing it. This is a purely physical, erotic pleasure, which is also spiritual. I think that this is what I'll miss when I stop singing, and also the joy of singing the songs of Hugo Wolf, because the blend of music and poetry in his songs, combined with the sound of my voice, was something special to me. So "the song, which out of the throat comes" has been worth it.

Still, I ask myself, "What have I done for the world, for other people all these many years?" Wasn't it grossly egotistical to be concerned only about myself and my vocal cords, just to produce a sound? Next to this, everything around me was unimportant: contacts with friends, my life as a wife and mother. As wife, I was surely impossible, and as mother, I wasn't really there to experience my son's childhood and adolescence.

But I've tried to make people happy with my singing, and to be the means by which they could experience something deeper and more meaningful. I'm grateful that I was given this musical talent and a voice, so that I could be a singer, and through a constant preoccupation with music and poetry, experience life more reflectively and spiritually, and with a sense of the profound connections between the physical and spiritual worlds.

The End of My Search

These are to be the last pages that I will write for this book. I'm sitting in an airplane in December 1993, and I'm on my way to New York. For the first time, I'm not going there to sing, since I already gave my farewell recital in March. This time I'm going to accept the honor of being named "Musician of the Year" by *Musical America*. The honor makes me very happy, even though it reminds me of my age.

This flight to New York is especially pleasant because, for the first time, I don't have to take care of my voice! I can go to the theater and enjoy New York to my heart's content and without fear of drafts. I especially love this city just before Christmas because of all the decorations and Santa Clauses. The Salvation Army workers ring bells on every street corner, asking for small donations for the poor, and the Christmas tree in Rockefeller Center is magnificent, especially because they add extra branches, or so I've been told.

Up here in the plane, I feel as if I'm in the world that Dali painted once: huge elephants fly in the light blue sky, while people fight wars down on the earth. In Dali's picture, there are black ruins and warriors seen against a blood-red background. I think how singers and other artists always stand a bit outside real life. Interpretive artists like singers give consolation and edification. Creative artists like painters and composers hold up a mirror before mankind.

Cave paintings, which are so admired today, show that artists were already at work thousands of years ago. Because of these paintings, we know what people wore and how they lived. They report the facts. Today we go to museums to look at pictures painted in bygone eras, and likewise to concert halls and opera houses to hear what composers wrote hundred of years ago. But few of us want to be confronted with the mirror image of our own time— our noise and our own torn-up souls—in modern atonal music. In painting and in music, we flee from the present to search for the feeling of harmony we need so badly, and we hope to find this in the past.

Many years ago, I went to a concert of Stockhausen's music in New York. His is a music that I can neither understand nor judge. I can only describe its effect on me. In its intensity, I almost felt as if I were being destroyed. I was shaken up internally by the experience, not in the same way as I'm shaken up by the music of Beethoven, Bruckner, or Wagner. Stockhausen's music almost made me ill! My nerves were tense, and I couldn't relax. Certainly that is what he wanted, and it's surely very important for us to see our times reflected in the artist's mirror as it is held up before us. But isn't it only human to want to flee from the chaos that exists in nature and in society, or soften it with art? Don't we want to overcome the disharmony in ourselves? Shouldn't art be the bridge to finding a better self and the way we begin to overcome our helpless sadness? As Pfitzner says in *Palestrina*, "Man weint, weil man geboren ist." (One cries because one is born.)

I ask myself question after question, and I search for answers in books about physics and metaphysics. I think how all of us search for the same thing—to overcome the disharmony between our inner and outer selves in whatever way we can. Perhaps that's why I always loved to portray characters on the opera stage who were searching, most of all, Kundry. And in recitals, I loved best to sing *Die Winterreise*, a piece I like to call a "search for salvation." My ears have gotten used to the strange sounds I have to make when I sing modern music, and surely future generations will understand all this. Often genius composers are prophets who are far ahead of their times, and only a few revolutionary pioneers can understand them while they live. Some composers search, and look beyond their own times. They are precursors, like Mahler. Others, like Mozart, are a fulfillment, but such composers are rare.

I love the times of change and retrospection, when new things are created on the base of the traditional, because every step has a profound meaning. I love Mahler, Bartók, and Ligeti. I love Proust, Rilke, and Thomas Bernhard. I love Monet, Kubin, and Feininger, just to name a few. But above all, I ask myself if, just once, the physical sciences like biology and physics will connect with spiritual transcendence and mystery. After my lifelong preoccupation with music and the beautiful voice with which I was gifted, I've realized that the singing voice, although a material thing, can touch what lies beyond the material, and I truly believe that music, as the Composer in *Ariadne* says, is "die heiligste unter den Künsten" (the holiest of the arts).

In 1816, Franz Schubert composed a song based on a poem dedicated to him by Johann Baptist Mayrhofer called "Geheimnis" (Mystery). It begins "Sag an, wer lehrt dich Lieder" (Tell me, who taught you these songs), and the last verse is:

> So geht es auch dem Sänger,
> Er singt, erstaunt in sich;
> Was still ein Gott bereitet,
> Befremdet ihn wie dich.
>
> [So is it also with the singer,
> He sings, amazed at himself;
> What in silence a god made,
> Amazes him as well as you.]

If, through art, one soul can speak to another, by which I mean the best and truest part of a person can speak to that part of another person, then surely art is a necessity. And perhaps these inter-spiritual currents between people are the most valuable connections that we can make on this earth. And knowing that I have experienced this connection is perhaps the end of my search.

Talking with My Voice

Voice: Well, I don't think it is at all nice of you to tell everyone how much you are looking forward to not singing anymore and starting a new life without me. Have I not served you faithfully for almost fifty years? You are extremely ungrateful! It almost seems as though we are an old married couple, and now I am not good enough for you anymore.

Christa: But I don't mean it like that at all! I'm deeply grateful to you for working with me so faithfully all these years. But wouldn't you also like to retire and not have to sing anymore? You are not all that young either, you know!

Voice: I must admit that I am a little tired, and you, of course, notice it too, especially when you force me to talk too much. After all, I was designed for talking, like the vocal cords of normal people. But I always had to sing and make a beautiful sound. Even when you were a small child, you used me in a totally unnatural way—for singing opera arias and lieder and parts from oratorios, etc., etc.

Christa: But you could only make a beautiful sound because you were well trained in what we singers call technique. From the very beginning you were carefully and gently instructed, so that your cords vibrated correctly.

Voice: Yes, yes, but how often you strained me, especially when you used me too quickly in the mornings. After a good night's sleep, I like to wake up slowly and to start the day with gentle physical exercises. But you—you wanted me to scream out loud, or hit high notes, immediately. Terrible!

Christa: My God, don't get carried away! So sometimes I overslept. After all, you're quite robust, regardless of what you say, simply just one muscle—

Voice: Excuse me! Two muscles! And tiny ones!

Christa: OK, OK.

Voice: You know that I have always behaved well when you treated me right. But how often you strained me, especially when you sang soprano parts, something for which I really wasn't suited!

Christa: But think of how rewarding it was to overcome our joint difficulties, and how well we worked together. Wasn't it wonderful when we both carried on blissfully, never thinking about tomorrow? We poured out a huge sound over huge orchestras in huge opera houses. Wasn't that an indescribable pleasure?

Voice: Certainly, certainly. But do you remember how often you pinched me when you got carried away in your ecstasy and forgot to support me correctly with your breath?

Christa: Excuse me, that was seldom.

Voice: And on high notes, you didn't just pinch me, but you also pulled my cords too tight, so that I was very stiff afterwards!

Christa: But I always gave you enough time to recover.

Voice: Perhaps I didn't have to sing for a while, but you were always talking right away! What I really wanted was to make no sound at all. I just wanted to be left in peace for at least two or three days.

Christa: Now wait a minute! I really didn't speak very much at all. Ask my husband. Ask my family. Ask my friends. And I didn't talk to anyone on the phone, so I wouldn't have to speak louder than normal. And haven't I shocked my husband by sleeping with compresses full of stinking paste around my neck to improve your circulation and keep you warm at night?

Voice: Please, let's not speak about circulation! I remember with horror the time my capillary walls grew so thin that they burst.

Christa: I was frightened too, and probably more than you, because I wasn't sure what was going on.

Voice: Still, I was the one who was suffering.

Christa: And I couldn't use you to earn any money.

Voice: Hah! That's what you always thought about—money! I worked faithfully for you, and you did very well.

Christa: Please, don't be offended. When I found out how really sick you were, I suddenly realized how much I needed you, and I did everything I could so that you would be healthy again.

Voice: But, as usual, you didn't allow me enough time! You always tried to sing again too soon. Remember the recording of *Samson et Dalila*, or the two recordings of Schubert songs? Every time too early! You thought that just because I sounded fine, I was perfectly healthy again. A muscle has to have time to recover. That is why I bled over and over again. No, I don't want to think about that anymore. How stupid you were!

Christa: Thank God that time passed, but it took at least two years for you to come to love me again.

Voice: That's not true! I always loved you, and I still do. I just wanted to show you that I was easily hurt, and not at all as robust as you thought. But you did understand me finally.

Christa: Of course, we're like an old married couple. We came to understand each other in the end. And so I learned to treat you very carefully, and respect your idiosyncrasies, so now I think I can finally begin to call you my dear friend.

Voice: Absolutely right. That's how it should be. Finally I made you understand that you have to serve me, and not the other way round. Although I was given to you, you had to become my servant. I ruled over you and your whole life. You had to obey me! I was the prima donna—moody, unpredictable, and sensitive. When you tried to subjugate me to your will, I got my revenge. If I was the least bit swollen or tired, I simply wouldn't let you sing! I taught you to handle me carefully, like a raw egg, and pay attention to my wishes. But sometimes you tried to force me to sing anyway, regardless of how I felt. And you were lax in other ways, too. Confess!

Christa: Now, excuse me, but I never behaved badly. I have absolutely nothing on my conscience.

Voice: Really? And what about the evenings when you went out to those smoky places in Vienna for a few glasses of wine and I came home scratchy? And how many pills did you take for one thing or another that made me terribly dry? And always at night, you would leave the window open, so you could sleep better, but in the early morning, I would be the one to catch a chill from the cold air and terrible dampness. Thought about me all the time? Hah!

Christa: I remember those mornings well. You sounded like an angry raven instead of a sweet-tempered nightingale.

Voice: And what was that terrible thunder I used to hear?

Christa: A person does have to cough sometimes.

Voice: And what was that infernal rumbling?

Christa: I was just clearing my throat.

Voice: Just clearing your throat? There was this tiny speck of mucus on me. Did you have to overreact and give me such a terrible fright with that awful noise? And what did you manage to accomplish? You just coated me with more mucus. So then you would make that dreadful noise again, and I'd just get coated more and more. Certainly you knew it was hopeless!

Christa: What else could I do? I was standing out there in the middle of the stage in front of all those people. It's easy for you to talk. Nobody could see you! Everyone was looking at me, and who do you think they would blame if a note went wrong? Certainly not you!

Voice: It's true that I did notice you were nervous. Your breath was short and uneven, and I couldn't vibrate freely, and so I started to tremble. But your nerves I could live with. It was that rubbing that was so terrible. And those times when you shook and pinched me.

Christa: My God, you really are in a complaining mood this morning.

Voice: Well, I mean when you sneezed.

Christa: You mean when I had a head cold?

Voice: Or an allergy or whatever. But I tried to be forgiving, and you must admit I always behaved well at the beginning of a cold, and tried and tried, until I couldn't do anything anymore.

Christa: Singers are always having this kind of bad luck. But I always tried to stay healthy and not burden you with other people's germs. But, after a few days, both of us were completely healthy again, and you still refused to sing with me. Nothing sounded right.

Voice: Was it my fault that your ears were still blocked, and you couldn't hear me properly? Don't blame me!

Christa: But, really, you have to admit that for almost half a century, we worked well together. We depended on each other. Where would you be without my body? Your cords would have resonated differently. You would never have made such beautiful sounds without me.

Voice: Nonsense! I was the most important thing!

Christa: Wait a minute now! I deserve some credit too. You're really very thin and small, and without my strength, you would never have been able to sing wonderful parts like Leonore in *Fidelio*.

Voice: Hold on there! It's an open question whether or not that part was right for you.

Christa: Now don't be so contrary. You must admit that we loved each other, and now a little rest will do us both good.

Voice: Are you back to that again? Are you going to tell me again that you only want to use me to speak in the future?

Christa: Yes, aren't you happy to be free and not to have to work anymore?

Voice: Certainly, but I did enjoy vibrating on air, in spite of your behavior sometimes. And it was a pleasure to make sounds that seemed to come from heaven. I enjoyed listening to our sound, and to the way you connected it with the meaning of a beautiful text. It is wonderful to make such a sound!

Christa: I'm really grateful to hear you say that, and I always have been grateful. I always made an effort to keep my body healthy because I know you are no violin string, which I can loosen and tighten and change. I know you lived in me and not in a comfortably padded silk-lined case, protected from the weather and all kinds of physical shocks. I had to be your pro tector, and I know I didn't always do the best job.

Voice: The idea of taking me out and putting me in a silk-lined case is a tempting one, but I wouldn't like being changed like a piece of string!

Christa: Oh, but you couldn't be, because your vibrations are part of my individual sound, which is really unique in all the world, and that special sound could only be created by the two of us together.

Voice: I am happy that you realize this, and that you are grateful. But it is annoying when you behave as if I don't matter. You say that you are happy you won't need my services for singing after you have your "last scream," as you so disrespectfully call it, when you give your final farewell performance as Klytämnestra at the Vienna State Opera on December 14, 1994. See, I've memorized the date. You know that if you don't exercise me constantly after that, I won't be able to sing for you anymore. So please give up any ideas you may have in your head about coming back after that date and asking me to do you one last favor, and coming back again asking me one more time, and then again and again and again.

Christa: No, no! I solemnly promise that I won't cloud the memory of our work together. And perhaps now I can call you my dear one again—with all due respect, of course. And when I stop singing, I promise that I'll try to pass on everything I've learned from you to young singers, so that they know what a precious gift vocal cords like you are, and how to care for them so that they always make a beautiful sound. Everything beautiful in life has to be cared for, or it will be lost. Your vibrations, which came to life through my breath, are only a small part of singing. The other, most important part remains a secret, and all singers must discover that secret for themselves, just as each person must find his own happiness.

Voice: You said that very nicely, and I am close to tears. But let's not be maudlin. We did a lot of good work together, and had a lot of joy doing it, but everything comes to an end. Now you may finally use me like everybody else—to talk, to laugh, even to cough and clear your throat—as if that's nothing!

Finally Free

A Postscript

As I write these words, I am sitting at home, having uttered my last screams at the Vienna State Opera exactly four years ago. Finally, I take care of my house and my roses, cook for friends, have a social life, and, last but not least, live with my husband—and my dog and cat. I don't worry at all about my voice. I sleep with the windows open and go out in cold and windy weather. And I talk all the time. It's wonderful living without the word "must" and without a watch.

But I have to admit that only living is sometimes not so easy. For many, many years I traveled all the time, and packed and unpacked suitcases constantly. I was always working on my voice and learning new roles and songs. In short, I always had a goal. Now, free as a bird, there are times when I suddenly ask myself, "What are you *doing*, Christa? Have you nothing *serious* to do?" Perhaps this is why I feel it is my duty to share my experiences with young singers and to pass on the ideas I learned from so many great musicians.

I must say that I do miss some things very much. No longer do I sit waiting for my cue in the middle of an orchestra that is playing, for example, the glorious Mahler Second Symphony. I miss this world of beautiful sound very much. I also miss being in the electrifying presence of conductors like Leonard

Bernstein, and singing the words of beautiful poems. My dream world is gone, and now I live reality.

But because my soul is full of so many wonderful experiences from the past, I feel very rich and say, thank you, dear Lord, for giving me an exceptional talent.

Christa Ludwig
December, 1998

Reference Material

Repertory

Andreae, Volkmar
Cantata 169

Anonymous
Dornröschen (Good Fairy)
Deutsche Volkslieder (Arranged by Seidler-Winkler)

Auric, Georges
Songs

Bach, Johann Sebastian
Christmas Oratorio
"Der Herr segne euch" (Duet from "Der Herr denket an uns," BWV 196)
Magnificat
Mass in B Minor
St. John Passion
St. Matthew Passion

Bartók, Béla
Bluebeard's Castle (Judith)

Beethoven, Ludwig von
"Ah, Perfido!"
Fidelio (Leonore)
Lieder
Missa Solemnis
Symphony No. 9

Bellini, Vincenzo
Norma (Adalgisa)

Berg, Alban
Lieder Opus 2
Sieben frühe Lieder Opus 7
Wozzeck (Marie)

Berlioz, Hector
Les Troyens (Dido)
Les Nuits d'Été
Roméo et Juliette

Bernstein, Leonard
Candide (Old Lady)

Songfest
Song for Karl Böhm
Symphony No. 1 (Jeremiah)

Bizet, Georges
Carmen (Carmen, Mercédès)

Boito, Arrigo
Mefistofele (Elena)

Borodin, Alexander
Prince Igor (Kontchakovna)

Brahms, Johannes
Alto Rhapsody
Duets
Vier Ernste Gesänge
Lieder
Bratschen-Lieder
Deutsche Volkslieder
Zigeunerlieder

Bruckner, Anton
Mass No. 3 in F minor
Te Deum

Caplet, André
Spiegel Jesu

Cherubini, Luigi
"Dite almeno"

Czernik, Willy
Lieder (texts of Verlaine)

D'Albert, Eugen
Tiefland (Antonia)

Debussy, Claude
Chansons de Bilitis
Le Martyre de Saint Sebastian
Pelléas et Mélisande (Geneviève)

Dessau, Paul
Das Verhör des Lukullus (Courtesan, Woman)

267

Dvořák, Antonin
Biblische Lieder
Klänge aus Mähren
Zigeunermelodien

Egk, Werner
Lieder
Die Versuchung des Hl. Antonius

Einem, Gottfried von
Bald sing ich das Schweigen
Der Besuch der alten Dame (Claire)
Lieder

Falla, Manuel de
Songs

Flotow, Friedrich von
Martha (Nancy)

Franck, César
Nocturne

Gesualdo, Carlo
Madrigals

Giordano, Umberto
Andrea Chénier (Bersi)

Gluck, Christoph Willibald
Iphigénie en Aulide (Iphigénie)
Orfeo ed Euridice (Orfeo)

Gounod, Charles
Faust (Siebel)

Gulda, Friedrich
Galgenlieder
Lieder

Haas, Joseph
Das Jahr im Lied

Handel, George Frideric
"Ah, spietato" (from *Amadigi*)
"Care Selve" (from *Atalanta*)
Giulio Cesare (Cornelia)
Hercules (Dejanira)
Judas Maccabaeus
Messiah
"Oh, sleep why dost though leave me"
(from *Semele*)
Saul

Haydn, Joseph
The Creation

Hindemith, Paul
Ite, angeli veloces
Die Junge Magd
Requiem
Trakl Lieder

Honegger, Arthur
Antigone (Antigone)
Judith (Judith)
Romeo und Julia (Female Lover)

Humperdinck, Engelbert
Hänsel und Gretel (Gertrud, Die
Knusperhexe)

Janáček, Leos
Jenůfa (Mayor's Wife)

Jolivet, André
Songs

Kálmán, Emmerich
Gräfin Mariza (Ilonka, Marija)

Kodály, Zoltán
"Ballade der Kádár Kata"

Krenek, Ernst
Das Leben der Orest (Anastasia)

Liebermann, Rolf
Opus 1
Die Schule der Frauen (Georgette)
"Streitlied zwischen Leben und Tod"

Liszt, Franz
Christus
Lieder

Lortzing, Albert
Der Waffenschmied (Irmentraut)

Loewe, Karl
Ballads

Mahler, Gustav
Kindertotenlieder
Das klagende Lied
Des Knaben Wunderhorn
Das Lied von der Erde
Lieder
Lieder eines fahrenden Gesellen
Rückert Lieder
Symphony No. 2
Symphony No. 3
Symphony No. 8

Martin, Frank
Golgotha
Der Sturm (Miranda)

Massenet, Jules
Werther (Charlotte)

Mayuzumi, Toshiro
Sphenogramme

Mendelssohn, Felix
Elijah
Lieder

Menotti, Gian-Carlo
The Consul (Vera Boronel)

Milhaud, Darius
Songs

Monteverdi, Claudio
"Bel pastor, da cui bel guardo"
L'Incoronazione di Poppea (Ottavia)
"Tornate, o cari baci"

Mozart, Wolfgang Amadeus
Concert Arias
Così fan tutte (Dorabella)
Don Giovanni (Donna Elvira)
Lieder
Mass in C Major
Mass in C Minor
Le Nozze di Figaro (Cherubino, Marcellina)
Requiem
Scene with Rondo KV 505
Vesperae Solennes de Confessore
Die Zauberflöte (Zweite Dame)

Mussorgsky, Modest
Boris Godunov (Marina)
Khovanshchina (Marfa)

Nicolai, Otto
Die Lustigen Weiber von Windsor (Frau Reich)

Nono, Luigi
Memento

Offenbach, Jacques
Les Contes d'Hoffmann (Giulietta, Niklaus, Voice)

Orff, Carl
De temporum fine comoedia (Last Being)

Pergolesi, Giovanni Battista
Stabat Mater

Pfitzner, Hans
Lieder
Palestrina (Silla)

Pizzetti, Ildebrando
Assassinio nelle cattedrale (Seconda corifea)

Poulenc, François
Dialogues des Carmélites (Mme. de Croissy)

Puccini, Giacomo
Madama Butterfly (Kate, Suzuki)
Suor Angelica (Princess)
Tosca (Shepherd Boy)

Purcell, Henry
"Let Us Wander"
"Lost Is My Quiet"
"Sound the Trumpet"

Ravel, Maurice
Chansons madècasse
Shéhérezade

Reger, Max
An die Hoffnung
Lieder
Die Weihe der Nacht

Rachmaninoff, Sergei
Songs

Rossini, Gioacchino
Il Barbiere di Siviglia (Rosina)
La Cenerentola (Angelina)
"Duetto buffo di due gatti"
La Regata Veneziana
Songs

Saint-Saëns, Camille
"Un flûte invisible"
Samson et Dalila (Dalila)

Schmidt, Franz
Das Buch mit sieben Siegeln

Schönberg, Arnold
Gurre-Lieder

Schröder, Hermann
Hochzeitnacht im Paradis (Dolores)

Schubert, Franz
Duets

Der Hert auf dem Felsen
Lieder
Lieder der Mignon
Die Winterreise

Schumann, Robert
Duets
Frauenliebe und leben
Lieder
Liederkreis

Sieczynski, Rudolf
"Wien, Wien, nur du Allein"

Smetana, Bedřich
The Bartered Bride (Agnes)

Stolz, Robert
Lieder

Strauss, Johann
"Draussen in Sievering"
Die Fledermaus (Orlofsky)
Eine Nacht in Venedig (Ciboletta)
Die Zigeunerbaron (Mirabella)

Strauss, Richard
Ariadne auf Naxos (Ariadne, Dryade, Der Komponist)
Capriccio (Clairon)
Elektra (Dritte Mägde, Elektra's Recognition Scene, Klytämnestra)
Die Frau ohne Schatten (Falcon, Färberin)
Lieder
Der Rosenkavalier (Annina, Marschallin, Octavian, Zweite Adelige Waise)
Salome (Page)

Suppé, Franz von
Boccaccio (Petronella)

Tchaikovsky, Peter Ilyich
Eugene Onegin (Olga)

Queen of Spades (Countess)
Songs

Verdi, Giuseppe
Aida (Amneris, First Priestess)
Un Ballo in Maschera (Ulrica)
Don Carlo (Eboli)
Falstaff (Mistress Page, Mistress Quickly)
La Forza del Destino (Preziosilla)
Luisa Miller (Federica)
Macbeth (Lady Macbeth)
Requiem
Rigoletto (Giovanna, Maddalena)
La Traviata (Annina)
Il Trovatore (Azucena, Inez)

Wagner, Richard
Der Fliegende Holländer (Mary)
Götterdämmerung (Brünnhilde's Immolation Scene, Second Norn, Waltraute, Wellgunde)
Lohengrin (Ortrud)
Die Meistersinger von Nürnberg (Magdalena)
Parsifal (Kundry)
Das Rheingold (Erda, Fricka)
Rienzi (Adriano)
Siegfried (Erda)
Tannhäuser (Venus)
Tristan und Isolde (Brangäne)
Die Walküre (Fricka, Waltraute)
Wesendonck Lieder

Wagner-Régeny, Rudolf
Genesis

Wolf, Hugo
Italienisches Liederbuch
Lieder
Lieder der Mignon
Spanisches Liederbuch

Discography

Compiler's Note: This discography lists all of the studio recordings made by Christa Ludwig and released commercially along with the year in which each recording was made or first released. When the recording referenced is an American release, the American label and its parent company are given. Many of Miss Ludwig's live performances were taped and are available commercially. As many of these releases as possible are included.

Recent Collections

Les Introuvables de Christa Ludwig, EMI, 1991 (Reissue of studio recordings of lieder, opera, and orchestral pieces from 1957 onward)

Christa Ludwig, Walter Berry, TESSITURA, 1992 (Reissue of selections from RCA studio recordings made in 1963-4)

Ausgewählte Lieder, ORFEO, 1993 (Excerpts from recitals at the Salzburg Festival in 1963 and 1968)

Highlights 1955-1974, ORFEO, 1994 (Excerpts from Salzburg Festival opera performances)

Christa Ludwig 70th Birthday: A Tribute, DG, 1997 (Reissue of orchestral and lieder studio recordings)

Christa Ludwig: A 70th Birthday Tribute. The Classic 1964 Recordings, RCA, 1997

Opera and Operetta

BARTÓK, BÉLA
Bluebeard's Castle (Judith), LSO/Kertész, LONDON/DECCA, 1965

BEETHOVEN, LUDWIG VAN
Fidelio (Leonore), Philh/Klemperer, EMI, 1962
      BavSO/Karajan, ARKADIA, 1/12/63 (live)
      DOB/Böhm, CANYON, 10/20/63 (live)

BELLINI, VINCENZO
Norma (Adalgisa), Scala/Serafin, EMI, 1960

BERNSTEIN, LEONARD
Candide (Old Lady), LSO/Bernstein, DG, 1989

BIZET, GEORGES
Carmen (Carmen), BerSO/Stein, EMI, 1961 (in German)

DEBUSSY, CLAUDE
Pelléas et Mélisande (Geneviève), VPO/Abbado, DG, 1991

EINEM, GOTTFRIED VON
Der Besuch der alten Dame (Claire Zachanassian), VPO/Stein, AMADEO, 5/23/71 (live)

GIORDANO, UMBERTO
Andrea Chénier (Madelon), NPO/Chailly, DECCA, 1982/4

GLUCK, CHRISTOPH WILLIBALD
Iphigénie en Aulide (Iphigénie), VPO/Böhm, ORFEO, 8/3/62 (live, in German)

HANDEL, GEORG FRIEDRICH
Giulio Cesare (Cornelia), MPO/Leitner, MELODRAM, 3/20/66 (live, in German)

HUMPERDINCK, ENGELBERT
Hänsel und Gretel (Die Knusperhexe), MRO/Eichhorn, EURODISC, 1971
StkaD/Davis, PHILIPS, 1992
Hänsel und Gretel (Gertrud), ColGO/Pritchard, CBS, 1979

LIEBERMANN, ROLF
Die Schule der Frauen (Georgette), VPO/Szell, ORFEO, 8/17/57 (live)

MOZART, WOLFGANG AMADEUS
Così fan tutte (Dorabella), VPO/Böhm, LONDON/DECCA, 1955
VPO/Böhm, MELODRAM, 7/27/60 (live)
VPO/Böhm, GALA, 8/8/62 (live)
Philh/Böhm, EMI, 1962
Don Giovanni (Donna Elvira), NPhilh/Klemperer, EMI, 1966
Le Nozze di Figaro (Cherubino), VSO/Böhm, PHILIPS, 1956
VPO/Böhm, ORFEO, 7/30/57 (live)
Die Zauberflöte (Zweite Dame), VPO/Böhm, LONDON/DECCA, 1955
Philh/Klemperer; ANGEL/EMI, 1964

OFFENBACH, JACQUES
Les Contes d'Hoffmann (Mother), FNO/Ozawa, DG, 1989

ORFF, CARL
De temporum fine comoedia (Last Being), VPO/Karajan, DG, 1974

PIZZETTI, ILDEBRANDO
Assassinio nelle cattedrale (Seconda corifea), VPO/Karajan, DG, 3/9/60 (live, in German)

PFITZNER, HANS
Palestrina (Silla), VPO/Heger, MYTO, 12/16/64 (live)

PUCCINI, GIACOMO
Madama Butterfly (Suzuki), VPO/Karajan, DECCA, 1974
Suor Angelica (Princess), NPO/Bonynge, DECCA, 1973

SAINT-SAËNS, CAMILLE
Samson et Dalila (Dalila), MRO/Patané, EURODISC, 1973

SMETANA, BEDŘICH
The Bartered Bride (Agnes), Schuchter, HMV, 1954 (excerpt)

STRAUSS, JOHANN
Die Fledermaus (Orlofsky), Philh/Ackermann, EMI, 1960

STRAUSS, RICHARD
Capriccio (Clairon), Philh/Sawallisch, EMI, 1957/8
VPO/Prêtre, HANDELMANIA, 1964 (live)
Elektra (Klytämnestra), BosSO/Ozawa, PHILIPS, 1988 (live)

Die Frau ohne Schatten (Färberin), VPO/Karajan, DG, 6/11/64 (live)
Der Rosenkavalier (Annina), DOB/Hollreiser, EURODISC, 1964 (excerpts)
Der Rosenkavalier (Marschallin), VPO/Böhm, DG, 7/26/69 (live)
    VPO/Bernstein, CBS/SONY, 1971
Der Rosenkavalier (Octavian, Zweite Adelige Waise), Philh/Karajan, EMI, 1956
Der Rosenkavalier (Octavian), VPO/Krips, VOCE LUNA, 10/3/71 (live)
Salome (Page), HRS/Schröder, MYTO, 1952

VERDI, GIUSEPPE
Aida (First Priestess), HRS/Schröder, MYTO, 11/11/52 (live)
Un Ballo in Maschera (Ulrica), NPO/Solti, DECCA, 1984
Falstaff (Mistress Quickly), VPO/Karajan, PHILIPS, 1980
Macbeth (Lady Macbeth), VPO/Böhm, LEGATO CLASSICS, 1970 (live)
Il Trovatore (Azucena), VPO/Karajan, SERENISSIMA, 5/77 (live)

WAGNER, RICHARD
Götterdämmerung (Waltraute), VPO/Solti, LONDON/DECCA, 1964
Götterdämmerung (Waltraute and Second Norn), BPO/Karajan, DG, 1969
Götterdämmerung (Brünnhilde's Immolation Scene), NDR/Knappertsbush, ARKADIA,
    3/24/63 (live)
Lohengrin (Ortrud), VPO/Kempe, EMI, 1963
    Philh/Wallberg, 1958 [Excerpt in *Elisabeth Schwarzkopf: Romantic*
    Opera Arias, EMI, 1988]
Die Meistersinger von Nürnberg (Magdalena), DOB/Jochum, DG, 1975
Parsifal (Kundry), VPO/Karajan, ARKADIA, 4/1/66 (live)
    VPO/Solti, LONDON/DECCA, 1971
Das Rheingold (Fricka), MET/Levine, DG, 1988
Rienzi (Adriano), VSO/Krips, MELODRAM, 6/14/60 (live)
Tannhäuser (Venus), VPO/Karajan, DG, 1/8/63 (live)
    VPO/Solti, LONDON/DECCA, 1971
Tristan und Isolde (Brangäne), BFO/Böhm, PHILIPS/DG, 8/4/66 (live)
    DOB/Karajan, DG, 1971/2
Tristan und Isolde (Isolde's Liebestod), Philh/Klemperer, EMI, 1962 (excerpt)
    NDR/Knappertsbush, NUOVA ERA, 3/24/62
    (live, excerpt)
Die Walküre (Fricka), VPO/Solti, DECCA, 1965
    MET/Levine, DG, 1988

Opera Collections

Christa Ludwig Operatic Recital, DOB/Hollreiser, RCA, 1963-64
Christa Ludwig, Walter Berry: Scenes from Richard Strauss's Elektra, Die Frau ohne
Schatten, Der Rosenkavalier, DOB/Hollreiser, RCA, 1963-64
Samson et Dalila (excerpts) in *Grand Gala*, MRO/Eichhorn, EURODISC, 1974
Christa Ludwig Recital (excerpts from *Don Carlo* and *Aida*), VPO/Klobucar [*Don Carlo*
    5/25/67], MET/Cleva [*Aida*, 2/28/70], MELODRAM, 1990

Symphonies, Oratorios, and Other Concert Works

BACH, JOHANN SEBASTIAN
Christmas Oratorio, MBO/Richter, DG, 1965
Mass in B Minor, BPO/Karajan, DG, 1973
St. John Passion, BerSO/Forster, EMI, 1961
St. Matthew Passion, Philh/Klemperer, EMI, 1960
    VSO/Böhm, MYTO, 4/18/62 (live)
    BPO/Karajan, DG, 1972

BEETHOVEN, LUDWIG VAN
"Ah, Perfido!," LO/Whitney, 3/16/65 (live) [as Bonus Track on Fidelio, SFO/Böhm,
    MELODRAM, 11/29/68 (live)]
Missa Solemnis, Philh/Karajan, EMI, 1958
    VPO/Karajan, EMI, 8/18/59 (live)
    BPO/Karajan, DG, 1966
    BPO/Karajan, ARKADIA, 2/26/66 (live)
    BavRS/Sawallisch, ARKADIA, 5/23/70 (live)
    VPO/Böhm, DG, 1975
Symphony No. 9, Philh/Klemperer, EMI, 1957
    BPO/Karajan, CLAQUE, 1/1/68 (live)

BERLIOZ, HECTOR
Roméo et Juliette, VPO/Maazel, DECCA, 1973

BERNSTEIN, LEONARD
Symphony No. 1 "Jeremiah," IPO/Bernstein, DG, 1977

BRAHMS, JOHANNES
Alto Rhapsody, Philh/Klemperer, EMI, 1962
    VPO/Böhm, DG, 1976
    VPO/Böhm, 8/15/79 (live) [in The Vienna Philharmonic
    and Its Conductors, SF, 1995]

BRUCKNER, ANTON
Mass No. 3 in F minor, BerSO/Forster, EMI, 1963

FRANCK, CÉSAR
Nocturne, ODP/Barenboim, DG, 1976

HAYDN, JOSEPH
The Creation, BPO/Karajan, DG, 1966/8/9

MAHLER, GUSTAV
Kindertotenlieder, Philh/Vandernoot, EMI, 1958
    BPO/Karajan, DG, 1974
Des Knaben Wunderhorn, NYP/Bernstein, CBS, 1967/9
    Philh/Klemperer, EMI, 1964 (excerpts)
Das Lied von der Erde, Philh/Klemperer, EMI, 1964/6
    VSO/Kleiber, NUOVO ERA, 6/7/67 (live)
    BPO/Karajan, ARKADIA, 12/15/70 (live)
    BPO/Karajan, DG, 1973
    IPO/Bernstein, CBS, 1972
    CPO/Neumann, PRAGA, 4/7/83 (live)
Lieder eines fahrenden Gesellen, Philh/Boult, EMI, 1958

Rückert Songs, Philh/Klemperer, EMI, 1964 (excerpts)
    BPO/Karajan, DG, 1974
Symphony No. 2, VPO/Mehta, LONDON/DECCA, 1975
    NYP/Bernstein, DG, 1987 (live)
Symphony No. 3, NYP/Bernstein, DG, 1987 (live)

MOZART, WOLFGANG AMADEUS
Mass in C Minor, PRO/Grossmann, PREISER, 1958
Mass in C Major, PRO/Horenstein, VOX, 1958
Requiem, Philh/Giulini, EMI, 1963
    Philh/Giulini, EMI, 1978
Scene with Rondo (KV 505), SMO/Paumgartner, ORFEO, 8/25/63 (live)
Vesperae Solennes de Confessore, PMO/Horenstein, VOX, 1958

NONO, LUIGI
Memento, NDR/Maderna, ARKADIA, 2/26/53 (live)

PERGOLESI, GIOVANNI BATTISTA
Stabat Mater, BerRS/Maazel, PHILIPS, 1966

SCHÖNBERG, ARNOLD
Gurre-lieder, VSO/Krips, ARKADIA, 6/10/69 (live)

WAGNER, RICHARD
Wesendonck Lieder, Philh/Klemperer, EMI, 1962

VERDI, GIUSEPPE
Requiem, VPO/Karajan, ORFEO, 8/21/58 (live)
    Philh/Giulini, EMI, 1963
    VPO/Karajan, DG, 1972
    VPO/Karajan, 8/26/70 (live, excerpts) [in *Gundula Janowitz, Volume 1*, DORE-
    MI 1998]

Lieder

MAHLER, GUSTAV
Des Knaben Wunderhorn, Bernstein, CBS, 4/24/68 (live)

SCHUBERT, FRANZ
Die Winterreise, Levine, DG,1986

SCHUMANN, ROBERT
Frauenliebe und leben, Parsons, PRAGA, 5/28/66 (live)

WOLF, HUGO
Italienisches Liederbuch, Barenboim, DG, 1974/5

Lieder Collections

A Song Recital, Moore, EMI, 1957 (Brahms, Mahler, Schubert, Strauss, Wolf)
Mahler Songs—Album 2, Moore, EMI, 1959
Schubert Lieder, Parsons, EMI, 1961
A Most Unusual Song Recital, Moore, SERAPHIM/EMI, 1965 (Brahms, Reger, Rossini,
    Strauss)
The Shepherd on the Rock & Other Songs with Chamber Accompaniment, Parsons,
    ANGEL/EMI, 1965 (Brahms, Rachmaninoff, Ravel, Saint-Saëns, Schubert)

Ein Liederabend mit Christa Ludwig und Walter Berry, Werba, DG, 1968 (Schumann, Wolf)
Christa Ludwig Singt Brahms Lieder, Parsons, EMI, 1969
Schubert-Lieder, Gage, DG, 1973
Schubert-Lieder 2, Gage, DG, 1974
An Evening of Brahms Songs, Bernstein, CBS, 1977
Christa Ludwig à Royaumont, Spencer, TDF, 10/7/89 (live) [Brahms, Schubert, Wolf]
Farewell to Salzburg, Spencer, RCA, 1993 (Brahms, Mahler, Strauss)
Tribute to Vienna, Spencer, RCA, 4/24/94 (live) [Bernstein, Beethoven, Brahms, Mahler, Schubert, Strauss, Wolf]

Videos and Films

BEETHOVEN, LUDWIG VAN
Symphony No. 9; BPO/Karajan, UNITEL (USA Broadcast 12/31/75)
BERNSTEIN, LEONARD
Candide; LSO/Bernstein, DG, 12/13/89
Bernstein Conducts Bernstein: Chichester Psalms, Symphonies No. 1 and 2; IPO/Bernstein, KULTUR, 1977 (Symphony No. 1 recorded live on 8/22/77 in Berlin)
BRAHMS, JOHANNES
Lieder: Recital at the Tel Aviv Museum; Bernstein, UNITEL, 1972
MAHLER, GUSTAV
Das Lied von der Erde; IPO/ Bernstein, UNITEL, 1972
Rückert Songs: Vienna Philharmonic 150 Year Anniversary Concert; VPO/Muti, SONY, 3/22/92
Symphony No. 3; VPO/Bernstein, DG, 1972
MOZART, WOLFGANG AMADEUS
Così fan tutte (Dorabella); VPO/Böhm, UNITEL, 1969
Requiem; VPO/Böhm, UNITEL, 1972
PUCCINI, GIACOMO
Madama Butterfly (Suzuki): Film Directed by Jean-Pierre Ponnelle; VPO/Karajan, LONDON/DECCA 1974
SAINT-SAËNS, CAMILLE
Samson et Dalila ("Mon Coeur s'ouvre à ta voix"): Televised Charity Opera Gala from the Musikverein in Vienna; BEL CANTO SOCIETY, 9/4/88
VERDI, GIUSEPPE
Falstaff (Mistress Quickly): Salzburg Festival Production; VPO/Karajan, SONY 1982
WAGNER, RICHARD
Das Rheingold (Fricka): Metropolitan Opera Production; MET/Levine, DG, 1990
Die Walküre (Fricka): Metropolitan Opera Production; MET/Levine, DG, 1990
Götterdämmerung (Waltraute): Metropolitan Opera Production; MET/Levine, DG, 1990
VARIOUS COMPOSERS
A Toast to Vienna in 3/4 Time: Young People's Concert; NYP/Bernstein, SONY, 10/28/67 (Broadcast 12/25/67)
Bernstein at 70: Birthday Concert for Leonard Bernstein at Tanglewood; BSO/Ozawa (Mahler), BSO/Mauceri (Bernstein), UNITEL, 8/21/88
Tribute to Vienna: Farewell Lieder Recital in Vienna; Spencer, BMG, 4/24/94

Key to Orchestral Abbreviations

BavRS = Bavarian Radio Symphony
BavSO = Bavarian Symphony
BerRS = Berlin Radio Symphony
BerSO = Berlin Symphony
BFO = Bayreuth Festival Orchestra
BosSO = Boston Symphony
BPO = Berlin Philharmonic
BavRS = Bavarian Radio Symphony
BerRS = Berlin Radio Symphony
ColGO = Cologne Gürzenich
CPO = Czech Philharmonic Orchestra
DOB = Deutsche Oper Berlin
FNO = French National Orchestra
HRS = Hessian Radio Symphony
IPO = Israel Philharmonic
LO = Louisville Orchestra
LSO = London Symphony
MBO = Munich Bach Orchestra
MET = Metropolitan Opera
MPO = Munich Philharmonic
MRO = Munich Radio Orchestra
NDR = NDR (North German Radio)
Symphony
NPhilh = New Philharmonia
NPO = National Philharmonic

NYP = New York Philharmonic
ODP = Orchestre de Paris
Philh = Philharmonia
PRO = Pro Musica
Scala = Orchestra of La Scala, Milan
SFO = San Francisco Opera
SMO = Salzburg Mozart
StkaD = Staatskapelle Dresden
VPO = Vienna Philharmonic
VSO = Vienna Symphony

Key to Month Abbreviations

JA = January
FE = February
MA = March
AP = April
MY = May
JU = June
JL = July
AU = August
SE = September
OC = October
NO = November
DE = December

Important Dates and Awards

1928 Born March 16 in Berlin

1944 Received Abitur certificate in Giessen. (Signifies passing a university-qualifying examination.)

1945 Received first professional contract in Giessen.

1957 Married Walter Berry on September 29.

1959 Gave birth to son Wolfgang on March 4.

1963 Became Kammersängerin of the Vienna State Opera.

1967 Received Grammy Award as Best Classical Vocal Soloist.

1969 Awarded Österreichisches Ehrenkreuz für Kunst und Wissenschaft, Erster Klasse (Austrian Cross of Honor for Art and Science, First Class).

1972 Married Paul-Emile Deiber on March 3.
Became Honorary Member of the Vienna Konzerthaus Association on May 2.

1980 Received Silver Rose of the Vienna Philharmonic.

1988 Became Honorary Member of the Vienna State Opera on March 7.
Named Commandeur de l'Ordre des Arts et des Lettres, France on March 30

1989 Named Chevalier de Légion d'Honneur, France.

1994 Received Das Grosses Ehrenzeichen für Verdienste um die Republic Österreich (Highest Award of Merit from the Austrian Republic).
Named "Musician of the Year" by *Musical America*.
Gave final performance at the Vienna State Opera on December 14.

1995 Became Honorary Member of the Vienna Philharmonic on February 20.
Named Commandeur de l'Ordre National du Mérite, France on May 12.
Received the title of Professor from Senat in Berlin.

Selected Chronology

1945-52 GIESSEN AND FRANKFURT
Christa Ludwig received her first professional contract under her father's management in Giessen for the 1945-46 season. Here she sang opera and operetta arias in small concerts given in taverns and factories, because the opera house in Giessen had been totally destroyed in Allied bombings during the Second World War.

Beginning in the 1946-47 season, Miss Ludwig became a member of the Frankfurt Opera and sang a wide variety of roles in different cities (Offenbach, Hanau, Laufen, and at the Börse in Frankfurt itself) while the Frankfurt opera house was being rebuilt. Although she gave about 720 performances in six seasons, most of her roles were very small; only a few were more substantial. The role she sang most often was Prince Orlofsky in *Die Fledermaus* (77 performances).

Between 1946 and 1952, Miss Ludwig also sang innumerable small concerts and recitals, radio concerts, and concerts of modern music at the Donaueschingen Festival and elsewhere. Because performances of modern music had been forbidden under the Third Reich, a great flowering of interest in such music took place after the war. Her youth, her musical accuracy, and her low fees (according to Miss Ludwig) made her a very popular singer of such music. These performances also brought her to the attention of critics long before she began to sing important music in the standard repertoire.

Note: Although the original manuscript of this chronology contained over 60 pages, we are able to include only a small selection of performances here. Generally we chose debuts and first appearances in major roles.

1945-46 Season

FE 8	Giessen	First Lieder Recital: Songs to Heine texts; accompanied by Hans Göbel

1946-47 Season

OC 24	Offenbach	Debut with the Frankfurt Opera: *Die Fledermaus* (Orlofsky)
NO 22	Giessen	First Verdi *Requiem*
JA 12	Offenbach	*Un Ballo in Maschera* (Ulrica) with the Frankfurt Opera
MA 31	Frankfurt	*Les Contes d'Hoffmann* (Niklaus)

1947-48 Season

NO 22	Frankfurt	Radio Frankfurt Competition; awarded first prize (a concert on 12-30-47); sang "Mon Coeur s'ouvre à ta voix" (in German)

| DE 30 | Frankfurt | Frankfurt Radio Competition Prize Concert: *Wesendonck Lieder*; conducted by Winfried Zillig |

1948-49 Season

| FE 23 | Frankfurt | *Madama Butterfly* (Suzuki) |

1949-50 Season

| OC 13 | Giessen | Concert: "O don fatale" from *Don Carlos*, "Weiche Wotan" from *Das Rheingold*, Czernik Lieder (texts by Verlaine); conducted by Willy Czernik |
| FE 26 | Frankfurt | *Der Rosenkavalier* (First Octavian) |

1950-51 Season

| AP 18 | Frankfurt | Concert: First Mahler Symphony No. 2; Zillig |

1951-52 Season

| MA 7 | Frankfurt | *Carmen* (Mercédès); Zapf, Gonszar; Georg Solti |
| MA 31 | Frankfurt | *Carmen* (First Carmen); Windgassen, Ambrosius; Bitter |

1952-54 DARMSTADT

For two seasons (1952-53 and 1953-54), Christa Ludwig accepted a contract with the Darmstadt Opera, a smaller house than Frankfurt, because she could sing major roles there and work closely with the stage director Harro Dicks. Georg Solti, who was by then in charge in Frankfurt, brought Miss Ludwig back for several guest appearances. In addition, Miss Ludwig gave many concert and recital performances in Darmstadt, Frankfurt, and other smaller cities.

1952-53 Season

SE 17	Darmstadt	Debut at Darmstadt Opera: *Don Carlos* (First Eboli)
DE 15	Darmstadt	Recital: Debussy, Jolivet, Milhaud, Auric; Stock
DE 23	Darmstadt	*Carmen* (Carmen); Adam Fendt was the Don José in this Harro Dicks production

1953-54 Season

JL 18	Darmstadt	Honneger *Antigone* (Antigone)
AU 19	Frankfurt	*Tristan und Isolde* (First Brangäne); Aga Joesten was the Isolde
SE 22	Darmstadt	*Ariadne auf Naxos* (First Komponist)
NO 4	Darmstadt	Honegger *Judith* (Judith)
NO 8	Frankfurt	*Così fan tutte* (First Dorabella); Richter, Friedrich, Baldauf, Schmitt-Walter; Solti
DE 9	Darmstadt	*Les Contes d'Hoffmann* (First Giulietta)

1954-55 HANOVER, VIENNA, AND SALZBURG

Christa Ludwig was under contract with the opera in Hanover for one season (1954-55), and the year 1955 was very important in Miss Ludwig's professional life. She first sang with the Vienna State Opera in the Redoutensaal at the Hofburg in April (the first of 766 performances with the Vienna State Opera), and she made her debut in the newly rebuilt opera house there in December. She also debuted at the Salzburg Festival in the same year. These debuts mark the beginning of Christa Ludwig's international career, and she was soon singing opera, lieder, and concert works throughout the world. This chronology lists only selected performances. Unless otherwise noted, all opera performances in Vienna are at the State Opera and in New York at the Metropolitan Opera.

1954-55 Season

AU 28	Hanover	Debut at Hanover Opera: *Boris Godunov* (Marina)
SE 4	Hanover	*Tristan und Isolde* (Brangäne); Varnay, Suthaus, Kreppet
OC 11	Hanover	Concert: First *Das Lied von der Erde* with Johannes Schüler conducting
NO 24	Hanover	*Eugene Onegin* (Olga)
JA 4	Hanover	*Aida* (First Amneris)
MA 19	Hanover	*Wozzeck* (First Marie)
AP 14	Vienna	First performance with the State Opera at the Roudentsaal in the Hofburg: *Le Nozze di Figaro* (First Cherubino); Schöffler, Jurinac, Seefried, Kunz; Böhm
JU 11	Hanover	*Die Walküre* (First Fricka)

1955 Salzburg Festival

AU 6   Debut at the Salzburg Festival: *Ariadne auf Naxos* (Der Komponist); Zadek, Schock, Streich, Güden, Kunz; Böhm.
Also sang several performances of the Zweite Dame in *Die Zauberflöte* with Solti conducting.

1955-56 Season

DE 26	Vienna	Debut in newly rebuilt opera house: *Der Rosenkavalier* (Octavian); Konetzni, Güden, Czerwenka; Moralt
JA 7	Vienna	*Les Contes d'Hoffmann* (Niklaus); Schock, Streich, Welitsch, Stich-Randall; Hollreiser
FE 16	Vienna	*Tristan und Isolde* (Brangäne); Lustig, Böhme, Grob-Prandl; Cluytens
FE 19	Vienna	*Aida* (Amneris); Goltz, Gostic, Czerwenka, Böhme; Loibner
FE 23	Vienna	Vienna Symphony Concert at the Konzerthaus: *Judas Maccabaeus* (Handel); Stader, Patzak, Prey; Gillesberger
FE 28	Paris	Guest appearance with Frankfurt Opera: *Der Rosenkavalier* (Octavian); Reining, Steffek, Böhme; Solti
MA 17	Rome	Concert: Mahler Symphony No. 2; Maazel
MA 21	Vienna	Vienna Symphony Concert at the Konzerthaus: *Bluebeard's Castle*; Hurshell; Strauss
MA 23	Vienna	*Don Carlos* (Eboli); Greindl, Egenera, Friedrich, Hurshell; Rossi
AP 15	Vienna	Vienna Philharmonic Concert at the State Opera (first concert with the Vienna Philharmonic): *Missa Solemnis*; Zadek, Dermota, Wiener; Böhm
AP 22	Vienna	*Ariadne auf Naxos* (Der Komponist); Zadek, Gostic; Böhm
AP 29	Vienna	*Prince Igor* (Kontchakovna); Schöffler, Zadek, Dermota, Hurshell; Klobucar
MY 25	Vienna	Recital at the Konzerthaus: Works of Krenek; Patzak; accompanied by Krenek and Kamper
MY 29	Vienna	*Così fan tutte* (Dorabella) at the Hofburg; Seefried, Kunz, Dermota; Böhm
JU 17	Vienna	World premiere of the Frank Martin opera *Der Sturm* (Miranda); Wächter, Dermota, Koréh, Dirtl; Ansermet

1956 Salzburg Festival

JL 21		*Le Nozze di Figaro* (Cherubino); Fischer-Dieskau, Schwarzkopf, Seefried, Kunz; Böhm

AU 8   *Così fan tutte* (Dorabella); Seefried, Kunz, Dermota, Otto, Schöffler; Böhm
Also sang several performances of the Zweite Dame in *Die Zauberflöte* with Solti conducting.

1956-57 Season
NO 22   Vienna   *Carmen* (Carmen); Hopf, Berry, Scheyrer; Hollreiser
MA 15   Vienna   Vienna Symphony Concert at the Musikverein:
                     St. Matthew Passion; Patzak, Prey, Berry; Scherchen
MA 22   Vienna   *Il Barbiere di Siviglia* (Rosina) at the Hofburg; Kmentt,
                     Dönch, Czerwenka, Prey; Rossi
MY 16   Vienna   Recital at the Konzerthaus (first solo recital in Vienna):
                     Wolf, Mahler, Einem, Strauss; accompanied by Erik Werba
JU 18   Vienna   Vienna Symphony Concert at the Konzerthaus:
                     Liebermann *Streitliedzwischen Leben und Tod*, Wagner-
                     Régeny *Genesis*; Lipp, Patzak, Schöfer; Matacic
JU 21   Vienna   Vienna Symphony Concert at the Konzerthaus: Hindemith
                     Ite, angeli veloces (Hindemith); Patzak; Hindemith

1957 Salzburg Festival
AU 17   Liebermann *Die Schule der Frauen* (Georgette); Berry, Böhme, Rothenberger,
          Gedda, Pernerstorfer; Szell
Also sang several performances of Cherubino and Dorabella with Böhm conducting.

1957-58 Season
OC 18   London   Debut Recital at Wigmore Hall: Schubert, Brahms, Wolf,
                     Strauss, Mahler; Gerald Moore
FE 20   Chicago   Chicago Symphony Concert (American debut): *Das Lied
                     von der Erde*; Lewis; Reiner
MA 29   Vienna   Vienna Philharmonic Concert at the Musikverein:
                     Beethoven Symphony No. 9; Güden, Kmentt, Hotter;
                     Karajan
AP 10   Vienna   Vienna Symphony Concert at the Konzerthaus: Mahler
                     Symphony No. 2; Coertse; Maazel
MY 5   Brussels   Guest appearance with the Vienna State Opera at World's
                     Fair (sang special variations on "Voi che sapete"): *Le Nozze
                     di Figaro* (Cherubino); Wächter, Schwarzkopf, Seefried,
                     Kunz; Karajan
MY 20   Vienna   Recital at the Konzerthaus: Brahms; Werba

1958 Salzburg Festival
AU 13   *Don Carlos* (Eboli); Siepi, Fernandi, Bastianini, Jurinac; Karajan
AU 21   Vienna Philharmonic Concert: Verdi *Requiem*; Rysanek, Zampieri, Siepi;
          Karajan
Also sang several performances of Cherubino and Dorabella with Böhm conducting.

1958-59 Season
JA 7   Vienna   Vienna Symphony Concert at the Musikverein: Schmidt
                     Das Buch mit sieben Siegeln; Patzak, Berry, Lipp, Wunderlich;
                     Wallberg
MY 21   Vienna   Recital at the Musikverein: Schubert, Brahms; Werba
JU 10   Vienna   Musikverein Quarter Concert at the Musikverein: Egk *Die
                     Versuchung des heiligen Antonius*
JU 18   Vienna   Concert at the Konzerthaus: Gesualdo *Madrigals*; Horne,
                     Sjöstedt, Dickie, Berry; Hindemith

1959 Salzburg Festival
AU 19   Vienna Philharmonic Concert: *Missa Solemnis*; Price, Gedda, Zaccaria; Karajan
Also sang several performances of Dorabella with Böhm conducting.

1959-60 Season

OC 25	Vienna	New production by Günther Rennert: *La Cenerentola* (First Angelina); Kmentt, Berry, Dönch; Erede
NO 9	Chicago	American opera debut at the Lyric Opera of Chicago: *Così fan tutte* (Dorabella); Schwarzkopf, Simoneau, Berry; Krips
DE 10	New York	Metropolitan Opera debut: *Le Nozze di Figaro* (Cherubino); Borg, Amara, Tozzi, Söderström; Leinsdorf
DE 26	New York	*Der Rosenkavalier* (Octavian); Della Casa, Czerwenka, Söderström; Leinsdorf
JA 14	New York	*Aida* (Amneris); Amara, Uzunov, Scott, Flagello; Cleva
JA 21	New York	*Tristan und Isolde* (Brangäne); Liebl, Hines, Nilsson; Böhm
MA 9	Vienna	Pizzetti *Assassinio nelle cattedrale* (Seconda corifea); Hotter, Equiluz, Heater, Hurshell; Karajan
AP 26	Paris	Berlin Philharmonic Concert (first appearance with Berlin Philharmonic): Beethoven Symphony No. 9; Karajan
MY 18	Vienna	Dual Recital with Walter Berry at the Konzerthaus: Wolf, Schumann; Werba
JU 14	Vienna	Vienna Symphony Concert at the Musikverein: *Rienzi* (Adriano); Svanholm, Christiansen, Schöffler, Berry, Stich-Randall; Krips

1960 Salzburg Festival
JL 26   Vienna Philharmonic Concert (sang first notes at opening of the Large Festival Hall): "Gloria" from Mozart Mass in C Minor; Price, Kmentt; Karajan
Also sang several performances of Cherubino and Dorabella with Böhm conducting and of Eboli with Nello Santi conducting.

1960-61 Season

NO 16	Chicago	*Die Walküre* (Fricka) at the Lyric Opera: Vickers, Hotter, Brouwentijn, Nilsson; Matacic
DE 2	New York	American Opera Society Concert: Handel *Hercules* (Dejanira); Schwarzkopf, Berry, Verreau, Ludgin; Rescigno
JA 31	Vienna	Dual Recital with Berry at the Konzerthaus: Rossini, Purcell, Brahms, Schubert, Dvořák; Berry; Werba
MA 16	Vienna	Vienna Symphony Concert at the Konzerthaus: *Kindertotenlieder*; Fricsay
AP 1	Vienna	New Karajan production: *Parsifal* (First Kundry—Act 2 only); Wächter, Franc, Hotter, Uhl, Berry; Karajan
AP 13	London	London Philharmonia Concert: *Das Lied von der Erde*; Wunderlich; Klemperer
AP 17	London	Berlin Philharmonic Concert: Beethoven Symphony No. 9; Karajan
MY 18	Milan	*Der Rosenkavalier* (Octavian) at La Scala; Schwarzkopf, Edelmann, Rothenberger; Böhm

1961 Salzburg Festival
JL 28   *Der Rosenkavalier* (Octavian); Schwarzkopf, Edelmann, Wiener, Rothenberger; Böhm

AU 20   Vienna Philharmonic Concert: Bach Mass in B Minor; Price, Gedda, Souzay,
         Berry; Karajan
AU 28   Dual Recital with Berry: Monteverdi, Wolf, Dvořák; Werba
Also sang several performances of Dorabella with Böhm conducting.

1961-62 Season

SE 29	Berlin	Debut in premiere of new Wieland Wagner production during reopening week of the rebuilt Deutsche Oper: *Aida* (Amneris); Davy, Thomas, Greindl, Neralié; Böhm
OC 21	Chicago	*Mefistofele* (Elena) at the Lyric Opera; Christoff, Bergonzi, Ligabue; Votto
OC 30	Chicago	*La Forza del Destino* (Preziosilla) at the Lyric Opera; Farrell, Bergonzi, Guelfi, Christoff; Cillario
DE 5	Berlin	*Così fan tutte* (Dorabella) at the Deutsche Oper; Lear, Berry, Haefliger; Bour
DE 27	Berlin	New Wieland Wagner production at the Deutsche Oper: *Lohengrin* (First Ortrud); Thomas, Silja, Uhde; Hollreiser
JA 11	Vienna	Recital at the Musikverein: Wagner, Mahler, Wolf, Dvořák; Werba
MA 14	Berlin	*Der Rosenkavalier* (Octavian) at the Deutsche Oper; Crespin, Langdon, Köth; Schüler
MA 30	Vienna	Vienna Symphony Concert at the Musikverein: Schmidt *Das Buch mit sieben Siegeln*; Dermota, Berry, Muszely, Weymar, Kathol; Wallberg
AP 18	Vienna	Vienna Symphony Concert at the Musikverein: *St. Matthew Passion*; Wunderlich, Wiener, Lipp, Berry; Böhm
MY 5	Wiesbaden	First Appearance on Television: *Ariadne auf Naxos* (Der Komponist) at Wiesbaden May Festival; Zadek; Wallberg
MY 25	Vienna	New Karajan production: *Fidelio* (First Leonore); Vickers, Berry, Kreppel; Karajan
MY 29	Vienna	*La Forza del Destino* (Preziosilla); Scheyrer, Bastianini, Ferraro; Molinari-Pradelli
JU 16	Vienna	Vienna Symphony Concert at the Musikverein: Beethoven Symphony No. 9; Lipp, Kmentt, Berry; Sawallisch
AU 17	Lucerne	Dual Recital with Berry at the Lucerne Festival: Schumann, Ravel, Dvořák, Wolf; Werba

1962 Salzburg Festival

AU 3   *Iphigénie en Aulide* (Iphigénie); Steiner, Berry, Borkh, King; Böhm
AU 22   Vienna Philharmonic Concert: Beethoven Symphony No. 9; Grümmer,
         Häfliger, Berry; Klecki
Also sang several performances of Dorabella with Böhm conducting.

1962-63 Season

OC 5	Berlin	*Tristan und Isolde* (Brangäne) at the Deutsche Oper; Beirer, Mödl, Kreppel; Hollreiser
NO 7	Berlin	*Fidelio* (Leonore) at the Deutsche Oper; King, Greindl, Berry; Rother
DE 8	Vienna	Vienna Philharmonic Concert at the Musikverein: Bach *Magnificat*; Kmentt, Wächter; Karajan
JA 8	Vienna	New Karajan production: *Tannhäuser* (Venus); Frick, Beirer, Wächter, Kmentt; Karajan

JA 10	Innsbruck	Dual Recital with Berry at the Olympics: Brahms, Schumann; Werba
FE 10	London	London Philharmonia Concert: "Ah, Perfido!," Liebestod; Klemperer
MA 1	Berlin	Berlin Philharmonic Concert: Bach Magnificat; Karajan
MA 13	Amsterdam	Concert: Das Lied von der Erde; Lewis; Dorati
MA 24	Hamburg	NDR Symphony Concert: Liebestod, Immolation Scene; Knappertsbusch
AP 19	Berlin	Berlin Philharmonic Concert: Mahler Symphony No. 2; Gayer; Maazel
MY 19	Vienna	Wozzeck (Marie); Berry, Uhl; Ludwig
JU 15	Vienna	Götterdämmerung (Waltraute); Windgassen, Nilsson; Karajan
JU 16	Vienna	Berlin Radio Orchestra Concert at the Konzerthaus: Verdi Requiem; Lorengar, Gedda, Ghiaurov; Maazel
JU 23	London	London Philharmonia Concert: Verdi Requiem; Schwarzkopf, Gedda, Ghiaurov; Giulini
SE 1	Lucerne	Berlin Philharmonic Concert at the Lucerne Festival: Verdi Requiem; Price, Zampieri, Ghiaurov; Karajan
SE 4	Lucerne	Berlin Philharmonic Concert at the Lucerne Festival: Bach Magnificat; Karajan

1963 Salzburg Festival

| AU 10 | Salzburg Festival Solo Recital Debut: Mahler, Schumann, Brahms, Strauss; Werba |
| AU 25 | Salzburg Mozart Orchestra Concert: Mozart "Ch'Io mi scordi di te" (KV505); Geza Anda; Paumgartner |

Also sang several performances of Iphigénie and Dorabella with Böhm and in a performance of Beethoven's Ninth Symphony with Karajan and the Vienna Philharmonic.

1963-64 Season

OC 20	Tokyo	Guest with Deutsche Oper Berlin at opening of Nissei Theater: Fidelio (Leonore); King, Berry, Greindl; Böhm
OC 22	Tokyo	Deutsche Oper Berlin Concert: Immolation Scene; Böhm
NO 7	Tokyo	Deutsche Oper Berlin Concert: Beethoven Symphony No. 9; Böhm
NO 11	Tokyo	Dual Recital with Berry
DE 1	Munich	Debut during reopening week of the Bavarian State Opera: Fidelio (Leonore); Karajan
JA 26	Vienna	Recital at the Konzerthaus: Schubert, Wolf; Werba
MA 21	Vienna	Capriccio (First Clairon); Della Casa, Kerns, Kmentt, Berry, Wiener; Prêtre
MA 24	Vienna	Vienna Symphony Concert at the Musikverein: St. Matthew Passion; Prey, Wunderlich, Stich-Randall, Wiener; Richter
AP 23	Vienna	Vienna Symphony Concert at the Konzerthaus: Missa Solemnis; Lorengar, Ilosfalvy, Berry; Böhm
JU 11	Vienna	New Karajan production: Die Frau ohne Schatten (First Färberin); Thomas, Rysanek, Berry; Karajan

1964 Salzburg Festival

| JL 26 | Ariadne auf Naxos (First Ariadne); Thomas, Popp, Jurinac, Grist; Böhm |

JL 31   Recital of Hugo Wolf songs with Werba
Also sang several performances of Dorabella with Böhm conducting.

1964-65 Season

SE 8   Buenos Aires   *Bluebeard's Castle* (Judith) at the Teatro Colón; Berry;
                              Kertesz
SE 18   Buenos Aires   *Le Nozze di Figaro* (Cherubino) at the Teatro Colón; De Los
                              Angeles, Holm, Berry, Prey; Kertesz
OC 6   Buenos Aires   *Lohengrin* (Ortrud) at the Teatro Colón; De Los Angeles,
                              Uhl, Alexander, Crass; Schmidt-Isserstedt
OC 20   Buenos Aires   *Ariadne auf Naxos* (Der Komponist) at the Teatro Colón;
                              Hillbrecht, Holm, Uhl, Prey, Berry; Schmidt-Isserstedt
DE 16   Vienna   *Palestrina* (Silla); Frick, Wunderlich, Jurinac; Heger
DE 19   Vienna   Recital at the Musikverein: Wolf, Brahms; Werba
MA 5   New York   Dual Debut Recital with Berry at Carnegie Hall: Purcell,
                              Monteverdi, Wolf, Ravel, Schumann, Dvořák; Werba
MA 11   Detroit   Detroit Symphony Concert: *Alto Rhapsody*; Immolation
                              Scene; Ehrling
MA 16   Louisville   Louisville Orchestra Concert: "Ah, Perfido!," *Lieder eines
                              fahrenden Gesellen*; Whitney
MA 23   New York   American Opera Society Concert at Carnegie Hall:
                              Iphigénie en Aulide (Iphigénie); Berry, Allen, Cassilly;
                              Skrowaczewski
AP 10   Vienna   Vienna Symphony Concert at the Musikverein: *St. John
                              Passion*; Kmentt, Prey, Grümmer, Dickie, Berry; Richter
AP 27   Vienna   Vienna Philharmonic Concert at the State Opera:
                              Beethoven Symphony No. 9; Lipp, King, Wiener; Böhm
MY 16   Vienna   *Lohengrin* (Ortrud); Talvela, Thomas, Watson, Berry; Böhm
JU 4   Vienna   Vienna Philharmonic Concert at the Musikverein: *Orfeo ed
                              Euridice* (Orfeo); Lipp, Schädle; Krips
JU 13   Vienna   Recital at the Konzerthaus: Rossini, Egk, Gulda; Berry,
                              Werba, George, Kleinschuter; Gulda, Planyavsky
SE 1   Lucerne   Dual Recital with Berry at Lucerne Festival: Monteverdi,
                              Schubert, Wolf; Werba
SE 12   Epidaurus   Berlin Philharmonic Concert: Verdi *Requiem*; Karajan

1965-66 Season

SE 27   Barcelona   Vienna Philharmonic Concert: Mozart *Requiem*; Böhm
SE 29   Barcelona   Vienna Philharmonic Concert: Beethoven Symphony
                              No. 9; Böhm
DE 16   Vienna   Recital at the Musikverein: Schumann, Reger, Pfitzner;
                              Werba
FE 14   Vienna   New Otto Schenk production: *Carmen* (Carmen); King,
                              Wächter, Pilou; Maazel
FE 25   Berlin   Berlin Philharmonic Concert: *Missa Solemnis*; Janowitz,
                              Wunderlich, Berry; Karajan
MY 11   Drottningholm   *Così fan tutte* (Dorabella); Schwarzkopf, Sciutti, Kmentt,
                              Dönch; Koltay
MY 15   Berlin   Berlin Radio Symphony Concert: Pergolesi *Stabat Mater*;
                              Lear; Maazel

JU 16   Berlin   *Fidelio* (Leonore) at the Deutsche Oper; King, Berry, Lagger, Otto, Grobe; Maazel

1966 Bayreuth Festival
AU 4   Debut at the Bayreuth Festival: *Tristan und Isolde* (Brangäne); Nilsson, Windgassen, Talvela, Wächter; Böhm

1966 Salzburg Festival
AU 8   Dual recital of Wolf songs with Berry and Werba

1966-67 Season

OC 2	New York	New production during opening weeks of new Met at Lincoln Center: *Die Frau ohne Schatten* (Färberin); Rysanek, King, Berry; Böhm
OC 29	New York	Dual Recital with Berry at Hunter College: Purcell, Cherubini, Bach, Schubert, Brahms, Wolf, Schumann, Dvořák; Werba
DE 8	New York	New production designed by Wieland Wagner: *Lohengrin* (Ortrud); Kónya, Bjoner, Berry; Böhm
FE 24	Berlin	Berlin Philharmonic Concert: *Gurre-Lieder*; Jurinac, Kachel, Stolze, Talvela, Friedrichsen; Karajan
MA 19	Salzburg	Debut at the first Salzburg Easter Festival: *Die Walküre* (Fricka); Berlin Philharmonic; Karajan
MY 20	Vienna	Vienna Philharmonic Concert at the Musikverein: *Lieder eines fahrenden Gesellen*; Böhm
JU 1	Vienna	Recital at the Konzerthaus: Mahler, Wolf, Reger, Pfitzner, Strauss; Werba
JU 4	Vienna	Recital at the Musikverein: Brahms; Werba
JU 7	Vienna	Vienna Symphony Concert at the Konzerthaus: *Das Lied von der Erde*; Kmentt; Kleiber
JU 10	Vienna	Vienna Philharmonic Concert at the Musikverein (first concert with Leonard Bernstein): Mahler Symphony No. 2; Güden; Bernstein
JU 18	Vienna	Berlin Radio Orchestra Concert at the Konzerthaus: *Kindertotenlieder*; Maazel

1967 Bayreuth Festival
JL 28   *Parsifal* (Kundry); King, Stewart, Crass, Nienstedt; Boulez

1967 Salzburg Festival
AU 10   Recital of Brahms songs with Werba

1967-68 Season

SE 11	Montreal	Guest appearance with Vienna State Opera at Expo '67: *Der Rosenkavalier* (Octavian); Rysanek, Czerwenka, Loose; Krips
SE 19	Montreal	*Wozzeck* (Marie); Berry, Uhl; Hollreiser
OC 12	New York	New York Philharmonic Concert: *Des Knaben Wunderhorn*; Bernstein
OC 21	New York	Dual Recital with Berry at Metropolitan Museum of Art: Wolf; Werba
OC 26	Chicago	Chicago Symphony Concert: *Des Knaben Wunderhorn*, Immolation Scene; Berry; Wallenstein

OC 28	New York	New York Philharmonic Young People's Concert ("A Toast to Vienna in $^3/_4$ Time" televised 12/25/67): Berry; Bernstein
NO 21	New York	Karajan Ring Production: *Die Walküre* (Fricka); Vickers, Janowitz, Stewart, Nilsson; Karajan
DE 31	Berlin	Berlin Philharmonic Concert: Beethoven Symphony No. 9; Janowitz, Thomas, Berry; Karajan
JA 30	London	Covent Garden Debut: *Aida* (Amneris); Jones, Vickers, Rouleau, Shaw; Downes
AP 13	Vienna	New Otto Schenk production: *Der Rosenkavalier* (First Marschallin); Jones, Berry, Grist; Bernstein
AP 24	Vienna	Recital at the Konzerthaus: *Des Knaben Wunderhorn*; Berry; Bernstein

1968 Salzburg Festival

| JL 27 | Recital of songs by Mahler, Berg, Reger, Pfitzner, and Strauss with Werba |
| AU 12 | *Fidelio* (Leonore); Hotter, Wixell, King, Crass, Mathis, Grobe; Böhm |

1968-69 Season

OC 4	Berlin	Berlin Philharmonic Concert: Verdi *Requiem*; Lorengar, Bergonzi, Flagello; Maazel
NO 14	New York	Recital at Metropolitan Musem of Art: Brahms
NO 27	Los Angeles	Los Angeles Philharmonic Concert: *Bluebeard's Castle*; Berry; Mehta
JA 5	New York	Dual Recital with Berry at Philharmonic Hall (later renamed Avery Fisher Hall): Purcell, Mozart, Beethoven, Schubert
FE 24	New York	*Der Rosenkavalier* (Marschallin); Lear, Berry, Raskin; Böhm
AP 11	Vienna	Vienna Philharmonic Concert at the Musikverein: Andreae *Cantata 169*; Abbado
MY 2	Vienna	Vienna Symphony Concert at the Konzerthaus: Reger *An die Hoffnung*; Hollreiser
MY 20	Vienna	Dual Recital with Berry at the Musikverein: Wolf; Werba
MY 25	Vienna	Vienna Philharmonic Concert at the Musikverein: *Missa Solemnis*; Janowitz, Kmentt, Berry; Bernstein
JU 10	Vienna	Vienna Symphony Concert at the Konzerthaus: *Gurre-Lieder*; Sergi, Janowitz, Dickie; Krips

1969 Salzburg Festival

JL 26	*Der Rosenkavalier* (Marschallin); Adam, Troyanos, Wiener, Mathis; Böhm
AU 11	Recital of Schumann songs with Werba
AU 17	Vienna Philharmonic Concert: *Lieder eines fahrenden Gesellen*; Böhm

1969-70 Season

SE 19	Buenos Aires	*Der Rosenkavalier* (Octavian) at the Teatro Colón; Jurinac, Berry, Geszty; Leinsdorf
OC 4	Buenos Aires	Dual Recital with Berry: Wolf, Brahms, Schumann, Dvořák; Werba
OC 10	Buenos Aires	*Wozzeck* (Marie) at the Teatro Colón; Berry; Leinsdorf
DE 2	New York	Recital at Carnegie Hall: Schumann, Mahler; Otto Herz
JA 9	New York	Recital at Metropolitan Museum of Art: Brahms, Schubert; Werba
JA 17	New York	Recital at Hunter College: Reger, Berg, Dvořák, Strauss; Werba

MA 21	Salzburg	*Götterdämmerung* (Waltraute) at the Salzburg Easter Festival
AP 18	Vienna	*Macbeth* (First Lady Macbeth); Milnes, Ridderbusch, Cossutta; Böhm
MY 23	Rome	Bavarian Radio Symphony Concert in St. Peter's Basilica (first concert in the Basilica, directed by Franco Zeffirelli): *Missa Solemnis*; Bjöner, Domingo, Moll; Sawallisch
JL 5	Lenox	First performance at Boston Symphony Concert at Tanglewood (beginning of the "Swimming Pool Tour"): Mahler Symphony No. 2; Bernstein
JL 7	Ravinia	Chicago Symphony Concert: *Kindertotenlieder*; Kertesz
JL 9	Cuyahoga Falls	Cleveland Orchestra Concert: Mahler Symphony No. 2; Haywood; Bernstein
JL 11	Hollywood	Los Angeles Philharmonic Concert: Mozart, Gluck, Strauss (J); Krips
JL 14	Hollywood	Los Angeles Philharmonic Concert: *Kindertotenlieder*; Krips
JL 16	Detroit	Detroit Symphony Concert: *Lieder eines fahrenden Gesellen*
JL 18	Detroit	Detroit Symphony Concert: *Wesendonck Lieder*
JL 25	Ambler	Pittsburgh Symphony Concert: *Wesendonck Lieder*

1970 Salzburg Festival

AU 20	Recital of songs by Wolf and Schubert with Werba
AU 26	Vienna Philharmonic Concert: Verdi *Requiem*; Janowitz, Bergonzi, Raimondi; Karajan

1970-71 Season

NO 14	New York	New Nathaniel Merrill production: *Parsifal* (Kundry); Brilioth, Stewart, Siepi, Flagello, Macurdy; Leopold Ludwig
DE 6	New York	Recital at Carnegie Hall: Handel, Debussy, Dvořák, Loewe, Rachmaninoff, Wolf; Werba
DE 14	Berlin	Berlin Philharmonic Concert: *Das Lied von der Erde*; Spiess, Laubenthal; Karajan
DE 18	Vienna	Recital at the Musikverein: Handel, Debussy, Dvořák, Loewe, Wolf, Rachmaninoff; Werba
FE 19	New York	New Paul-Emile Deiber production: *Werther* (Charlotte); Di Giuseppe, Reardon, Blegen; Lombard
FE 23	New York	*Fidelio* (Last Leonore); Vickers, Dooley, Macurdy; Böhm
AP 28	Vienna	*Die Walküre* (Fricka); Thomas, Rysanek, Adam, Nilsson; Stein
MY 7	Vienna	Vienna Symphony Concert at the Konzerthaus: Immolation Scene; Hollreiser
MY 23	Vienna	World Premiere of Gottfried von Einem opera: *Der Besuch der Alten Dame* (Claire); Wächter, Zednik, Beirer; Stein
JU 22	Paris	Orchestre de Paris Concert (final concert for Karajan as Music Director): Verdi *Requiem*; Karajan
JL 25	Orange	Orchestre de Paris Concert: Verdi *Requiem*; Guilini

1971-72 Season

SE 11	San Francisco	Debut at San Francisco Opera: *Der Rosenkavalier* (Octavian); Jurinac, Donath, Jungwirth; Varviso
OC 2	Moscow	Vienna Philharmonic Concert: Beethoven Symphony No. 9; Donath, Thomas, Berry; Böhm

OC 3	Moscow	Guest with Vienna State Opera: *Der Rosenkavalier* (Octavian); Rysanek, Ridderbusch, De Groote; Krips
OC 31	New York	Recital at Carnegie Hall: Brahms; Doktor (viola); Bernstein
JA 12	Berlin	Recital: Mahler, Wolf, Schubert, Brahms, Strauss; Werba
JA 25	Paris	Orchestre de Paris Concert (first concert of new Music Director Solti): *Bluebeard's Castle* (Judith); Solti
FE 8	New York	New York Philharmonic Concert ("Informal Evening" at the Juilliard School): *Wozzeck* Fragments (Marie); Berg *Early Songs*; Boulez
FE 10	New York	New York Philharmonic Concert: Liszt Songs, *Wozzeck* Fragments (Marie); Boulez
FE 26	Flushing (NY)	Recital at Queens College: Mahler, Brahms, Strauss (R), Wagner, Saint-Saëns, Bizet, Strauss (J), Sieczynski; Herz
MA 25	Salzburg	*Tristan und Isolde* (Brangäne) at the Salzburg Easter Festival Vickers, Moll, Berry; Berlin Philharmonic; Karajan
MA 28	Salzburg	Berlin Philharmonic Concert at the Salzburg Easter Festival: *St. Matthew Passion*; Karajan
AP 19	Vienna	Recital at the Musikverein: Mahler, Berg, Schumann, Wolf; Werba
AP 23	Vienna	Vienna Philharmonic Concert at the Musikverein: Mahler Symphony No. 3; Schreier; Bernstein
MY 2	Vienna	Recital at the Konzerthaus: Brahms; Bernstein
MY 18	Tel Aviv	Debut at Israel Philharmonic Concert: *Das Lied von der Erde*; Kollo; Bernstein
MY 24	Tel Aviv	Recital at the Tel Aviv Museum: Brahms; Bernstein
JL 16	Orange	Orchestre de Paris Concert: Bach Mass in B Minor; Guilini
SE 4	Edinburgh	Berlin Philharmonic Concert at the Edinburgh Festival: *Das Lied von der Erde*; Kollo; Karajan

1972 Salzburg Festival

AU 15	Staatskapelle Dresden Concert: *Kindertotenlieder*; Böhm
AU 21	Recital of Schubert songs with Werba
AU 27	Berlin Philharmonic Concert: *Das Lied von der Erde*; Kollo; Karajan

1972-73 Season

OC 11	Paris	Debut at Palais Garnier: *Die Frau ohne Schatten* (Farbërin); Rysanek, King, Berry; Böhm
OC 18	Paris	Orchestre de Paris Concert: *Lieder eines fahrenden Gesellen*; Solti
DE 31	Vienna	*Die Fledermaus* (Orlofsky): Wächter, Moser, Zampieri, Holecek; Krips
JA 16	Vienna	Recital at the Musikverein: Schubert, Wolf; Werba
JA 28	New York	Recital at Avery Fisher Hall: Schubert, Schumann; Werba

1973 Salzburg Festival

Appeared only as the offstage prerecorded voice of one of the Last Beings in Carl Orff's *De temporum fine comoedia* with Karajan conducting.

1973-74 Season

| OC 27 | New York | *Les Troyens* (First Dido); Vickers, Dunn; Kubelik |
| JA 23 | Vienna | New Paul-Emile Deiber production: *Luisa Miller* (First Federica); Sukis, Taddei, Smith, Bonisolli; Erede |

FE 18 New York Cleveland Orchestra Concert at Carnegie Hall:
Kindertotenlieder; Maazel
FE 27 New York Recital at Avery Fisher Hall: Brahms, Schubert, Mahler,
Strauss; Ryan Edwards
MY 30 Paris *Elektra* (First Klytämnestra); Nilsson, Rysanek, Cassily,
Krause; Böhm
JU 17 Paris Orchestre de Paris Concert: *Das Lied von der Erde* (Mahler);
Solti
JU 24 Vienna Berlin Philharmonic Concert at the Musikverein: Verdi
Requiem; Freni, Pavarotti, van Dam; Karajan

1974 Salzburg Festival
JL 27 Recital of Wolf songs with Werba
AU 16 *Die Frau ohne Schatten* (Färberin); King, Rysanek, Berry, Hesse; Böhm. Last
Färberin on August 30

1974-75 Season
SE 28 Hamburg *Khovanshchina* (First Marfa)
FE 8 Vienna Vienna Philharmonic Concert at the Musikverein: Mahler
Symphony No. 2; Cotrubas; Mehta
AP 24 Vienna Recital at the Musikverein: Mahler, Wolf; Werba
JU 6 Vienna *Elektra* (Klytämnestra); Nilsson, Rysanek, Beirer, Adam;
Böhm

1975 Salzburg Festival
AU 11 Sang last Eboli with Karajan.

1975-76 Season
NO 6 Milan Concert at La Scala: *Des Knaben Wunderhorn*; Mehta
JA 23 Paris *Der Rosenkavalier* (Marschallin); Sotin, Minton, Popp;
Stein
MA 23 London *Carmen* (Carmen); Vickers, Cotrubas, Diaz; Lopez-Cobos
JU 6 Vienna Vienna Philharmonic Concert at the Musikverein: *Alto
Rhapsody*; Böhm
JU 28 Paris Orchestre de Paris Concert: *Des Knaben Wunderhorn*; Boulez

1976 Salzburg Festival
AU 21 Recital of songs by Berg, Pfitzner, Strauss, and Wolf with Werba

1976-77 Season
OC 17 Vienna *Les Troyens* (Dido); Chauvet, Lilowa; Albrecht
DE 6 Paris *Das Rheingold* (First Fricka); Adam, Mazura; Solti
DE 18 Paris *Die Walküre* (Fricka); Hoffmann, Dernesch, Adam, Jones;
Solti
MA 15 Vienna Recital at the Musikverein: Reger, Berg, Pfitzner, Wolf,
Strauss; Werba
MY 8 Vienna Karajan's return to Vienna: *Il Trovatore* (Azucena);
Cappuccilli, Price, Pavarotti, Van Dam; Karajan
AU 22 Berlin Israel Philharmonic Concert at the Philharmonic:
Bernstein Symphony No. 1; Bernstein

1977-78 Season
JA 5 Paris Orchestre de Paris Concert: *Kindertotenlieder*; Bernstein

JA 29	New York	Recital at Avery Fisher Hall: Beethoven, Schubert, Wolf, Mahler, Berg; Geoffrey Parsons
MA 17	Paris	New Günther Rennert production: *L'Incoronazione di Poppea* (Ottavia); Jones, Vickers, Ghiaurov; Rudel
JU 6	Vienna	Recital at the Musikverein: Wolf; Werba
AU 25	Vienna (VI)	Leonard Bernstein 60th Birthday Gala at Wolf Trap: "Lamentation" from Bernstein Symphony No. 1, Selections from *Songfest*; National Symphony Orchestra; Aaron Copland

1978 Salzburg Festival

| AU 13 | Vienna Philharmonic Concert: Mahler Symphony No. 3; Abbado |

1978-94 CONCERTS AND RECITALS

Although Christa Ludwig was as celebrated for her lieder recitals and concert work as she was for her operatic roles throughout her professional life, her first performance of Schubert's *Die Winterreise* during the 1978-79 season marks the beginning of a gradual concentration on recital and concert work. Although Miss Ludwig sang hundreds of performances during her professional life, this chronology lists mainly the recitals and concerts in Vienna, Salzburg, and New York, since such a selection gives a good idea of the range of her repertory.

1978-79 Season

NO 12	Vienna	Recital at the Musikverein: first performance of *Die Winterreise*; Werba
FE 17	New York	Cleveland Orchestra Concert at Carnegie Hall: Ravel *Shéhérezade*; Maazel
FE 25	New York	Recital at Avery Fisher Hall: Brahms, Wagner, Mahler, Strauss; John Wustman
AP 2	New York	*Parsifal* (Kundry); Vickers, Weikl, Talvela, Shinall, Plishka; Levine
JU 6	Vienna	*Un Ballo in Maschera* (Ulrica); Bonisolli, Paskalis, Arroyo, Grist; Patané
SE 6	Edinburgh	Recital at the Edinburgh Festival

1979 Salzburg Festival

| AU 15 | Vienna Philharmonic Concert: *Alto Rhapsody*; Böhm |
| AU 27 | Concert in honor of Karl Böhm's 80th Birthday: Bernstein Song for Karl Böhm with James Levine at the piano |

1979-80 Season

OC 21	New York	Recital at Avery Fisher Hall: Schumann, Brahms, Liszt, Wolf; Trampler; Wustman
NO 14	Vienna	Recital at the Musikverein: Schubert; Werba
NO 24	Vienna	Vienna Philharmonic Concert at the Musikverein: *Des Knaben Wunderhorn*; Mackerras
FE 24	Vienna	*Falstaff* (First Quickly); Saràbia, Weikl, Ramiro, Lorengar, Ghazarian, Miltschewa; Solti
AP 15	Vienna	Recital at the Konzerthaus: Wagner, Liszt, Pfitzner, Schumann, Dvořák; Werba
AP 24	Chicago	Chicago Symphony Concert: Mahler Symphony No. 2; Buchanan; Solti

JU 7   Vienna   Vienna Philharmonic Concert at the Musikverein: Reger
Die Weihe der Nacht; Mehta

1980 *Salzburg Festival*
AU 21   *Die Winterreise* with Werba

1980-81 Season

DE 21	Vienna	ORF Symphony Concert at the Musikverein: *Kindertotenlieder*; Neumann
MA 22	Vienna	*Das Rheingold* (Erda); Sotin, Fassbaender, Hornik; Mehta
AP 1	Vienna	Recital at the Musikverein: Mahler, Reger, Wolf, Chopin, Brahms, Bernstein; Werba
MY 6	Vienna	London Symphony Concert at the Konzerthaus: *Les Nuits d'Été*; Prêtre
MY 12	Berlin	Berlin Philharmonic Concert: Reger *Die Weihe der Nacht*, *Alto Rhapsody*; Lopez-Cobos
JU 12	Rome	Concert for Pope John Paul II at the Vatican: Bernstein Symphony No. 1; Saint Cecilia Orchestra; Bernstein

1981 *Salzburg Festival*

JL 25		Vienna Philharmonic Concert: Bruckner *Te Deum*; Moser, Araiza, Berry; Karajan
JL 26		New Karajan production: *Falstaff* (Quickly); Taddei, Panerai, Araiza, Kabaivanska, Perry, Schmidt; Karajan
AU 22		Recital of songs by Liszt, Mahler, Wolf, and Strauss with Werba
AU 26		Vienna Philharmonic Concert: Mozart *Requiem*; Popp, Schreier, Berry; Levine

1981-82 Season

SE 10	New York	New York Philharmonic Concert: *Kindertotenlieder*; Mehta
SE 17	New York	New York Philharmonic Concert: Mahler Symphony No. 2; Battle; Mehta
NO 2	Vienna	Recital at the Konzerthaus: Mendelssohn, Einem, Berg, Wolf; Werba
NO 15	New York	Recital at Avery Fisher Hall: Schubert; Laurence Davis
FE 18	Vienna	ORF Symphony Concert at the Musikverein: *Das Lied von der Erde*; Hollweg; Neumann
MA 22	Vienna	Recital at the Musikverein: Mozart, Mendelssohn, Schubert, Beethoven, Schumann, Tchaikovsky, Wolf; Wussow; Werba
JU 6	Vienna	Vienna Philharmonic Concert at the Musikverein: Mahler Symphony No. 2; Blegen; Levine
JU 13	Vienna	Recital at the Musikverein: Wolf; Werba

1982 *Salzburg Festival*
AU 10   Recital of songs with texts by Goethe, accompanied by Werba

1982-83 Season

SE 15	Turin	First recital with Charles Spencer: *Die Winterreise*
NO 22	Vienna	Queen of Spades (First Countess); Kollo, Ligendza; Kitaenko
NO 24	Vienna	Recital at the Musikverein: *Die Winterreise*; Werba

MA 6	New York	Concert at the Metropolitan Opera House: *Die Winterreise*; Levine
MY 8	Vienna	Recital at the Musikverein: Brahms; Führlinger; Werba
MY 13	Vienna	ORF Symphony Concert at the Musikverein: *Alto Rhapsody*; Zagrosek
JL 9	Vienna	Recital at the Schönnbrun Palace: Schubert, Brahms, Liszt, Mahler; Werba

1983-84 Season

DE 15	Nice	New Paul-Emile Deiber production: *Dialogues des Carmélites* (First Mme. de Croissy); Esham, Blanc, Pruett, Resik; Périsson
MY 21	Paris	Recital: Lieder on texts by Goethe with Paul-Emile Deiber and Erik Werba
JU 11	Vienna	Recital at the Musikverein: Strauss, Debussy, Liszt, Mahler, Berg, Egk; Werba
JU 17	Vienna	Vienna Symphony Concert at the Musikverein: Debussy *Le Martyre de Saint Sebastian*; Ghazarian; Deiber, Raymond; Prêtre

1984 Salzburg Festival

AU 7   Recital of songs by Strauss and Wolf with Werba

1984-85 Season

NO 11	New York	Recital at Avery Fisher Hall: Strauss, Wolf; Levine
DE 1	New York	*Elektra* (Klytämnestra); Vinzing, Meier, Estes, Cassilly; Levine
AP 25	Chicago	Chicago Symphony Concert: *Falstaff* (Quickly); Sarabia, Brendel, Ricciarelli, Battle, Murray; Solti
MY 17	Vienna	Concert at the Vienna State Opera: *Siegfried* (Erda); Bernstein
AU 14	Berlin	European Community Youth Orchestra Concert: Mahler Symphony No. 2; Mattila; Abbado

1985-86 Season

NO 1	Vienna	London Symphony Concert at the Konzerthaus: *Das Lied von der Erde*; Raffeiner; Boulez
NO 16	Vienna	Recital at the Konzerthaus: Liszt, Schumann, Berg, Mahler; Spencer
MY 15	Vienna	Recital at the Musikverein: Dvořák, Brahms, Wolf, Mendelssohn, Debussy, Strauss; Werba
MY 31	Berlin	Berlin Philharmonic Concert: Mahler Symphony No. 3; Levine

1986 Salzburg Festival

AU 4   Vienna Philharmonic Concert: Mahler Symphony No. 8; Greenberg, Alexander, Blase, Norman, Hollweg, Weikl, Rydl; Maazel

AU 11   ORF Symphony Concert: Martin *Golgotha*; Moser, Schreier, Fischer-Dieskau, Peeters; Zagrosek

AU 15   Recital of songs by Brahms, Schubert, Liszt, and Mahler with Werba

1986-87 Season

| DE 13 | Vienna | Vienna Philharmonic Concert at the Musikverein: *Des Knaben Wunderhorn*; Levine |

| AP 12 | New York | Recital at Avery Fisher Hall: Brahms, Liszt, Strauss, Berg, Debussy, Mahler; Levine |
| AP 16 | New York | New York Philharmonic Concert: Mahler Symphony No. 2; Hendricks; Bernstein |

1987 Salzburg Festival

| AU 22 | | First concert of Vienna Philharmonic tour: Bernstein Symphony No. 1; Bernstein. Also SE 4 (Lucerne Festival), 15 (Hollywood Bowl), 18 (Concord), 20 (Chicago), 22 (Ann Arbor), 24 (Carnegie Hall), 26 (Avery Fisher Hall) |
| AU 29 | | Recital of Wolf songs with Spencer |

1987-88 Season

NO 25	New York	New York Philharmonic Concert: Mahler Symphony No. 3; Bernstein
DE 9	Boston	Boston Symphony Concert: Elektra (Klytämnestra); Behrens, Secunde, King, Matthews; Ozawa
MY 26	Vienna	Recital at the Musikverein: Strauss, Wolf; Spencer
JU 11	Vienna	Pelléas et Mélisande (First Geneviève); Le Roux, Von Stade; Abbado
AU 12	Vienna	Vienna Chamber Orchestra Concert at the Konzerthaus: St. John Passion; Marshall, Schreier, Bär, Hermann; Hagen-Groll
AU 25	Lenox	Leonard Bernstein 70th Birthday Gala with the Boston Symphony at Tanglewood: Mahler "Des Antonius von Padua Fishpredigt"; Ozawa; Bernstein "I Am Easily Assimilated" from Candide; Mauceri
AU 26	Lenox	Boston Symphony Concert at Tanglewood: Final Movement of Mahler Symphony No. 2; Alexander; Ozawa

1988 Salzburg Festival

| JL 31 | | Die Winterreise; Levine |

1988-89 Season

SE 8	Pompeii	Elektra (Klytämnestra)
OC 21	New York	New Otto Schenk production of Wagner's Ring: Götterdämmerung (Waltraute); Behrens, Krämer; Levine
DE 8	Vienna	Sinfonia Varsovia Concert at the Konzerthaus: Messiah; Viljkainen, Blochwitz, Schöne; Menuhin
JA 11	Las Palmas	Concert: Kindertotenlieder; Ashkenazy
FE 18	Vienna	Recital at the Konzerthaus: Schubert, Brahms; Spencer
FE 21	Jerusalem	Israel Philharmonic Concert: Mahler Symphony No. 2; Levine
MA 24	New York	Die Walküre (Fricka); Lakes, Norman, Morris, Behrens; Levine
MA 27	New York	Das Rheingold (Fricka); Sotin, Wlaschiha; Levine
AP 14	New York	Recital at Avery Fisher Hall: Schubert, Brahms; Levine
JU 8	Vienna	Vienna Symphony Concert at the Konzerthaus: Bach Mass in B Minor; Auger, Thomas, George; Menuhin
JU 24	Vienna	Vienna Symphony Concert at the Konzerthaus: Mahler Symphony No. 8; Varady, Poschner-Klebel, Klepper, Hintermeier, Leech, Nimsgern, Schenk; Prêtre

1989 Salzburg Festival

AU 19	Vienna Philharmonic Concert: Mahler Symphony No. 2; Battle; Levine
AU 27	Recital of songs by Mahler, Einem, and Strauss wtih Spencer

1989-90 Season

OC 3	Vienna	Recital at the Konzerthaus: *Die Winterreise*; Spencer
OC 7	Royaumont	Recital at the Abbey: Schubert, Brahms, Wolf; Spencer
DE 12	London	London Symphony Concert: *Candide* (Old Lady); Anderson, Hadley, Green; Bernstein
MA 20	New York	Recital at Carnegie Hall: *Die Winterreise*; Levine
JU 3	Vienna	Recital at the Musikverein: Reger, Pfitzner, Mahler, Einem, Wolf; Spencer
JL 7	Berlin	Berlin Philharmonic Concert: Mahler Symphony No. 2; Sweet; Maazel
JL 12	Kiel	Schleswig-Holstein Festival Concert: Mahler Symphony No. 3; Eschenbach
AU 2	Nice	Gustav Mahler Youth Orchestra Concert: *Kindertotenlieder*; Abbado. Also AU 4 (Orange), 7 (West Berlin), 8 (East Berlin)
AU 11	Vienna	Recital at the Vienna State Opera: Schubert, Mahler; Spencer

1990 Salzburg Festival

AU 19	Recital of songs by Schumann and Brahms with Spencer

1990-91 Season

SE 27	Tokyo	First Recital in Far Eastern Tour with Spencer
NO 14	New York	Bernstein Memorial Concert: Mahler "Ich bin der Welt abhanden gekommen"; Levine
AP 9	Vienna	Recital at the Konzerthaus: Schubert, Brahms; Spencer
JU 29	Lenox	Tanglewood Recital: Schubert, Mahler, Brahms, Strauss; Davis
JL 5	Ravinia	Chicago Symphony Concert: *Das Lied von der Erde*; Levine
JL 8	Ravinia	Recital: *Die Winterreise*; Levine
JL 28	Sapporo	Recital: Mendelssohn, Bernstein; Spencer

1991-92 Season

MA 12	Vienna	Recital at the Konzerthaus: Liszt, Brahms, Wolf, Schumann; Spencer
MA 22	Vienna	Vienna Philharmonic 150th Anniversary Concert at the Musikverein: *Rückert Lieder*; Muti
MY 12	Vienna	Recital at the Musikverein: *Die Winterreise*; Spencer

1993-94 FAREWELL PERFORMANCES

Christa Ludwig gave a series of farewell performances in 1993 and 1994. In addition to those listed below, farewell performances were also given in: Milan, Cologne, Bonn, Stuttgart, Zurich, Heidelberg, Valencia, Monaco, Lisbon, Lille, London, Munich, Lausanne, Amsterdam, Athens, Graz, Hamburg, Auvers-sur-Oise, Dresden, Schleswig-Holstein Festival, Carinthian Summer Festival, Hong Kong, Taipei, Osaka, Nagoya, Brussels, and Zurich.

1992-93 Season

FE 19	Paris	Farewell Recital at Theatre des Champs Élysées: Schubert, Mahler, Schumann, Wolf, Strauss; Spencer
MA 20	New York	Farewell Recital at Carnegie Hall: Brahms, Mahler, Schumann, Strauss, Wolf; Levine
AP 3	New York	American farewell on Metropolitan Opera radio broadcast: *Die Walküre* (Fricka); Lakes, Gessendorf, Morris, Jones; Levine

1993 Salzburg Festival

JL 24	Farewell Vienna Philharmonic Concert: Mahler Symphony No. 2; Studer; Maazel
AU 9	Farewell Recital: Brahms, Mahler, Schumann, Strauss; Spencer

1993-94 Season

OC 13	London	First Farewell Recital at Wigmore Hall: *Die Winterreise*; Spencer
OC 18	London	Second Farewell Recital at Wigmore Hall with Charles Spencer
FE 17	Berlin	Farewell performance at the Deutsche Oper: *Elektra* (Klytämnestra); Jones, Lechner, Neumann, Feldhoff; Kout
FE 16	London	London Symphony Concert: Mahler Symphony No. 3; Levine
AP 19	Vienna	First Farewell Recital at the Musikverein: *Die Winterreise*; Spencer
AP 24	Vienna	Second Farewell Recital at the Musikverein: Beethoven, Schubert, Mahler, Wolf; Spencer
MY 20	Berlin	Recital (only performance at the Staatsoper Unter den Linden): *Die Winterreise*, accompanied by Tzimon Barto
MY 27	Vienna	Farewell Vienna Symphony Concert at the Konzerthaus: "Der Abschied" from *Das Lied von der Erde*; Bertini
SE 13	Berlin	Farewell Recital: Schubert, Mahler, Bernstein, Wolf, Strauss; Spencer
OC 28	Tokyo	Farewell Recital in the Far East with Charles Spencer
DE 14	Vienna	Final farewell performance: *Elektra* (Klytämnestra); Behrens, Patchell, Zednik, Grundheber; Hollreiser

Acknowledgements

Erwin Barta of the Vienna Konzerthaus, Hannagret Büker, Bill Clark, Peter Csobádi, Peter Diggins, Madelyn Elliott, Frankfurt Opera, Roger Gilkeson, Gunther Gottschalk, Monica Greipel of the Musikverein in Vienna, Dr. Helge Grünewald of the Berlin Philharmonic, Hanover Opera, Peter Heilker of the Bavarian State Opera, Mark Horowitz of the Library of Congress, R. C. Jacobs, Carol Siri Johnson, Harry Kraut, Thomas Lindner, Daniel Lombard of Musicaglotz, Professor Kate McCoy, Thomas Moody, Richard Morrison, Christiane Peter, Geoff Peterson of the Metropolitan Annals Project, Chris Putnam of Colbert Artists Management, William Russell, Heinz Rüttel of the Theater Collection of the Darmstadt State Theater, Howard Sanner, Anke Schneider-Hilsdorf of the Deutsche Oper in Berlin, Maria L. Serantoni of the Lyric Opera of Chicago, Paul Skonberg, Gail Slobodien, Charles Spencer, Robert Tuggle of the Metropolitan Opera Archives, Craig Urquhart, the Vienna Philharmonic, and Paul Wathen

Special thanks to Tom Kaufman and Carol Domeraski and to anyone who was inadvertently forgotten

Index